Midrash, Mishnah, and Gemara

Midrash, Mishnah, and Gemara

The Jewish Predilection
for Justified Law

David Weiss Halivni

Harvard University Press
Cambridge, Massachusetts
and London, England
1986

Printed in the United States of America
10 9 8 7 6 5 4 3 2 1

This book is printed on acid-free paper, and its binding materials
have been chosen for strength and durability.

Library of Congress Cataloging-in-Publication Data

Halivni, David.
Midrash, Mishnah, and Gemara.

Bibliography: p.
Includes index.
1. Jewish law—Philosophy. I. Title.
BM520.6.H3 1986 296.1′206 85-17676
ISBN 0-674-57370-6 (alk. paper)

As God drove Adam and Eve out of paradise and saw them leaving, His heart went out to them and He gave them the smile of a child.

When God took away prophecy from Israel, He felt pity for them and gave them the Talmud.

Acknowledgments

WRITING A BOOK, like any other major human activity, requires the assistance of many individuals in different capacities, from the one who initially encourages the author to write the book to the one who helps him complete the technical details. All deserve to be publicly thanked.

In order to avoid an inordinately long list, I will, however, content myself here with singling out for thanks only a few, those who have most tangibly and concretely contributed to either the writing or the publishing of the book. They are the following: the administration of the Institute for Advanced Studies of the Hebrew University in Jerusalem, where, during my tenure as a fellow in 1980–1981, this book was conceived and partially written; Professor Steven T. Katz of Cornell University, who, with his characteristic camaraderie, took an interest in the manuscript as soon as he heard of it and offered valuable suggestions; Margaretta Fulton, Senior Editor at Harvard University Press, who helped me forge the final manuscript; Mary Ellen Geer, Manuscript Editor at Harvard University Press, who edited the manuscript and supervised the book through the various stages of proof; Emily Biederman, who, during my teaching year in Jerusalem in 1984–1985, proved to be (and I hope will remain) an invaluable friend and assistant. Her enormous patience and sensitivity made what otherwise would have been an arduous task into a joyous adventure.

To all others, my heartfelt appreciation.

Note on Transliteration

The Hebrew letter *het,* often transliterated as *h* with a dot under it, is here transliterated throughout as *ch.*

Contents

Midrash, Mishnah, and Gemara

Introduction

THIS BOOK WAS WRITTEN at a time when my critical commentary on the Talmud (called *Sources and Traditions*) had achieved half its goal: it covered half of the Talmud text. That commentary discusses in great detail more than a thousand different subjects and touches fleetingly in the notes on ten times that number. It avoids being disjointed because it follows the order of the Talmud and thus has a consecutive thread. It is further united by the several very important historical facts it implies, principally that the present text of the Talmud most often evolved from a different preceding text, and that in the process of evolution the present text absorbed both transmissional changes and redactional changes.

I became very interested in these redactional changes. Transmissional changes enter the text without the transmitter's awareness. In contrast, redactional changes are consciously made for the sake of improving the text, either contextually or aesthetically. Transmissional changes are understandable, though unpredictable. They are mechanical changes, made unwittingly by the transmitter. A person, for instance, may genuinely think he heard the word "can" and transmit it that way, whereas in fact the word "can't" was said. Not all mechanical changes are a result of faulty hearing; they may also result from faulty speech. The speaker may think he said "can't," but the word he actually spoke was "can." Transmissional changes are simply a part of human susceptibility to error. Redactional changes, on the other hand, are made purposefully by the redactors. When the purpose of these changes is to improve content or correct defects, the question arises: who is responsible for these defects? Did the original authors release defective texts? This is most unlikely; more plausibly, the texts became defective during the interval between the time of the authors and the time of the redactors.

However, texts, and oral texts in particular, become defective only if they are not carefully preserved, if they are not faithfully and reliably transmitted. In this case, we would have to assume that during the Talmudic period certain texts (those that required redactional changes) composed by some of the great sages were transmitted haphazardly, in an incomplete and defective state. Some texts eventually may even have disappeared altogether: neglecting to preserve texts properly leads not only to defectiveness but also to disappearance. It is extremely unlikely that this kind of neglect would have taken place without the tacit approval of the authorities; it appears that they did not mind the neglect of certain texts whose attribution to the most authoritative sources was not doubted. They must have assumed that these most authoritative sources themselves did not care to have some of their texts disseminated; these texts were not considered worthy of being preserved, and were allowed to suffer neglect or disappearance.

All this sounds strange and runs counter to the general belief that every statement of the sages was meticulously preserved—until one notices that the overwhelming majority of redactional changes occurred in the discursive passages of the Talmud, the ones that contain arguments and discussions, rather than in the apodictic passages, the ones that contain fixed law. Apodictic passages apparently needed no improvement; they were not defective. Such a substantial difference could not have taken place accidentally. There must have been a conscious decision to preserve carefully the fixed law and to neglect benignly the argumentational material. After a conclusion was reached, the means of arriving at it, the arguments that went into making it, seemed no longer important. This should not surprise us; it is exactly the way the authors of the Mishnah and the Braitha (ca. 50–200 C.E.) practiced transmission.

The Mishnah and the Braitha (Tannaitic material not included in the Mishnah) consist almost entirely of fixed law; they contain very little discursive material. This is so despite the almost certain fact that the authors of the Mishnah and Braitha too discussed and argued (sometimes fiercely) before they arrived at conclusions. It can be assumed a priori that conclusions are always preceded by discussions and arguments. In addition, occasionally one encounters enough arguments in the Mishnah and Braitha to indicate that there were initially many more that were not subsequently preserved. Apparently, to the authors of the Mishnah and Braitha, law was to be officially transmitted only in the apodictic form. Arguments and discussions were necessary—indeed, indispensable—but only as a means of arriving at decisions, not as ends in themselves. Once the end was achieved, the means was left to wither away, to be forgotten. What remained, however, was often defective and truncated. This state also prevailed throughout the Amoraic period (200–427 C.E.) until the redactors of the Talmud (who I believe lived and flourished after 427) came to the aid of the discursive material and affirmed it worthy to be preserved. The redactors added discursive passages of their own and tried hard to reconstruct and complete defective discursive (occasionally even nondiscursive) material that survived from previous generations, both Tannaitic (mainly Braitha) and Amoraic. Because of their proximity to the Amoraic period, they were more successful in reconstructing the discussions of this period than those of the Tannaim.

The role of the redactors of the Talmud (whom I call Stammaim, which is Aramaic for "anonyms") continued to fascinate me. They were more than editors—that is, they did not just correct and arrange contents and style in conformity with set standards; they were partners in creation. They provided lengthy explanatory notes, completed defective statements, and supplemented the text with passages of their own. Above all, they initiated a new (rather, old and new) awareness that the discursive too deserves to be preserved, that how one arrives at a conclusion has importance beyond the pedagogic lesson of knowing how to arrive at new conclusions in the future. Disputation is an activity of the human mind and as such deserves to be known, studied, and explored. The redactors became masters of this genre of learning and influenced subsequent rabbinic learning up to this day.

I asked myself about the origin of this awareness—did it have an antecedent, and if so, what was it? Were the redactors the innovators of this genre of learning, or did they merely revive earlier precedents that the authors of the Mishnah and Braitha eclipsed? I came to the conclusion that there was an antecedent, and that it was to be found in Midreshei Halakhah, collections of biblical commentaries containing a large portion of law culled from biblical verse. In the process of culling, Midreshei Halakhah resorted to argument and disputation. Midreshei Halakhah helped the Gemara—the final product of the redactors of the Talmud—to overcome the negative spell that the authors of the Mishnah and Braitha had cast on the discursive and to make it a legitimate part of the transmission. The Gemara, though much more argumentational than Midreshei Halakhah, is nevertheless close enough in nature to invoke the latter in its defense against the charges that it deviated from the authoritative Mishnaic form. Midrashic form, too, deviated from Mishnaic form.

To understand further the contribution of the redactors of the Talmud and their dependence on Midreshei Halakhah, I extended the inquiry into Midrashic form, the form used when law is tied to Scripture. How and when did this form come into being? What was its genesis? How does it relate to the Mishnaic form, the form used when law is arranged topically without scriptural reference? Which form is older and which younger? Are they complementary or counter to each other? The road eventually led me to the Bible, specifically to those clauses in the Bible that resemble Midrash: the "motive clauses," or subordinate sentences in which the motivation or reason for the commandment is given.

What all these have in common—motive clauses, Midreshei Halakhah, and Gemara—is their proclivity for vindicatory law, for law that is justified, against law that is autocratically prescribed. This proclivity is, to be sure, not shared equally. Most laws in the Bible do not have supporting motive clauses. The hermeneutic justification of the Midreshei Halakhah is not as vindicatory as the usual logical reasoning of the Gemara. Yet in contrast with the apodictic Mishnah, they all seem to have a preference for law that is expressly reasonable, that seeks to win the hearts of those to whom the laws are addressed. They seem to convey that Jewish law cannot be imposed from above, to be blindly obeyed. Jewish law is justificatory, often revealing its own *raison d'être.* Apodictic Mishnah, on the other hand, constitutes a deviation from this overall trend of vindicatory law. It runs counter to Jewish apperception, which favors laws that justify themselves, either logically or scripturally. No wonder Mishnaic form was relatively short-lived, lasting only about 130 years. Mishnaic form initially emerged as a response to the particular political and religious conditions that prevailed in Palestine during the period following the destruction of the Temple. During the second century it was supported and upheld by the Patriarchate family, particularly by R. Judah Hanassi. After his death (ca. 220–221 C.E.) Mishnaic form was gradually abandoned, and the Jewish apperception for justificatory law prevailed.

The initial impetus for writing this book was the desire to understand more fully and completely the contribution of the redactors of the Talmud, the Stammaim. It was this desire to appreciate the redactors' innovations along with their indebtedness to their predecessors that made me reexamine the nature of both Midrashic and Mishnaic forms, place them in their proper historical perspective, and relate them to the source of all Jewish knowledge, the Bible. (I also show in Chapter 7 the influence of the redactors on later generations in regard to sensitive religious issues.) The other starting point of this book is the distinction between the apodictic and the vindicatory modes in transmitted law, which served as a criterion for determining the scope of this study. Only those elements in the literature that had relevance to this central distinction were studied. And it is through this distinction that one appreciates the full impact of the redactors' revival of—and their almost conclusively tilting the scales in favor of—the discursive. Indeed, the apodictic Mishnaic form never regained even a fraction of its former glory; it became relatively unused. Later attempts like that of Maimonides to restore Mishnaic form met with fierce opposition. The redactors would not have succeeded had Jewish apperception been on the side of the apodictic. They rode, as it were, on the crest of Jewish inclination for the vindicatory. The discovery that Jewish apperception since the time of the Bible favored justificatory law was an unexpected result of this study. It is also its most important observation.

II

In a passage in the *Laws* (722D–723B), Plato extols the value of accompanying codes of law and discrete laws with justificatory clauses. He compares the legislator to the physician: the free physician treating a free man explains and persuades, whereas the "servile physician treating slaves issues brusque injunctions." To prevent law from being "brusque injunctions," one ought to add to each law a reason, a justification that states the rationale for the law. The law will then persuade and win the hearts of those whose obedience it seeks.

Yet ancient law in general is apodictic, without justification and without persuasion. Its style is categorical, demanding, and commanding. Its tone seems to be in accord with the critics of Plato, such as the famous Greek philosopher quoted by Seneca (*Writings* 94.38) who declares, "I censor Plato, because he added justifications to the laws. Let the law be like the voice that reaches us from heaven. Command and do not argue. Tell me what I have to do. I do not want to learn. I want to obey." Plato's argument for persuasion in law was apparently not very persuasive.

Ancient Near Eastern law in particular is devoid of any trace of desire to convince or to win hearts. It enjoins, prescribes, and orders, expecting to be heeded solely on the strength of being an official decree. It solicits no consent (through justification) from those to whom it is directed. It rests entirely on its own absolute powers.

It is true that there is an occasional though rare reference in ancient Near Eastern law to a just god who demands just laws, which may serve as a motive or as a justification for the laws themselves. God is his own justification, and laws issued by Him or associated with Him (ensuing as they do from His infinite wisdom) carry their own built-in justification. Ur Engur, the king of Ur (ca. 2400 B.C.E.), boasts that he has made justice prevail according to the just laws of Shamash (Sun God and the god of light and learning); Lipit Ishtar, the Akkadian king of Isin (ca. 1930 B.C.E.), describes himself in the prologue and epilogue of his Law Code as the wise Shepherd who had established justice in Sumer and in Akkad in accordance with the words of the gods. Hammurabi (ca. 1752 B.C.E.), in his great Code, followed suit. Indeed, "the closing sentences of the epilogue are but a version in Akkadian of the corresponding portion of the epilogue of Lipit Ishtar."[1] The mention of a god in the prologue and epilogue may have come in lieu of justification; an attribution of divine origin to a law simultaneously justifies that law. It would follow, then, that the codes of these kings were not totally devoid of justification.

Nevertheless, it seems to be the consensus of scholars that the references to a god in the prologue and epilogue of these codes ought not to be taken as a sign that these codes were intended to be divine documents, emanating from on high and thus carrying a built-in justification. The mention of a god in the prologue and epilogue is not intended to make a divine claim (for these laws); rather, he appears as custodian, guarantor, of law (any just law). The ultimate authority of Near Eastern law (so radically different from biblical law) is the king and his administration, or, more accurately, the necessity of having law and order to combat chaos.[2] That authority mandated a categorical acceptance on the part of the populace. No additional justification or reason was necessary.

In 1934 A. Alt[3] caused a scholarly stir with his distinction between apodictic and casuistic laws—the former denoting an absolute pronouncement, the latter denoting a conditional one incorporating an "if" clause. The law in Exod. 21:18–19 ("If men quarrel and a man smite his fellow man with a stone or with his fist and he did not die but kept to his bed, if he rises again and walks abroad upon his staff, then he that smote him shall be freed; only he shall pay for the loss of his time and for his cure") is a typical example of casuistic law. Such laws are formulated in exact language, dry and professional. On the other hand, the law in Exod. 22:17 ("You should not suffer a sorceress to live") is a typical example of apodictic law. It is categorical, absolute, without ifs or buts. In comparing Mesopotamian law with biblical law, Alt concluded that the casuistic form is typical of the former—similar forms in the Bible are taken from there—whereas the apodictic form in the Bible is of biblical origin. Subsequent scholars questioned this distinction on the grounds that some Near Eastern laws (especially Hittite law) are not casuistic, while biblical law is composed of both apodictic and casuistic forms.

Without taking sides on the substance of this issue[4] (which at most covers only a portion of biblical law, that is, civil law), I would like to point out that logically this distinction between apodictic and casuistic law is not very appropriate. An "if" clause is not necessarily less apodictic in the dictionary sense of the word apodictic, namely, "necessary truths," "absolutely certain." Logically, an "if" clause possesses the same relationship of its words to one another and/or to the whole that a non-"if" clause possesses, except that the former's assertion is only hypothetical. However, when that assertion actually does occur—and the law is designed for precisely that eventuality—the difference between it and the non-"if" clause disappears. Moreover, the difference is merely formal, and the forms are interchangeable. The law in Exod. 22:17 could have read (similarly, for instance, to the law in Deut. 17:2): "If there is found among you a sorceress . . . you shall not suffer her to live." Conversely, the law in Exod. 21:18–19 could have read something like this: "He that smites his fellow man who did not die but kept his bed and rose again [he that smote] shall pay for the loss of time and cure. He shall not be put to death." Alt's distinction is essentially syntactic and stylistic. It distinguishes between an eventuality that has occurred and one that is about to occur.

Logically and substantively it would be better to contrast the apodictic with the vindicatory, the former denoting categorical pronouncements, the latter justificatory statements. (Note that both pronouncement and statement could be conditional or nonconditional. See, for instance, Deut. 22:8: "When you build a new house, you shall make a parapet for your roof, so that you do not bring bloodguilt on your house if anyone should fall from it." The pronouncement that "you shall make a parapet for your roof" is apodictic, even though the clause "if" [or when] you build a new house is conditional; whereas the entire second half beginning with "so that" is a justificatory statement, justifying the pronouncement.) The distinction between apodictic and justificatory is basic and substantial. General law (including, for instance, the Twelve Tablets)[5] is apodictic, offering no justification or reason. It is expressed categorically, in precise and terse language. Jewish law, including biblical law, in contrast to other ancient Near Eastern law, is vindicatory. It offers a justification or reason that is either particular (applying to an individual law) or collective (grouping together a series of laws as divine commandments). Even the civil law of Exod. 21–23:18, which has its counterpart in Near Eastern law, both in content and in form, is justified by virtue of having been placed between explicit divine commandments (it is preceded by the giving of the Torah) and by having in its preface the words of God:

"These are the ordinances which thou [Moses] shall put before them [the Israelites]."[6] The preface makes this law a divine mandate.

Jewish apperception, I hope to show, suffers categorical imperatives only when issued forth from the Divine as He exercises divine authority, claiming obedience because of His divine deeds. Otherwise, it tends to the vindicatory. This vindicatory predisposition persisted throughout the ages, with the exception of the Mishnah at its early stage. It is part of the purpose of this book to trace, from the Bible onward, the vicissitudes of this unique characteristic of Jewish law.

Chapter 1

The Biblical Period

A POPULAR MIDRASHIC HOMILY raises the question: "Why does the Torah begin with the account of creation and not with Exod. 12:1, the first commandment given to Israel?"[1] The author of this question, in his perception of the nature of law, was closer to Seneca than he was to Plato. Like the famous Greek philosopher quoted by Seneca, the author of this homily perceived law as being totally apodictic, in no need of preambles or other justificatory means.[2] The story of creation, the events of the Patriarchal families, the exodus of the Israelites from Egypt—all of which precede the verses in Exodus 12—are to the author of this homily a burdensome preface, a superfluous justification. "Like a voice that reaches us from heaven," the laws are self-sufficient. Since the Torah's main purpose is to teach law (that, at least, is the assumption of the author of the homily), the Torah should have begun with the first declarative public law.

An early rabbinic tradition that found its way into later literature divides biblical law into two categories: those without humanly discernible reasons and those whose reasons can be discovered.[3] Seizing upon the biblical use of synonyms for the word *law,* the tradition appropriated (with minimal contextual support) the root חקק (*chakak*) to designate the former category and the root שפט (*shafat*) to designate the latter,[4] thus tracing back to the Bible the distinction between justified laws and laws without reasons. This apparent compromise is, in fact, closer to the view that holds that biblical laws were apodictically formulated, except that man may subsequently discover the rationale for some of the laws (which can be said of nonbiblical law as well). Law (including biblical law) is, however, even according to this tradition, basically without justification.

The notion that Mosaic laws are apodictic—that phrases such as "so spoke the Lord," and "I am your God" preceding or following commandments in the Bible indicate that the laws of the Bible are offered without reason and demand obedience without justification—seems to have been widespread in the ancient world among different cultures. An Arabic fragment[5] translated and published by R. Walzer reports Galen, the Greek physician and writer, as having said ("any time before 192"):[6] "They compare those who practice medicine without specific knowledge to Moses who framed laws for the tribe of the Jews, since it is his method in his books to write without offering proofs, saying 'God commanded,' 'God spoke'" (this comparison of medicine to legislation was inspired by the line from Plato quoted in the Introduction). It is quite likely that R. Yitzchak, a Palestinian scholar around the turn of the fourth century C.E. who was probably the author of the Midrashic homily[7] quoted earlier, was reacting to Galen's charges when he explained (Babylonian Talmud [henceforth cited as B.T.] Sanhedrin 21b):

> מפני מה לא נתגלו טעמי תורה? שהרי שתי מקראות נתגלו טעמן ונכשל בהם גדול העולם.
>
> Why were the reasons for the commandments of the Torah not revealed? Because in two instances where the reasons were revealed [Deut. 17:16–17], they misled the great of the world [Solomon].

According to R. Yitzchak, the lack of justification for biblical laws does not arise from the arbitrariness of these laws, but from the fear that giving reasons might induce people to draw the wrong conclusions. But he grants Galen's assumption that biblical laws are without justification.

A cursory reading of the Bible will reveal, however, that biblical law is not devoid of reasons. There are many "motive clauses" (more than one hundred in Deuteronomy alone), subordinate sentences in which the motivation or reason for the commandment is given.[8] Motive clauses are usually introduced with the words "for" (*ki*), "that" (*lema'an*), "lest" (*pen*), or "therefore" (*al ken*). In the Decalogue, for instance, in Exod. 20:1–17, there are three motive clauses beginning with the word *ki* ("You should not bow down to them nor serve them for I am the Lord your God," verse 5; "You should not take the name of the Lord your God in vain, for the Lord will not hold him guiltless," verse 7; "The seventh day is the Sabbath . . . for in six days the Lord made Heaven and earth," verses 10–11); one with *lema'an* ("Honor your father and mother that your days may be long upon the land"); and one with *al ken* ("Therefore the Lord blessed the Sabbath day and hallowed it," verse 11). Other phrases introduce motive clauses as well, such as *bevigdo vah* ("because he has dealt deceitfully with her," Exod. 21:8). Sometimes the reason is not explicitly stated but is discernible in the context; Lev. 18:12 is a good example of such implicit motive clauses. Perhaps the first commandment in the Decalogue ("I am the Lord your God who brought you out of the Land of Egypt, out of the house of bondage") is an implicit motive clause for the rest of the commandments in the Decalogue (because I took you out of Egypt, you have to obey me).[9]

Motive clauses in the Bible have recently been subject of three studies, two of them book-length,[10] which identify, locate, and classify the clauses. There is no need to duplicate their findings here; suffice it to say that there are motive clauses in all sections of the Bible, though with varying frequency. Deuteronomy understandably has the largest number, the Cultic Decalogue the smallest. B. Gemser, who first called attention to the phenomenon of motive clauses in the Bible, divides them into four types: explanatory, ethical, religious (both cultic and theological), and historical—a sign of their richness and variety.

It is noteworthy that the motive clauses discussed by scholars involve, on the whole, individual motives that suit a particular commandment.[11] But along with the individual motives there are also expressly general motives, serving as an overall justification for God to issue commandments. That right is granted Him by virtue of His being the creator of the universe, with a special claim on the Israelites because He led them out of Egypt. These two themes serve as both general and individual motives. The observance of the Sabbath, for instance, is motivated in the first Decalogue by God's creation of the world in six days and His having rested on the seventh, and in the second Decalogue by His having taken the Israelites out of Egypt.

The creation theme is not a very frequent motive in the Bible as compared with the exodus motive; the former theme appears only a few times in certain sections of the Bible, whereas the theme of redemption is found in all sections. In one instance, the exodus from Egypt serves as the motive for the commandment to be holy, which in turn is used elsewhere as an independent justification for issuing individual commands: "For I am the Lord that brought you up out of the Land of Egypt to be your God. You shall, therefore, be holy for I am holy" (Lev. 11:45). Nevertheless, the creation theme deserves our attention because ontologically the God of creation supersedes the God of redemption. Without creation there is no possibility of redemption. Mention should also be made of the covenant theme: God entered into a covenant relationship with Abraham, which entitles God to impose laws on Abraham's children (Gen. 17:8–9). This is, however, much less frequent as a motive than the creation and exodus themes and occupies a less central position in the Bible. In this chapter, therefore, I focus on the creation and redemption themes only.

An important distinction between the motive for a particular and individual commandment and the motive for general commandments is that the motive for the former is rarely complete and self-sufficient; it almost always needs further elucidation and supplementary explanation. Such a motive often rests on an assumption that transcends the individual commandment, and the relation between the two may require further explanation. Take, for example, what seems to be a quite satisfying individual motive clause, that of Deuteronomy 10:19: "Love, therefore, the stranger, for you were strangers in the Land of Egypt." Having been strangers in the land of Egypt, however, is not sufficient reason for loving the stranger. One has to add: you have known the unpleasantness of being a stranger ("You know the heart of a stranger," Exod. 23:9) and are duty-bound not to cause others such unpleasantness. The duty not to cause unpleasantness transcends the individual commandment of loving the stranger. The motive is applicable to the whole range of human relationships, and it is derived from a basic moral commitment that is not reducible to particulars.

The motive for general commandments, on the other hand, is more or less self-sufficient, requiring a minimum of supplementary explanation. Given ancient Near Eastern realities concerning the obligations of the freed man to his former owner, God's right as the deliverer of the Israelites from their former owner, the Egyptians, to impose laws upon them is firmly established and legally binding. (This is not, however, the interpretation in rabbinic law: the rabbis saw in references to Israel's deliverance more a moral force than a legal one.) "For to me the people of Israel are servants, they are my servants whom I brought out from the land of Egypt" (Lev. 25:55). This entitles God to impose laws upon the Israelites as He sees fit; no additional explanation is needed.

God as creator makes an even stronger claim: since He has called man and the universe into being, man owes Him obedience and is subject to His commandments. In His capacity as the creator, God could have imposed laws on any nation; but He chose to exercise His sovereignty over Abraham's children because of the covenant He entered into with them. He singled them out by miraculously taking them out of slavery, freeing them from bondage. Thus the two principal general motives, God as the creator (the beginning of the world) and God as the redeemer (the beginning of the national Jewish history), act as one.

The creation story and the description (in great detail) of the events that led to the redemption from Egypt are thus a kind of preamble to the laws of the Bible, contained in Exodus 12 and thereafter, while at the same time they also serve as the motives for individual commandments. Exodus 12 itself, which up to verse 20 is almost all law, is punctuated (in verses 11–14 and 17) with references to the exodus as a motive for the laws therein. Phrases like "I am the Lord" or "So spoke the Lord," or the mention of God as the lawgiver are not assertions of arbitrariness, as Galen and others have thought, but rather a brief recapitulation of God's right to issue commandments as implied in the preamble. The few portions of the Bible that have no motives—that make reference neither to creation nor exodus, and contain no phrases such as "I am the Lord" (in fact, they hardly mention God's name)—deal with civil laws (for example, parts of Exodus 21–22). They bear, both in content and in form, an extraordinary resemblance to Mesopotamian law. The apodictic nature of these passages is partly modified by the placement of civil laws in the midst of other commandments whose justification is affirmed either through motive clauses or through references to the preamble. Some (such as Exodus 21:1) are introduced by an additional verse which absorbs them into the overall system of biblical law. Thus, even these sections are not wholly devoid of justification.

This, then, is the answer to the question raised by the popular homily quoted at the beginning of the chapter. The Torah could not have begun with Exodus 12, because biblical law would then have been without preamble, without a rationale, and thus counter to the Bible's inner spirit.

The presence of motive clauses in the Bible is significant beyond the explanation they offer. They add up to an assertion that biblical law is not categorically imperative, that it seeks to justify itself, though the justification is sporadic and sometimes logically not very tight. This characteristic of biblical law can best be appreciated by comparing it with ancient Near Eastern law. Gemser compared biblical law with ten collections of ancient Near Eastern law and concluded: "In absolutely none of these lawbooks or codes or collections can one single instance of motive clause be discovered. The motive clause is clearly and definitely a peculiarity of Israel's or Old Testament law."[12] This peculiarity expresses a basic trait of Jewish law, which tends to be justificatory (one could say "democratic"), to explain itself rather than to impose, as opposed to the autocratic attitude of the ancient Near East. Biblical law, by providing instances of its motives, signifies that it reckons with the will of the people to whom the laws are directed; it seeks their approval, solicits their consent, thereby manifesting that it is not indifferent to man. This, in turn, is rooted in the unique biblical relationship between God and man, where "God is in search of man,"[13] desiring, as it were, man's approbation. In contrast, ancient Near Eastern law shows no concern for the will of the people to whom the laws are directed. The laws are to be obeyed; they need not be understood. Motives are not necessary. The law's authority is derived from the need to have law and order, and it is the king and his entourage who decide what law and order are; the people are not privy to that decision. The Bible, on the other hand, invites the receiver of the law to join in grasping the beneficent effect of the law, thereby bestowing dignity upon him and giving him a sense that he is a partner in the law.

A different—and one may say a very important—kind of motive is the exegetical motive. One predicates his claim by showing that it is contained in an earlier, more authoritative text and quotes the text in support. This genre is very common in rabbinic and sectarian literature. The canonization of the Bible and its attendant authority undoubtedly gave subsequent literature a special impetus to use the exegetical motive.[14] But the exegetical motive is not restricted to post-biblical literature; it is already found in Joshua 8:31. When a text becomes binding even before canonization, it serves for future legislators as a source on which to base their new legislation.

The formula used in Joshua to designate this genre is "as it is written in the law of Moses." This formula, or one similar to it, is repeated thirteen times in the Bible, of which all but one (2 Kings 14:6) are in the late books of Ezra and Nehemiah. In rabbinic literature the most common formulas for the exegetical motives are *shene'emar* ("as it says") followed by a scriptural reference (the usual form in the Mishnah), or *melammed* ("it comes to teach") or *maggid* ("it declares") followed by a law (the usual form in the Halakhic Midrashim). In the Damascus Scroll (and in other texts of the Dead Sea sect, notably the Rule Scrolls),[15] the formula is a variation of *shene'emar,* namely, *asher amar.* It seems that in rabbinic literature a distinction is made between *kakatuv* ("as it is written") and *shene'emar* ("as it says") or *melammed* ("it comes to teach") or *maggid* ("it declares"). The latter three expressions adduce something new, something that is not explicitly stated in the text,[16] whereas "as it is written" does not adduce anything that is not already explicit in the text. One does not say, "Do not kill a human being, as it says 'Thou shalt not kill.'" One would have to say: "As it is written, 'Thou shalt not kill.'"

The motive clause and the exegetical motive are substantially different, principally because the motive clause appeals to logic, however weak that logic might be,[17] while the exegetical motive appeals to authority. Yet if it were not for the biblical mode of providing a motive, the exegetical motive would not have come into being, and rabbinic laws, like the laws of the ancient Near East, would have been motiveless. The two kinds of motives, though different, are related.

II

The date of sectarian literature, based on the Dead Sea Scrolls, is usually given as the second century B.C.E. I have said nothing about the development of Jewish law, let alone the formula employed in motives, during the period from the canonization[18] of the Torah to the second century B.C.E. No corresponding literature of that period is available; most of the Apocrypha and the Pseudepigrapha were written during the second century or later.[19] But we may assume a priori that there was exegetical activity[20] going on during that period, and that some of the conclusions reached through that activity found their way into later *halakhah* (Jewish religious law). This assumption is also supported by the phrase in Ezra 7:10 "to seek the law of the Lord," which in Hebrew includes the root *drash* and the word *torah. Drash* in the Bible does not, as a rule, mean exegesis, exposition of a text. Rather, it means seeking information—theological or otherwise—without reference to a text.[21] However, the combination of *drash* and *torah* connotes an exegetical activity similar to that engaged in by the rabbis of the Talmud.[22]

Midrash (the noun constructed from the root *drash*) as an institution did not begin in the second century B.C.E.; it is much older. Its specific nature, however, remained obscure until the second century. This obscurity is further compounded by the fact that in some sectarian circles, such as those that produced the Temple Scroll or Chapter 49 of the Book of Jubilees, the exegetical results were integrated into the Bible proper, employing biblical style and language. We cannot discern from reading them where Bible ends and where their added Midrash begins. In contrast to rabbinic and most of the Dead Sea literature, where there is (in the former almost always and in the latter quite often) a distinct differentiation between the old and the new, in the Temple Scroll[23] or Chapter 49 of Jubilees[24] there is no explicit differentiation between the ancient layers, those that constitute the Bible of old, and the Midrash that they later accreted. On the surface they are indistinguishable, and were so even when, as I hope to prove in the next chapter, the Temple Scroll incorporated a proto-rabbinic *drashah* (a particular application of Midrash). This, incidentally, also tells us that there was not necessarily a unilinear development from integrating exegetical results into the Bible proper to using specific formulas to indicate an accretion. Some groups integrated, while others used specific formulas to designate the additions.

The differences among the groups concerning how to incorporate additions perhaps reflect their respective perceptions of God's nearness to man. Midrash represents distance from God, a clinging to the words of the past at a time when the living present word is not forthcoming any longer. It constitutes a substitute for direct intervention, through either revelation or prophecy. Midrash seeks (that is the literal meaning of the root *drash*) rather than being "seized" and "told." Midrash emerged after prophecy ceased. Canonization (even in its early, imperfect state) dried up the flow of direct information from God to man (or was it the other way around, that the drying up was responsible for the canonization?), forcing man to rely on Midrash, an intellectual endeavor that anchors the present in the past. It divines God's will from words uttered by Him in the past, since man can no longer talk to, or be addressed by, Him now. Results obtained through Midrash, which enjoys only derivative status, had to be designated clearly as such and not integrated into Scripture proper. Thus arose the special Midrashic terminology.

On the other hand, sectarian groups who claimed that God spoke to and was intimate with them could avail themselves of direct contact with God whenever the need for instruction arose. They did not resort to Midrash, seeking no implicit meaning from among the words of the past. Since the Bible for them was still in the making, no specially designated formula was necessary to distinguish between recent additions and messages of old. They were all words of the living God.

I began by showing that "motive clauses"—subordinate sentences in which the motivation or reason for the commandment is given—are a unique characteristic of the Bible, found rarely if at all in Near Eastern law. This characteristic reflects Jewish apperception of justificatory law, that a law should not be categorically imperative but rather vindicatory, seeking to justify itself through either individual or general reasons. Vindication indicates that God, as it were, is interested in man's opinion, that He seeks man's approval. I further asserted that Midrash (narrowly confined in definition to when—and only when—an actual quotation is cited) represents a continuation of the biblical motive clause, except that its justification is now primarily exegetical (that is, it makes its claim by showing that it is contained in an earlier, more authoritative text). If biblical law had followed the pattern of Near Eastern law, if it too were without motive clauses, Halakhic Midrash might not have come into being. Post-biblical law would have been as apodictic (motiveless) as Near Eastern law, and Midrash would not have been necessary. The biblical motive clause is, in a sense, the father of Midrash.

We can now turn to the relationship between Midrash and Mishnah. I would first like to add, however, that I follow the rabbinic model of using the term "Midrash" only when an actual quotation from the Bible is cited.[25] I do so because I feel that this promotes clarity and allows for subtle distinctions within explicatory activity. Implicit comments that do not mention the text to which they refer, the kind of comments that are found in abundance in the Bible itself, should properly be called "inner-biblical exegesis"[26] and not Midrash. Later prophets were naturally influenced by earlier prophets, and some of their prophecies were shaped both in content and in form by their predecessors. Yet this should not make them *darshanim,* authors of Midrash. Chronicles, for instance, should not be viewed as Midrash on Kings, as many scholars claim, even in those sections where Chronicles reacts to, elaborates on, or harmonizes the contradictions in Kings. For a passage to qualify as Midrash, the formula "as it is written" should be employed. Without that formula, Chronicles merely shares some of Kings' themes. Midrash, like commentary, ought to refer to exact chapter and verse. Influence should not be enough, nor should stimulation, nor even indirect reference;[27] direct quotation is necessary. Indeed, for those exegetical instances without direct quotation, a more suitable term should be devised.[28]

Chapter 2

The Post-Biblical Period

NOT SO LONG AGO, if one asked which of the two forms of study is older, the Midrashic form (in which specific biblical citations are made) or the Mishnaic form (which arranges the laws topically without scriptural reference), the nearly unanimous answer would have been that the Midrashic form is older. Only Isaac Halevy, the author of *Dorot Ha-Rishonim,* claimed that in early times laws were transmitted without reference to Scripture.[1] His view was ignored, however, because of his ferocious polemical tone and his obvious tendentiousness in seeking a scientific basis for the antiquity of the Mishnah and thereby for the oral law.[2] Most scholars agreed with N. Krochmal[3] that after Ezra, during the period of *sofrim* (scribes), the oral law was studied and transmitted in conjunction with Scripture, and those who performed this Midrashic activity were called scribes, that is, "explicators of the Book." Whatever disagreement there was among scholars concerned the date when the Midrashic form changed into the Mishnaic form.

A wide range of opinion existed concerning this date. J. Z. Lauterbach argued that the change took place in 190 B.C.E., at the time of Yose ben Yoezer.[4] D. Z. Hoffmann[5] attributed the change to the Shammaites and the Hillelites (first century C.E.), while C. Albeck[6] apparently thought that the change was effected by the sages of Yabneh during the reign of R. Gamaliel the Second, around 90 C.E.

The idea that the Midrashic form is older than the Mishnaic form has come under increased questioning. First, Y. Kaufmann[7] cogently argued that the *sofrim* lived not only in the period between Ezra (fifth century) and the "pairs" (first century B.C.E.), but continued in later periods as well. The term *sofrim* (literally, enumerators or scribes)[8] refers to individuals who occupied themselves with the study and teachings of the

Book, an activity that existed in most ages; they represent too general a phenomenon to deduce anything specific about Midrash. Following Kaufmann, E. E. Urbach[9] noted that other ancient peoples had codes that consist of apodictic, fixed laws (derived from custom[10] and decree) without the burden of exegetical justification; he assumed that the Jews were probably no exception, and that Midrash must be a later form. Furthermore, scholars since the time of H. Graetz[11] have quoted the famous statement in the Palestinian Talmud (henceforth cited as P.T.) Pesachim 6:1 (33a), concerning the reaction of the Benel Bateyra to Hillel—

אע״פ שהיה יושב ודורש להם כל היום, לא קיבלו ממנו.

("Even though he [Hillel] would exposite Midrash abundantly [to prove his point], they did not accept his conclusions")—as an indication that at the time of the Benei Bateyra in the first century B.C.E., Midrashic method was not yet an accepted means of settling a legal argument. It was too new at the time to yield final authority.

It appeared that a new consensus was emerging, according to which Midrash was not firmly established as an authoritative means of deriving halakhah until after the destruction of the Temple—which corresponds to the period of the Tannaim, whose *drashoth* (plural of *drashah*) are actually recorded in the Mishnah and the Midreshei Halakhah. (Midrash, as I am using the term, is the generic name for midrashic activity, while drashah is a particular instance of such activity.) Few, if any, explicit drashoth are recorded in the name of the sages who flourished before Hillel (ca. 30 B.C.E.–9 C.E.). This was so, it seemed to those of the new consensus, because before Hillel the sages did not engage in Halakhic Midrash. (That is, they did not deduce a new law from the text explicitly through exegetical means. I emphasize the matter of an explicit statement; for surely they derived laws from Scripture, the ultimate authority. However, when they transmitted these laws, they dropped the scriptural proof texts. Intra-biblical influence without express acknowledgment is quite common among biblical authors.)[12] The emerging consensus was that the Midrash was pioneered by Hillel, and that after Hillel almost a century passed before Midrash became firmly established.

Recently this consensus too has been questioned. By implication the question was asked: Can we be sure that the drashoth attributed to rabbis who lived long before the times of the editors of the Mishnah and the Midreshei Halakhah were actually stated by them and are not later additions by the editors, composed by the latter or by rabbis who lived close to their times? (Even where the halakhah and drashah are intertwined, the possibility still exists that the intertwining too was done by the editor.) For example, in Mishnah Shekalim, end of the sixth chapter, a drashah is attributed to Yehoiada the High Priest during the reign of Joash (835–798 B.C.E.):

זה מדרש דרש יהוידע כהן גדול

("Yehoiada the High Priest gave this exposition [Midrash]"). By all admissions Yehoiada did not formulate the drashah as it is stated.[13] It bears the stamp of a later harmonization between a text in Leviticus and a text in 2 Kings, describing Yehoiada's activity. (Note in particular the phrase in the Mishnah here:

נמצאו שני כתובים קיימים

["thus both Scriptures are fulfilled"], which may well be consistent with the style of the school of R. Akiba.)[14] Yet it is offered in all earnestness as a drashah by Yehoiada. A rabbinic editor of the second half of the second century C.E. would not (and did not) hesitate to add a drashah to a law, transmitting it in the name of a given sage, if he thought the drashah to be the basis of the law, without stating that the formulation of the drashah was his own. In this he was not alone; we know that many ancient editors altered and added to the texts at their disposal.[15] Whence the certainty that the credit for the pioneering Midrashic activity, or at least for strengthening it, is not due to the editors of Mishnah and Midreshei Halakhah or to their older colleagues, who modestly attributed Midrashic activity to earlier sages or merely attached their drashoth to earlier halakhoth?

A similar objection, but in reverse, can be raised against the view of Lauterbach and others, who deduce from the fact that Yose ben Yoezer testified (Eduyoth 8:4):

העיד ר׳ יוסי בן יועזר "...ודיקרב במיתא, מסתאב".

("and he that touches a corpse becomes unclean") without scriptural support that at the time of Yose ben Yoezer the Mishnaic form was already extant. The possibility exists that originally Yose ben Yoezer cited scriptural support and that the Midrashic form was then the accepted form, but that later on, when the Midrashic form was changed to Mishnaic form, the scriptural support was omitted.

This solipsistic attitude is a counterreaction to the overcredulousness of earlier scholars (and to their counterparts today) who considered historically authentic a statement by an Amora or even by a Gaon[16] concerning what took place centuries earlier, on the grounds that he must have had an early reliable tradition or else he would not have said what he said. Lauterbach is particularly guilty in this respect.[17] He felt triumphant after he had proved to his satisfaction that a statement (P.T. Moed Katan 3:7 [83b]) by the fourth century scholar Hezekiah indicates that at first laws were embedded in Midrash. However, he did not quote the right reading,[18] and his interpretation of the phrase *ve'od Torah* to mean "in connection with Torah" (with Midrash) is almost certainly wrong.[19] But all this is beside the point. Suppose it is true that Hezekiah made a statement[20] about an event that took place 500 years earlier—does that qualify as reliable history? Lauterbach treats similarly a statement by Rav in B.T. Temurah 15b. It is this statement of Rav's mentioning the name Yose ben Yoezer that gave Lauterbach the idea that the change to Mishnaic form took place in the time of Yose ben Yoezer. Again one wonders—even in the case of Rav, who transmitted much historical material—why this should be considered proof in the absence of corroborating contemporary evidence. (Thus Lauterbach's conclusion is unjustified regardless of the validity of his interpretation of Rav's phrase

היו למידין תורה כמשה רבינו

to mean "that they taught in the same manner in which Moses taught," namely, Midrashically. In fact, his interpretation is not correct.)[21]

The pendulum has now swung back. Extremism breeds extremism, often in the opposite direction. We have moved from relying on dubious statements by Amoraim concerning events that took place centuries earlier to denying the veracity of the drashoth attributed in the Mishnah and Midreshei Halakhah to Tannaim who lived a few generations before the editors.

I share this current skepticism, but have no wish to travel the whole length of the road back to credulity. I believe we can show that Midrash already existed in the second century before the common era. The evidence does not come from explicit or implicit statements by noncontemporary authorities but from contemporary realia, reflecting conditions that existed only during the second century B.C.E. or earlier, and from contemporary sectarian literature—with whose rediscovery we have, of late, been so lavishly blessed. What follows will be four examples, three similar ones of drashoth in the Mishnah amd Midreshei Halakhah that could not have been drafted after the second century B.C.E., and one where the second-century Temple Scroll actually quotes a drashah found in the Mishnah and Midreshei Halakhah.

II

I start with the examples from realia, even though I suspect the example from the Temple Scroll is more surprising. I do so for two reasons. First, because of the nature of this study, which traces the transmission of the oral law, we ought to start with examples from this kind of law, namely, Mishnah and Midreshei Halakhah. Second, it so happens that the examples from realia are found in the Mishnah (and there are parallel examples in Midreshei Halakhah), one in Tractate Bikkurim and one in Tractate Sanhedrin, and realia contain a greater degree of certainty than literary evidence.

Mishnah Bikkurim 1:8 reads:

נטמאו בעזרה, נופץ ואינו קורא.

If the Bikkurim [offering of the first fruits to the Temple] were defiled in the Temple *Court,* he scatters [the fruit (does not have to bring new fruit. While over the defiled fruit)] he does not recite the obligatory Bikkurim blessing.

The Mishnah Bikkurim continues:

ומניין שהוא חייב באחריותן עד שיביא להר הבית? שנאמר ראשית ביכורי אדמתך תביא בית ה׳ אלהיך-מלמד שהוא חייב באחריותן עד שיביא להר הבית.

Whence do we learn that a man is answerable for them until they are brought to the Temple *Mount?* Because it is written, "the first of the first-fruits of your land you shall bring into the House of the Lord your God" [Exod. 23:19] which teaches that a man is answerable for them until they are brought to the Temple *Mount.*

This continuation contains the biblical support for the defilement law, saying that after the man brought the fruit to the Temple *Court* he was not responsible for its care, as it is written (Exod. 23:19): "The first of the first fruits of the Land you shall bring into the House of the Lord, your God." The problem with this continuation is that the expression it uses is not *azarah,* "Temple *Court*" (as in the first Mishnah Bikkurim) but *har ha-bayit,* "Temple *Mount.*" In rabbinic literature,[22] Temple Mount and Temple Court are not the same place; Temple Mount refers to a *section* of the Temple complex, to the incline that led to the Courts and the Temple itself and not (as in the Bible; see Jer. 26:18; Isa. 2:2, 10:32; Mic. 3:1, 4:12) to the whole Temple complex. The Mishnah Bikkurim, however, uses these two terms almost interchangeably. There is no doubt that if the fruits were defiled, stolen, or lost on the Temple Mount as defined in rabbinic literature – a place bustling with all kinds of activity[23] – one had the responsibility to bring new fruits; that is, there is no doubt that the intent of the continuation of the Mishnah Bikkurim is that one is responsible for the fruits until one has brought them to the Israelite Court (*ezrat yisra'el*). There the priest takes them, crosses the Priestly Court (*ezrat kohanim*), and "puts them in front of the altar of the Lord, your God" (Deut. 26:4). This is also supported in the parallel source, the Mekhilta D'Rashbi (ed. Epstein and Melamed, p. 219) where we read:

> תביא בית ה׳ אלהיך, מלמד שהוא חייב בטיפול הבאתן עד שיביאם לבית הבחירה.

> "Bring them to the House of the Lord" comes to teach that he is responsible for their care until he brought them to the chosen house.

"Chosen house" is a synonym for the Temple itself, not for the Temple Mount.

If the intention of the continuation of the Mishnah Bikkurim is that one is responsible for the first fruits until they are brought to the Temple Court, why then does the continuation use the term "Temple Mount" and not – in accordance with its intention – the term "Temple Court," which would be consistent with the first Mishnah Bikkurim for which it provides the scriptural support? The Gaon of Vilna[24] did in fact emend the text of the continuation of Mishnah Bikkurim and omitted in the continuation the word "mount," leaving only "until he has brought them to the House," corresponding to the version in the Mekhilta D'Rashbi, which is "chosen house."

Clearly, during the time when the continuation of the Mishnah Bikkurim was composed, the Temple proper too was referred to (as in the Bible) as the Temple Mount. The author of the continuation lived at an early period when the term "Temple Mount" was appropriate as a reference to any place in the Temple complex. When was that period? It could not have been after the time of Herod (37–4 B.C.E.), for the Jews who lived in the period after Herod had beautified and enlarged the Temple area[25] would not have confused the Temple Mount with the Temple proper. This Mishnah Bikkurim, that is, the drashah in the continuation, must be pre-Herodian, and most likely even older. It dates back to a time when the biblical usage of the term "Temple Mount" was still in vogue as being synonymous with the Temple proper.

If Yadin's understanding of the word "city" in the Temple Scroll and his perception of the Temple Scroll sect's image of the Temple[26] are correct,[27] then that sect did not designate the Temple Mount as a separate entity. It does not mention it. Moreover, the Temple Scroll states (p. 46, line 9):

> ועשית חיל סביב למקדש רחב מאה באמה אשר יהיה מבדיל בין מקדש הקודש לעיר.
>
> Make a rampart around the Temple, a hundred cubits wide, which will separate the holy Temple and the city.

This description of the boundary of the Temple differs from the description in the Mishnah. Whereas in the Mishnah, in Midoth 2:3, the rampart separates the Women's Court and the Temple Mount, in the Temple Scroll the rampart separates the Temple from the city. In the second century (during the time of the composition of the Temple Scroll), the Temple Mount was not significant enough to merit separate notation.

A similar date can be assigned to the Mishnah in Chagigah 1:1:

> איזהו קטן? כל שאינו יכול לרכוב על כתפיו של אביו ולעלות מירושלים להר הבית. דברי בית שמאי. ובית הלל אומרים כל שאינו יכול לאחוז בידו של אביו ולעלות מירושלים להר הבית.
>
> Who is deemed a child? Any that cannot ride on his father's shoulders and go up from Jerusalem to the Temple Mount. So the school of Shammai, and the school of Hillel say: Any that cannot hold his father's hand and go up [on his feet] from Jerusalem to the Temple Mount.

Here, too, when the Mishnah says "Temple Mount" it means "Temple Court," the place where one is supposed to come and make an offering during the three pilgrimage holidays. By merely going up the Temple Mount, one has not fulfilled the command "to appear before the Lord" (Exod. 23:14; Deut. 16:16). One has to appear at the Court of the Priests, where the first stages of sacrifice take place.[28] The Mishnah, like the Bible, calls the Courts, the actual Temple facilities, "Temple Mount" because of their elevated position. The mount did not yet constitute a separate sacred place, and its nomenclature was employed broadly to include the actual Temple premises. The Temple Mount became a distinct sacred place only starting with the Herod's refurbishing and enlargement. The pre-Herodian date of this Mishnah accords well with the fact that both the Shammaites and the Hillelites, first-century scholars, quoted the identical phrase,

> לעלות מירושלים להר הבית

("to go up from Jerusalem to the Temple Mount"). This identicalness is a sign that the phrase that constitutes a part of the definition of who is deemed a child is older than the Houses of Hillel and Shammai. The ability to go from Jerusalem to the Temple Mount was an uncontested requirement at the time of the Shammaites and the Hillelites; they disagreed only as to whether riding on one's father's shoulders was considered "going up" or not. One may safely place the time of the composition of the definition at around the first century before the common era, pre-Herod, not much after the composition of the Temple Scroll.[29]

It is plausible, therefore, that the Mishnah in Bikkurim, which uses the expression "the house of the Lord, your God," as a proof text for the law that one has to bring the bikkurim to the Temple Mount, and which uses (as does the Bible) "the Temple Mount" as a synonym for the Temple proper, was composed no later than the second century B.C.E.

III

The second example from realia for the antiquity of the simple Midrash is from the first Mishnah in the sixth chapter of Sanhedrin:

> בית הסקילה היה חוץ לבית דין שנאמר הוצא את המקלל (אל מחוץ למחנה).

> The place of stoning was outside the Court, as it is written [Lev. 24:14], Bring forth him that cursed outside the Camp.

Both Talmuds raise the problem of the discrepancy between "outside the court" (stated in the law) and "outside the camp" (stated in the supporting scriptural text). Outside the court is not necessarily also outside the camp (that is, outside the city limits). The stoning place could conceivably be in the middle of the camp (within city limits) while at the same time being outside the court. The Talmud interprets "outside the court" as meaning far away from the court, stretching all the way to the end of the camp. This interpretation seems quite forced. It is also unnecessary to express such a simple idea as "outside the camp" in such a roundabout way. The most plausible solution is that the author of the drashah in the Mishnah lived at a time when the court was situated at the gate, at the edge of town, as in biblical times. Outside the court was thus also outside the camp (outside the city), in one direction. When the author of the drashah said "outside the court," he was referring to that direction which makes outside the court automatically outside the camp or outside the city; hence the scriptural support "outside the camp."

Later, however, the location of the court changed. We read that the court was situated at the highest point in town. Commenting on Deut. 25:7: "And if the man like not to take his brother's wife, then his brother's wife shall go up to the gate unto the elders," the Sifrei Deut., *piska* [paragraph] 289 (p. 308), basing itself on the words "go up" and interchanging "court" for "gate," says

מצוה בבית דין שיהא בגבוה שבעיר.

> It is proper for the court to be situated at the highest point in town.

Consequently, the drashah of the Mishnah also changed. The Sifrei Numbers, piska 114 (p. 123), comments on a similar scriptural text, that of Num. 15:36, saying:

מלמד שכל חייבי מיתות, נהרגין חוץ לבית דין.

> It comes to teach that all people who are to be executed are killed outside the court.

The purport of this drashah, unlike that of the Mishnah, is not so much to tell us where the place of execution is situated as it is to prohibit execution in the court chambers. The purpose of the drashah is probably to distinguish typical execution from the case of the woman who was not a virgin at marriage, who is stoned "at the doorway of her father's house" (Deut. 22:21). Other culprits condemned to stoning are executed in the open, outside the court. A similar change, though less noticeable, on the identical scriptural text is to be found in the Sifra, Emor, chap. 19:1 (104c):

מלמד שבית דין מבפנים ובית הסקילה מבחוץ.

> It comes to teach that the court is situated inside [the camp] and the place of stoning outside [the camp].

The purport here again is to state that the court and the place of execution do not share the same area. This drashah does not solely prescribe geographically the place of execution, but also prescribes the location of the court. "Outside the court," during the time when these two drashoth —that of the Sifra and that of the Sifrei—were composed, was not identical to "outside the camp"; it would have been in the middle of the camp. The drashah, therefore, took on the negative meaning of not being inside the court.

While the Midreshei Halakhah changed the purport of the original drashah still preserved in the Mishnah, the *targumim* (Aramaic translations of the Bible)[30] sometimes added the words *beit dina* to the word *sha'ar* ("gate") when it appears in the Bible in the sense of court, implying "the gate of the court." They could reconcile gate with court only by adding the words "the gate of the court." In their time court and gate held no close association.[31]

Unfortunately, we do not know when the court changed from the location at the gate to the location at the highest point of town, when the judges ceased to sit at the gate and moved to the town. The best guess is that this move occurred in the wake of the significant increase in the Jewish population under Hashmonean rule, with the concomitant development of communal institutions both in the cities and in the villages. Sitting at the gate was an oriental custom, and when Palestine was hellenized this old custom must have slowly fallen by the wayside. Intense hellenization occurred in Palestine for the first time during the reign of the Ptolemies, in the third century B.C.E. The process of moving the court from the gate to the town would not, however, have been immediate; such moves take a long time. Most likely it was later, during the expansion of the Hashmonean state, when this move finally took place.[32] It is reasonable, therefore, to assume that the move from gate to town took place sometime between the mid-second century and mid-first century B.C.E. Accordingly, the date of the drashah in the Mishnah Sanhedrin—which knows only of the courts sitting at the gate—must perforce be earlier than the first century B.C.E.

IV

Mention should also be made of a third example from the Mishnah in support of the antiquity of the Midrashic form. This example is not based on realia but on literary analysis, which constitutes weaker evidence. Its inclusion here is prompted by the paradox that this very same Mishnah was used by some scholars to prove almost the opposite, that the change from Midrashic to Mishnaic form took place as early as the time of Yose ben Yoezer (ca. 190 B.C.E.). At least as a way of refuting them, this example ought to be included here.

In the Mishnah in Eduyoth 8:4, it is stated:

העיד ר׳ יוסי בן יועזר ... ודיקרב במיתא, מסתאב, וקרו ליה יוסי שריא.

Yose ben Yoezer testified . . . that he that touches a corpse becomes unclean. And they called him Yose the permitter.

This testimony of Yose ben Yoezer is obviously truncated. As the B.T. Abodah Zarah 37b already pointed out, the testimony in its present state is merely an Aramaic rendition of Num. 19:16: "And whosoever in the open field touches one that is slain with a sword, or one that dies of himself . . . shall be unclean seven days." The testimony of Yose ben Yoezer must have contained more than an Aramaic rendition of a biblical verse. Furthermore, for repeating a biblical verse in Aramaic his colleagues would not have called him disapprovingly "Yose the Permitter." Something was obviously omitted. The general scholarly consensus[33] follows the suggestion of the Babylonian Talmud (ad loc.)—with some variation—that the testimony ended with a missing negative statement to the effect that whosoever touches a corpse is unclean but not he who touches a man who touched a corpse, or he who touches an object that came in contact with a corpse. The scholars cite a similar statement in the Sifra, Vayikra, Chova 12:1 (22d), in the name of the "early elders," whom Lauterbach[34] and J. N. Epstein[35] identify as sofrim who flourished before the time of Yose ben Yoezer. That statement, however, differs in that the early elders advanced exegetical support (from Lev. 5:2–3) for their contention (as attested by the Sifra), while Yose ben Yoezer did not (as attested by the Mishnah). Lauterbach and Epstein see in this difference an indication that the change from Midrashic to Mishnaic form took place during the time of Yose ben Yoezer; that during the time of the early elders, laws were still transmitted with exegetical proofs, Midrashically, whereas later, during the time of Yose ben Yoezer (or soon thereafter), they were transmitted without exegetical proof, Mishnaically.

I do not accept either the assumptions of Lauterbach and Epstein or their conclusion. For one thing, I do not identify the early elders with the sofrim because I do not think the early elders were that early, predating the second century B.C.E.[36] I also do not share their view of the sofrim as being limited to the pre–Yose ben Yoezer period; the term may very well refer to any group of people, in any period, who were engaged in the teaching and spreading of Torah. Second, I do not believe that one can obtain the original formulation of the sages solely from quotations in the Mishnah and Midreshei Halakhah, which were subject to change. In our example from the Sifra, it is possible (though not likely) that originally the early elders stated the law without the exegetical increment and that it was added later. The drashah, however, is so intertwined that it is difficult to separate the law from the exegesis. The other possibility is that originally Yose ben Yoezer (and perhaps others too) "testified" the law in Midrashic form, and then when Midrashic form changed to Mishnaic form, at a later period, the exegesis was omitted from his testimony. Third, I am not certain that the generally accepted interpretation of the Mishnah in Eduyoth is correct. That interpretation should add, besides the missing negative statement, the words "for seven days" (or similar qualifying words)[37] to the available statement. For again, as the Babylonian Talmud points out, Numbers 19:22 explicitly says: "Whosoever the unclean person touches, shall be unclean." Therefore, one cannot state categorically: "He who touches a man who touches a corpse (or he who touches an object that came in contact with a corpse) is not unclean" without specifying the condition or duration of the uncleanliness. While the addition of the missing negative statement is necessitated by the context, these additional words in the available statement are not dictated by the initial statement.

I am inclined to interpret the Mishnah in such a way that the missing negative statement would not exclude "he who touches a man who touched a corpse" (or he who touches an object that came into contact with a corpse), but rather one who had no contact whatsoever, even remotely, with a corpse, one who afterwards remains totally clean. The Mishnah means to exclude he who becomes a proselyte; he is clean and does not need "to be sprinkled on the third and seventh days following before he becomes clean." This is the view of the Shammaites. The Hillelites, as recorded in Mishnah Pesahim 8:8, are of the following opinion:

הפורש מן הערלה כפורש מן הקבר.

> He that separates himself from his uncircumcision is as one that separates himself from a grave.

Yose ben Yoezer agreed with the Shammaites that only he who touches a corpse is unclean (but not a proselyte).[38]

An additional advantage of this interpretation is that it makes it somewhat easier to understand why the negative statement (but not a proselyte), which is the essential feature of the testimony, was subsequently omitted. During the ascendancy of the Hillelites,[39] it became intolerable to them that the testimony of Yose ben Yoezer contradicted their opinion. They omitted the contradiction but could not, apparently, omit the whole section dealing with the touching of a corpse since that was already incorporated by tradition. It was known that the testimony of Yose ben Yoezer was triadic,[40] consisting of three parts. The Hillelites retained the least controversial section of the third part, the citation of the biblical verse.[41]

All this is highly conjectural. To complete what is missing and to explain the motive behind the omission always involves a guessing game. Nevertheless, whatever the content of the missing negative statement was, it seems to me that originally the positive statement (whosoever touches a corpse is unclean) was a part of a full-fledged drashah consisting of law and proof text. For only thus can one explain why Yose ben

Yoezer repeated (in Aramaic) a biblical verse almost verbatim. His addition is the missing negative statement: that whosoever touches a man that touched a corpse (or he who touches an object that came into contact with a corpse) is not unclean or that the proselyte is not unclean. He could have given that testimony without repeating the biblical verse (and this, incidentally, would also have been more in line with the other testimonies in Mishnah Eduyoth). However, he repeated the biblical verse for emphasis, as is customary in drashoth. Originally Yose ben Yoezer composed (or repeated) a drashah more or less as follows: Whosoever touches a man that touched a corpse (or he who touches an object that came into contact with a corpse) is not unclean for seven days as it is written Whosoever . . . touches one that is slain . . . shall be unclean seven days—(only) he who touches a corpse is unclean but not he who touches a man that touched a corpse (or he who touches an object that came into contact with a corpse) (or according to our interpretation, Yose ben Yoezer testified: one who becomes a proselyte is not unclean as it is written . . . only he who touches a corpse is unclean but not he who becomes a proselyte). The repetition of the biblical verse emphasizes that the biblical formulation is exclusive, that it precludes anything that is not identical with it. During the time of Yose ben Yoezer, the principal mode of transmitting laws was the Midrashic form. This testimony too was originally dressed in the Midrashic garb. The other two testimonies of Yose ben Yoezer were either thus originally transmitted or, because of their peculiar nature, were not biblically related. Later, when for whatever reason it was decided to omit the essential feature of Yose ben Yoezer's third testimony (the negative statement) but to retain a semblance thereof (which may have been decided prior to the decision to change from Midrashic to Mishnaic form), all that was left was the repetition of the biblical verse. Even in this truncated form one recognizes its Midrashic quality.

If one can adduce anything, it is that, contrary to Lauterbach and Epstein, the Midrashic form was still the dominant mode of transmission during the time of Yose ben Yoezer. The change to Mishnaic form came centuries later.

V

We come now to the fourth example of simple Midrash that can be dated as early as the second century B.C.E. This example comes from the Temple Scroll.

In the Temple Scroll discovered, edited, and annotated by Yigal Yadin, we read (p. 66, lines 8–9 of the text) the following:

כי יפתה איש נערה בתולה אשר לוא אורשה והיא רויה לו מן החוק
ושכב עמה ונמצא ונתן האיש השוכב עמה לאבי הנערה חמשים כסף.
ולוא תהיה לאשה תחת אשר ענה. לוא יוכל לשלחה כול ימיו.

If a person seduces a maiden, a virgin who had not been[42] betrothed and *she is eligible to* [*marry*] *him according to the law,* and he lies with her and is caught, let the man who lies with her give to the father of the maiden fifty pieces of silver. And she becomes his wife because he has tortured her. He cannot ever send her away.

There are many problems with this text, all duly noted by Yadin. The principal problem[43] is that the author combines two distinct categories, that of "rape" and that of "enticement," which in the Torah are written separately (the case of enticement in Exod. 22:15 and the case of rape in Deut. 22:28–29) and contain different provisions. This problem has been somewhat exaggerated, since the early commentators, including Philo (*Sp. Leg.* III, 65–70), Josephus (*Ant.* IV, 8, 23), and some Tannaitic sources,[44] also approximated the two, a fact that apparently escaped modern scholars dealing with the subject.[45] The degree of approximation, however, differs. Philo and Josephus mention no distinction between the two, while the rabbis could not ignore the fact that the provision "he may never send her away" is written only in connection with rape.

But this problem is not my concern here. I am concerned with the author's addition to the biblical text of the phrase "and she is eligible to [marry] him." Yadin[46] expresses amazement at the similarity between this phrase and that of the Mishnah Ketuboth 3:5 (found also in the parallels in Mekhilta and in Sifrei Deuteronomy on the respective scriptural verses):

ולו תהיה לאשה — אשה הראויה לו

And she will become his wife, in [the case of] a woman who is eligible to [marry] him.

If we adopt the reading of the Kaufmann manuscript[47] of the Mishnah and some others, the similarity is even closer. The reading there is

ולו תהיה לאשה — שהיא ראויה לו

which is a negligible variant, a difference in only one letter.

What accounts for the almost identical language of the Mishnah and Midreshei Halakhah and the Temple Scroll? Yadin (pp. 400–401) posits the familiar three possibilities: (1) that the Temple Scroll took this law from proto-Mishnah or Midreshei Halakhah; (2) that the Mishnah and Midreshei Halakhah took this law from the Temple Scroll; (3) that both took the law from what he calls "an early written Halakhic tradition." He concludes, however, that further investigation is necessary.

It seems to me that we can say with a high degree of certainty that the phrase "and she is eligible to [marry] him" comes to the Temple Scroll from sources antecedent to the Mishnah and Midreshei Halakhah, and not the reverse. The word "eligible" in the sense in which it is used here, namely, potentially worthy or ready, is found only in rabbinic literature (where it is very common)[48] and nowhere else. To be sure, the word is found also in Esther 2:9 (a late book):

ואת שבע הנערות הראיות לתת לה

("And the seven maids chosen to be given her"). But there it is used not in the sense of eligibility but rather as the Septuagint translates it: *apodedeigmena,* "destined," "obligatory." Its use in the sense of eligibility is unique to rabbinic literature in the passive participal form. (The usage of the Septuagint may have served as a transition between the standard usage of the root *ra'ah* and the usage made in rabbinic literature of the passive participle.)[49] The Temple Scroll borrowed this usage from proto-rabbinic sources. Perhaps the emphasis in the Temple Scroll that she is eligible to marry him "according to the Law" reflects the position that only religious ineligibility precludes marriage, not personal incompatibility, much like the Mishnah: "Even if she was lame, even if she was blind, even if she was afflicted with boils," he must marry her.

Moreover, it can be demonstrated that the whole phrase, and not only this term, was borrowed from the drashah of the Mishnah and Midreshei Halakhah. But first let us consider what is meant by the expression "she is eligible to marry him according to the law." Yadin interprets the phrase to mean that a "man cannot marry a girl if she is not eligible to marry him according to the laws of the Torah as understood by the sect." I take this to imply that, according to Yadin, this phrase means that if, for example, a man seduces his sister, the law "that she should become his wife," does not apply. Otherwise, Amnon's fate after he seduced his sister Tamar (2 Sam. 13) would have been different and more favorable to him; indeed, he would have accomplished his goal.

But is there a need to tell us that? Yadin himself calls this law a self-evident one. The law must have been very important to the sectarians; otherwise they would not have crossed sectarian lines as the aforesaid borrowing indicates. That one is not allowed to marry his sister is a commonplace, and the sectarians were even stricter in matters of incest than the rabbis. Is it conceivable that someone would assume that a brother who has seduced his sister has to marry her—so that it was necessary to add the phrase "according to the law" to disabuse him of this assumption? No one would make such a mistake.[50]

The purport of this phrase is clearly something else. Again, we have to turn to the Mishnah and Midreshei Halakhah for guidance. In the preface to the drashah, the Mishnah (and with minor differences the Midreshei Halakhah also) says:

נמצא בה דבר ערוה או שאינה ראויה לבוא בישראל, אינו רשאי לקיימה שנאמר ולו תהיה לאשה — שהיא ראויה לו.

> If she was found unchaste or was not fit to be taken in marriage by an Israelite he may not continue [his union] with her, for it is written, And she shall be to him for a wife [Deut. 22:29]—a wife that is fit for him.

The first part, "if she was found unchaste," refers to postnuptial events and does not concern us here. The second part,"or was not fit to be taken in marriage by an Israelite," however, is the key to the understanding of the whole phrase. It explains the necessity for the drashah to teach us that if the seduced woman was not worthy to enter the community of Israel, that is, a woman of illegitimate birth or an Egyptian woman, the seducer could not marry her. A consanguineous relationship is equal and mutual: a brother cannot marry a sister for the identical reason, no more and no less, that a sister cannot marry a brother. Seducing her does not alter their blood relationship, and there is no need to state that specifically. But if the barrier to the marriage is the woman's unworthy social status, that she is "unworthy of entering the community of Israel," one might indeed assume—and, I would add, with some justification—that by seducing her a man has forfeited his high social status, becoming equal to her and thus subject to the obligation to marry her. Against such an assumption, the drashah deduces from the verse "and she becomes his wife" that only if "she was eligible to [marry] him" prior to the incident is he obliged to marry her now. The incident did not elevate her social status nor reduce his; their social status remains the same, and any ban against their marriage remains, therefore, in force.

The Temple Scroll here is actually quoting the drashah of the Mishnah and Midreshei Halakhah. If it were not quoting the drashah, the word *lo,* "to [marry] him," would not have been used. The Temple Scroll did not have to say this for the sake of clarity; on the contrary, it confounds matters by raising another issue, that of consanguineous relationship. The expression is there because it is a part of the drashah that the Temple

Scroll is quoting. More accurately, it is there because the *verse* quoted by the drashah contains this expression.[51]

Since the Temple Scroll dates from the latter part of the second century,[52] one must conclude that proto-rabbinic drashoth existed as early as the second century B.C.E.

VI

The word "simple" is crucial to this discussion of Midrash, for only the simple Midrash—the one that springs forth easily from the text, as against the "complex," heavy one that requires the assistance of hermeneutic principles—is old, before the time of Hillel. It is sometimes difficult to draw the line between simple and complex Midrash. Nevertheless, at their extremities the distinction is quite clear. When nothing beyond the text before us is necessary to obtain the drashah, the result is a simple Midrash; when the drashah has to resort to a specific hermeneutic principle, or to additional texts from elsewhere, the result is a complex Midrash.[53] The drashoth quoted in this chapter belong to the category of simple Midrash. The ones that Hillel advanced—before the Benei Beteyra (*gezeirah shavah, kal v'chomer,* and so on)—belong to the category of complex Midrash. Most drashoth in the Mishnah are simple ones, whereas most of those in the Midreshei Halakhah are complex. Simple Midrash probably came into existence with the canonization of the Torah, and perhaps even before. Simple Midrash may already have been referred to in Ezra 7:10, in the combination of *darash* with *torah* which carries a different connotation (closer to that of the rabbis) than when not combined with the word *torah.*[54] The Benei Beteyra did not object to simple Midrash but only to complex Midrash, mainly because the existence of the latter was relatively new to them and carried little authority.[55]

I should add that there are two kinds of Midrash. One begins with a verse of Scripture and proceeds—by way of the formula "it comes to teach" or "it declares"—to the law derived from the Scripture. The other—which I shall call Mishnaic Midrash—begins with a law and proceeds to the verse that supports it, typically introducing the Scripture with the formula "as it says." In the Mishnah there are hardly any drashoth with the formula "it comes to teach" and none with "it declares," whereas in the Midreshei Halakhah such drashoth appear in large numbers.[56]

My thesis, that the simple Midrash already existed in the second century B.C.E. (in the sense that the law was transmitted with, and not only originated in, the appropriate Scripture), refers to both types of Midrash. This claim is not made on the basis of the first two examples quoted above. In the example from the Temple Scroll, we have no way of knowing from what Midrashic types the phrase "and she is eligible to [marry] him" was quoted, since this phrase is found in both types. The case is similar regarding the drashah on place of execution. Although this drashah is quoted in Midreshei Halakhah in the later version, so that it would appear that the earlier version was of the Mishnaic Midrash type, it is still possible that originally the Midreshei Halakhah too had the drashah in the same way as it is found in the Mishnah, only to have changed later. I make my claim, rather, on the basis of the third example, the one from Mishnah Bikkurim. Further support can be derived from the Damascus Scroll, which employs the formula אשר אמר (*asher amar*)[57] followed by a scriptural verse both before and after it states the law (roughly corresponding to our two types).

The drashah of the Mishnah in Bikkurim has both types; that is, it uses both the formula "as it says" before a scriptural verse and "it comes to teach" after a verse. As far as I can ascertain, it is the only instance in Midrashic literature where a drashah employs both types simultaneously. If we accept the thesis—which I think we must—that the drashah of this Mishnah dates back to not later than the second century, we have also to accept the antiquity of both types. In a later period no one would have combined that law with its proof text in either type.

VII

For the sake of completeness, I should add briefly that this example from the Temple Scroll is a unique one. I am aware of no other example from any other sectarian text that contains a proto-rabbinic drashah. Yadin, however, pairs this example with one that appears in the Temple Scroll (p. 50, lines 10–19):

> ואשה כי תהיה מלאה וימות ילדה במעיה, כול הימים אשר הוא בתוכה מת תטמא כקבר.

> A woman if she becomes pregnant and the child dies in her womb, all the days that the dead child is in her womb, she will defile as a tomb.

Yadin (vol. 1, pp. 400–401) sees in both of these examples from the Temple Scroll an equal confirmation of the existence of a very early (crystallized) halakhah, to which later authors of early halakhah were resorting—both to its content and to its legal halakhic language.

I must confess I see nothing unusual in this second example. The views expressed there are each as expected: the rabbis in the Mishnah and Midreshei Halakhah exclude from defilement a woman whose child died in her womb, while the sectarians of the Temple Scroll include her. It is not to be expected that the sectarians would come up with such a rabbinic notion as "an encased defiling object does not defile." The rabbis based this notion on the biblical wording in Num. 19:16. We hear of no contrary rabbinic view, not even a possibility to that effect. The rabbis' exclusion is stated categorically. The only rabbinic source that may mislead is the Sifrei Zutta (ed. C. S. Horovitz, Leipzig 1977), p. 312):

יכול כל הימים שהחכמה טמא אף האשה תהא טמאה — אמרת הוא יתחטא פרט לזה.

> You may think that the mother is unclean for the same number of days that the midwife is unclean. [Do not think so.] The Torah says: He will have to cleanse himself—[only he, the cases enumerated in the Torah] not she [not in her case].

The possibility that the Sifrei Zutta raises here is unlike that of the Temple Scroll; it does not raise the possibility that a woman who carried a dead child in her womb is unclean for seven days. Only when—as Horovitz points out (p. 312)—the midwife touched the dead child and became unclean for seven days during which she touched the mother, might one have thought that the mother too is unclean for seven days. At any rate, Yadin should have alluded to the Sifrei Zutta.

According to R. Akiba, the words "in the open fields" (Num. 19:16) are not the source for exclusion from defilement of a woman whose child died in the womb (which is the view of R. Ishmael). These words came to include a stone that seals a tomb or a buttressing stone as causes of defilement. One should not deduce from this that R. Akiba, contrary to R. Ishmael, holds that a woman whose child died in her womb is unclean for seven days. Halakhically, in the matter of the mother's cleanliness, there is no difference between R. Ishmael and R. Akiba. Both are of the opinion that she is not unclean. The difference between them is in the biblical source for that exclusion: according to R. Ishmael, the biblical source is the phrase "in the open fields," while according to R. Akiba it is the phrase "slain with a sword." This is attested to by the Sifrei Zutta. First it says:

אשר יגע — לרבות הגולל אשר יגע — לרבות הדופק.

> "Whosoever touches" includes the stone that seals a tomb; "whosoever touches" includes the buttressing stone.

This is the view of R. Akiba. Then it continues:

בחלל חרב, בחלל שדרכו ליהרג־בחרב, פרט לאשה שמת עוברה בתוך מעיה.

"Slain with a sword" implies the corpse [of one] who might ordinarily be slain with a sword, to the exclusion of a woman whose child died in her womb.

It is clear, then, that R. Akiba also subscribes to the view of R. Ishmael that the woman is not unclean for seven days. The differences between them are only exegetical.

I do not know on what basis Yadin says (vol. 1, p. 336): "The likeness in language on the one hand and the contrast between the laws on the other, attests to a palpable controversy, and there is no doubt that the Tannaites knew of laws such as these in the Scroll." I recognize no sign of polemic here on either side, and I do not see any evidence to support the contention that the rabbis knew laws like those of the Temple Scroll. Nor do I perceive any particular linguistic similarity other than what is necessary to describe the case. Since the case is quite common and observable, its description inevitably contains similar expressions. In short, nothing relevant to our subject, the interconnection between the Temple Scroll and rabbinic literature, is evidenced in this second example.[58]

Chapter 3

The Mishnaic Period

I HAVE BEEN ARGUING for the antiquity of the simple halakhic Midrash, in contrast to the comparatively late complex Midrash. What, then, about the Mishnaic form, the form that transmits pure law without scriptural reference? Is it also early, contemporary with Midrashic form, or is it late, as previous scholars have assumed, postdating the Midrashic form?

The evidence by way of analogy to the Damascus Scroll would argue in favor of making both forms early. Both forms are found in the Damascus Scroll and in some other sectarian books, particularly the Rule Scrolls.[1] Moreover, in other cultures early law was terse, staccato, akin to the Mishnaic form. Why assume that the Jews, that is, the Pharisaic Jews, were different in this respect? If they were different from other peoples and from the sectarians, traces of the reason for their difference ought to have survived.

Indeed such traces did survive. In an oft-quoted but misunderstood section of the Scolion to the Fast Scroll (ed. H. Lichtenstein, p. 75),[2] the author describes the festival of the fourth of Tammuz, when the Book of Decrees of the Sadducees was removed, as follows:

> מפני שהיה כתוב ומונח לצדוקים ספר גזרות, (אלו שהן נסקלין), אלו שהן נשרפין, אלו שהן נהרגין, אלו שהן נחנקין ומי שהוא אומר להם מניין שזה חייב סקילה וזה חייב שריפה וזה חייב הרגה וזה חייב חניקה, אין יודעין להביא ראיה מן התורה אלא שכתוב ומונח להן ספר גזירות.

Because the Sadducees had in their possession a Book of Decrees written and deposited (which contained a list of the crimes whose perpetrators were either to be) stoned, burnt, beheaded, or strangled. And when someone asked them [the Sadducees] from where do you know that such a person is liable to be burnt, this person liable to be beheaded, and this person liable to be strangled—they did not know the source in the Torah, only that they possessed a book of decrees, written and deposited.

I am quoting from a manuscript designated by the editor as Ms. P. De-Rossi 117, which he considers the best. Some manuscripts read

אמרו להם חכמים והלא כתוב על פי התורה אשר יורוך וגו׳

("The Sages told them: it is written [Deut. 17:11] according to the law which they shall teach you") instead of the phrase

אלא שכתוב ומונח להם ספר גזירות

("Only that they possessed a book of decrees, written and deposited"). Either way, the complaint of the Pharisees against the Book of Decrees (executions) of the Sadducees was not as we might have expected—that they were killing innocent people, people who according to Pharisaic law were not guilty of a capital crime, or at least that they were meting out the wrong punishments. Instead, they complained that the Sadducees did not know the sources in the Torah for their decrees.[3] The Pharisees did not feel that the executions were wrong; but in their view even justified executions could not be carried out unless their basis in the Torah was cited.[4] It was not enough that the decrees once had a source in the Torah, presumably when they were promulgated, that was subsequently forgotten. The Pharisees—at least according to the author of the Scolion—interpreted the verse in Deut. 17:11, "according to the law which they shall teach you," literally: a person cannot be convicted of a capital crime until a source, a rubric, in the Torah is cited that justifies the conviction. The Sadducees could not produce citations for their decrees about capital offences; they merely clung to tradition. They received the tradition from their forefathers, who presumably knew the Torah citations. "Only that they possessed [through inheritance?] a book of decrees." But this was not enough for the Pharisees. Each law, particularly those related to capital offences, had to be connected with its Torah source. This is why law among the Jews, in contrast to other peoples, was transmitted Midrashically, in order to preserve its visible link with the Torah, the source of the law.[5]

To the passage quoted above, the Scolion (not found in Ms. P.) adds:

מלמד שאין כותבין הלכות בספר.

("It [the story of this festival] comes to teach that one does not write fixed laws in a book"). Presumably the purport of this addition is to explain the objection of the Pharisees to the Book of Decrees of the Sadducees. They did not object to the contents, but merely to having them written down. Clearly the addition is a late gloss stemming from a time when the Mishnah, consisting of fixed laws without biblical references, was already well established and when the interdiction against writing down was still in effect.[6] It necessarily postdates what was said in the passage quoted earlier, that the objection was based on the Sadducees' inability to provide scriptural support for the decrees and not on the writing of such decrees. In the time of the glossator, transmitting laws without biblical reference was a well-established norm, and thus he felt compelled to change the objection from lack of biblical references to the mere act of putting laws down in writing.[7]

Indirectly this gloss leads us to compare the change from Midrashic to Mishnaic form to the change from oral to written transmission, echoes of which are still heard in the Talmud. Both changes needed special dispensations. The dispensation for the change from the oral to the written was based on the realization[8] that oral literature could not survive, and one may surmise that a similar dispensation was at the basis of the change from Midrashic to Mishnaic form. To facilitate memory, the rabbis reduced the laws to their bare statement without noting their source in the Bible; it was too burdensome to remember both the laws and their appropriate scriptural sources. For the sake of a higher purpose, one is allowed to forgo a minor interdiction[9] such as the one against writing down laws or that against transmitting them without biblical references.

It seems clear that the change from Midrashic to Mishnaic form did not take place before the destruction of the Temple in 70 C.E. The author of the Scolion of the Fast Scroll (and certainly the glossator) did not live before the destruction of the Temple. Most of the Scolion material dates from a much later period, probably from the second century and beyond.[10] One should not, of course, assume a single author for the entire Scolion; it is a composite document, written by many authors from different periods. Our passage may well be one of the oldest. But even the oldest part cannot predate the destruction of the Temple, that is, the time of the composition of the Fast Scroll itself. When an author of even a single commentary on the scroll considers transmitting fixed laws without biblical reference a Sadducean trait, this is an indication that the change to the Mishnaic form did not take place until after the destruction of the Temple.

I should add that the use of the Scolion as evidence for the lateness of the Mishnah does not depend on the accuracy of the Scolion's interpretation of the event recorded in the Fast Scroll. Even if the interpretation were completely imaginary, it would still indicate that the author of the Scolion did not yet have Mishnah. A Jew who lived after the formation of the Mishnah would not have considered it a sin to transmit fixed laws without scriptural support; that was exactly what the rabbis of his time were doing. He would certainly not have viewed it as a Sadducean trait (whether it actually was or not). Thus the author of the Scolion must have been living at a time when the Midrashic form was still the accepted mode of transmission while the Mishnaic form was considered deviational, and he projected that deviation back in time onto the Sadducees. Interestingly enough, R. Leszynsky argued just the opposite. He took for granted that the Mishnah is early and claimed that the author of the Scolion confused the position of the sects by mistakenly attributing a Book of Decrees to the Sadducees, whereas, Leszynsky continued, the Sadducees followed the written law and had no additional book while, as attested by the Mishnah Sanhedrin, the Pharisees had such books.[11] Apparently, mistaken projections onto the past are not an exclusive trait of scholars of any particular period.

Another proof that the Mishnaic form did not predate the destruction of the Temple is a passage in Josephus, *Antiquities* IV, 196–197. In this instance we can be more specific and say that the Mishnaic form does not predate the early nineties, since Josephus completed the *Antiquities* (in Rome) in 93–94.[12] Josephus begins his summary of the laws of the Pentateuch with an apology for having changed the biblical order and arranged the laws according to subject (*kata genos*). "I have thought it necessary," Josephus states, "to make this preliminary observation, lest perchance any of my countrymen who read this work should reproach me at all for having gone astray." During the time of the Mishnah, no Jew would have reproached another for having arranged the laws according to subject, whether their format was divorced from the Bible, like the Mishnah, or made reference to the Bible, like a Midrash. Arrangement according to subject would have then been almost the norm. If Josephus was apprehensive about it, he must have lived at a time when Jews[13] still considered anyone who deviated from the biblical order and, as in the Mishnah, arranged the laws according to subject as having gone astray. Josephus thus predated the Mishnaic method.

Josephus counteracts the expected criticism by claiming that the biblical order is not sacrosanct, that it was not intended to serve as a model for posterity. The writings of Moses, he says, "were left behind in a scattered state just as he received them from God." Those who did not learn the laws from God, however, are free to arrange them in whatever form they deem convenient or efficient. Josephus' claim was eventually shared by the rabbis, and the people became accustomed to new arrangements of the laws of the Bible. But at the time when Josephus was writing this passage of the *Antiquities* in the early nineties, the people were not yet accustomed to new arrangements, and he felt constrained to explain himself.

The rabbis of the Mishnah—like Josephus—not only did not follow the biblical sequence of subjects, they also occasionally changed the order within a given subject. The sequence of the drinking ordeal of the Sotah (the suspected adultress), for example, is different in the Mishnah from the account in the Bible (see M. Sotah, chapter 2; compare Numbers, 5). The rabbis apparently did not consider biblical consecution as binding.[14] Josephus, however, lived at a time when the Midrashic form was the exclusive mode of Jewish learning; Mishnaic form was either unknown or unacceptable. The laws were arranged scripturally, following more or less the contours of the biblical text. No dispensation was as yet granted to change the biblical order for the sake of facilitating memorization, and certainly not for the reason for which Josephus wanted to change it, namely, literary and aesthetic considerations. It is no wonder he was apprehensive that his countrymen would call him a heretic.

I have omitted the possibility that Josephus' apprehension stemmed from the fear of being accused of not drawing the proper distinction between Written Law and Oral Law. New arrangements when presented as Oral Law, separate and in juxtaposition with laws that are not found in the Bible, like the Mishnah, are permitted and even encouraged; whereas new arangements—such as those Josephus employed—that resemble the biblical order and yet have different subject divisions (that is, they are similar but not the same) might be censured because they may confuse people into thinking that they are studying the Bible itself. I do not believe this distinction is valid, however; people are not that easily confused. Moreover, Josephus could have avoided that confusion by simply stating at the outset that what follows is not the Written Law but a paraphrase thereof. And if he were worried about confusion, he would not have claimed the right to alter the order handed down by Moses. Such a claim would only have increased the people's confusion and disapprobation of him.

I suggest that the root of Josephus' concern was that the people, conservative in nature, might consider any change, even in arrangement, as heretical. He therefore sought to convince his fellow Jews—as the rabbis of the Mishnah did so successfully years later—that the biblical order is not prescriptive, but rather represents a particular, one-time occurrence permitting each generation to arrange the Laws according to its needs and taste.

II

It is not clear how soon after Josephus wrote the *Antiquities* (ca. 93–94 C.E.) that the change to the Mishnaic form took place. He may have been out of touch with the Jewish community in Palestine for some time, and the change may have occurred during that period. I am inclined to believe, however, that the change to the Mishnaic method took place in Yabneh, during the reign of R. Gamaliel the Second, around the end of the first century C.E.

I base my claim principally on the statement in the B.T. Berakhoth 28a[15] that "[Mishnah] Eduyoth was taught [i.e., composed] [in Yabneh] on that day [when R. Gamaliel was temporarily removed from his Patriarchate]":

תנא, עדיות בו ביום נשנית.

I believe this statement is historically reliable because it dates back to Tannaitic times. The prefatory words used here indicate that what follows is of Tannaitic origin; the specific term *tanna* implies that what follows is part of a larger passage from the Mishnah or a Braitha that was quoted before the term *tanna.*[16] In this instance, what follows is a continuation of the previously described incident between R. Gamaliel and R. Joshua, much the same as the passage quoted a few lines earlier is a part of the larger story of the incident, as attested by the P.T. Berakhoth 4:1 (7c) and demanded by the context. Thus, whatever date and place "on that day" may refer to elsewhere, here it refers to the end of the first century and to Yabneh. I am aware that the term *tanna* is not Tannaitic but comes from "the sages of the Gemara" and, as such, could be very late;[17] therefore, the connection between the composition of Mishnah Eduyoth and the time of R. Gamaliel the Second could be of late origin and thus suspect. Nevertheless, here I think it is genuinely Tannaitic since the Gemara in Berakhoth carefully distinguishes between this "on that day," for which it has an explicit Tannaitic tradition (namely, its attachment to the larger story), and the other instances for which it has no explicit tradition (or only a nebulous tradition). When the identification was mere conjecture, it was expressed in Aramaic.[18]

One could argue that the attachment of this statement to the larger story was made in late Tannaitic times, by which time they did not know exactly what happened two or more generations before in Yabneh. But as we have seen, the author of the Scolion to the Fast Scroll and Josephus did not yet know the Mishnaic form. Thus, if Mishnah Eduyoth was not composed in Yabneh during the latter part of the first century C.E., it must have been composed later, closer to late Tannaitic times. In that case, the late Tannaim would have known the accuracy of the tractate's historical accounts. Furthermore, the historicity of "on that day" is confirmed indirectly by a passage in Tosefta Eduyoth. The Tosefta begins, "When the sages gathered at the vineyard of Yabneh." The drashah that follows does not have as close a connection with the contents of Mishnah Eduyoth as others have argued, but both this drashah and Mishnah Eduyoth were composed in Yabneh at about the same time.

The Tosefta reads:

> כשנכנסו חכמים בכרם ביבנה אמרו עתידה שעה שיהא אדם מבקש דבר מדברי תורה ואינו מוציא, מדברי סופרים ואינו מוציא, שנאמר לכן הנה ימים באים וגו׳ ולא ימצאו דבר ה׳ וכו׳ שלא יהא דבר מדברי תורה דומה לחבירו. אמרו נתחיל מהלל ושמאי. שמאי אומר וכו׳.
>
> When the sages gathered at the vineyard of Yabneh, they said: There will be a time when a person will seek a word from the teaching of the Torah and will not find [it], and a word of the teaching of the rabbis [scribes] and will not find [it], as it is written "Therefore behold the coming of days when . . . you will not find the word of God . . . [when] one word of the Torah will not be like the other" [Amos 8:11–12]. They said: Let us begin with Hillel and Shammai. Shammai says . . .

Some modern scholars, including Albeck, assumed that the second part of this passage in the Tosefta, beginning "They said: Let us begin with Hillel and Shammai," was an attempt to ward off, to forestall, the coming of a time when a person will seek a word of the teachings of the Torah, of the rabbis, and will not find it. These scholars therefore interpreted this passage to mean that the sages in Yabneh were saying: "Let us do something to prevent that time from coming. Let us arrange the laws differently from the way in which they were arranged heretofore. Let us arrange them (according to names?) in a manner that will make them easier to remember, assuring thereby their preservation. Toward that goal, let us begin with Hillel and Shammai. Shammai said, etc." Following this interpretation of the Tosefta, it was only a small step for Albeck to identify the new arrangement as the first stage in the change from Midrashic to Mishnaic form, the second stage being the shift from names to topics as the organizing principle. That this took place in Yabneh is attested by the opening sentence, "When the sages gathered at the vineyard of Yabneh."

I do not think, however, that the second part of this passage in the Tosefta is a preventive measure against the coming of a time when a person will seek a word of the teaching of the Torah, of the rabbis, and will not find it. Rather, it introduced a new subject. For the coming of such a time was prophesied by Amos, and prophecies, generally, are not reversible. Also, in the parallel sources (Sifrei Deut., piska 48 [p. 112], and B.T. Shabbath 138b) only the first half of the Tosefta passage is quoted. It is unlikely that the authors of the parallel sources would quote only the gloomy aspect of that prophecy without including the attempt to offset it, if that were the intent of the second half. The fact that this second half is not quoted indicates that it is an independent statement.

It should be noted that Tosafoth Rid (Shabbath ad loc.) has a different reading in the Tosefta. Instead of

נתחיל מהלל ושמאי, שמאי אומר וכו׳

("Let us begin with Hillel and Shammai"), it reads

תחלת כל דבר שמאי אומר וכו׳

("Beginning of all things [disagreements], Shammai says . . ."). Thus Tosafoth Rid conceives of this not as an antidote to the gloomy prophecy, but rather as an elaboration of the theme of forgetting the Torah, placing the blame on the Shammaites and Hillelites and their masters, Shammai and Hillel. Echoing the famous statement by R. Yose (T. Chagigah 2:9, and parallels), Tosafoth Rid explains:

> תחלת המחלוקת היא זו שנחלקו בה שמאי והלל הקדמונים ואחר כך נתרבו מחלוקת תלמידיהן ב״ש וב״ה וזהו ושוטטו לבקש דבר ה׳. שבתחילה היתה כל התורה ברורה בלי מחלוקת ... עד שגברו השמדות בישראל ולא יכלו לעסוק בתורה כראוי. ומתוך כך נתרבו הספקות והמחלוקות בישראל.

> The first of all disagreements is that between Shammai and Hillel the elders. After that many disagreements increased among their students the Houses of Shammai and Hillel. This is the meaning of the verse "there will be a time when a person will seek a word of God..."

> [Amos 8:11-12]. At the beginning, the Torah was clear without disagreements until the persecution overcame Israel and they could not properly study the Torah, because of that, doubts and disagreements increased in Israel.

According to the Tosafoth Rid, then, Amos prophesied the coming of a time when one will not find a word of the Torah, or a word of the rabbis. The Tosefta connected this time with the period of the Shammaites and Hillelites when, because of their fierce disagreements, the Torah was almost forgotten. Amos proposed no remedy to overcome this.

I prefer, however, to view the second half of this passage of the Tosefta as independent of the first. The first part deals with the prophecy of Amos, the second with the disagreement of the Shammaites and the Hillelites (a substantial part of the contents of Mishnah Eduyoth). The second "they said" should be taken to mean "they also said," beginning a new subject. The connection between the two parts is the fact that both were enunciated by the sages when they gathered in the vineyard at Yabneh.[19] Indirectly we learn that Mishnah Eduyoth—at least that part which deals with the disagreements of the Shammaites and Hillelites—was composed in Yabneh. This is why I hold that the change to the Mishnaic form took place in Yabneh around the end of the first century, even though I do not agree with the reading and interpretation that Albeck and others have given the Tosefta.[20]

It should be noted, incidentally, that both Mishnah and Tosefta Eduyoth give reasons near the beginning why dissenting views ought to be recorded. The bluntness of the question ("Why do they record the opinions of the individual against those of the majority?") and the applicability of the answer to almost all dissenting views suggest that at the beginning they indeed recorded all dissenting views—a practice abandoned later on, during the editorship of R. Judah Hanassi, who not only did not record all views but sometimes even split the same statement into two and included in his code only the part that he thought appropriate for his purpose.[21] This abandonment is probably due to the large number of dissenting views accumulated during the course of time, which made the recording of all of them impractical. The recording had to be restricted to those views that had special importance, halakhic or otherwise. It follows, then, that during the time when Mishnah and Tosefta Eduyoth were composed, the compilation of the Mishnah was still young. Dissenters were few, so all of the dissenting views could be included. Since that Mishnah and Tosefta most likely date from the period of Yabneh, this further supports my thesis that the change to the Mishnaic form took place during the reign of R. Gamaliel the Second at Yabneh.

The theory that the change to the Mishnaic form took place in Yabneh also gives the best explanation for the timing of the editing of Mishnah Aboth. Scholars[22] have long contended that Mishnah Aboth is divided into several layers. The oldest layer (consisting of 1:1–16, 2:8, 10–14) lists the "chain of tradition" from Moses to the five disciples of R. Yochanan ben Zakkai (accompanied by a triadic statement attributed to each post-biblical member of the chain). It was composed by these five disciples (or by their disciples) around the first quarter of the second century for the purpose of strengthening their authority, showing themselves to be direct successors of Moses, who received the Torah from Sinai. It is hardly a coincidence that these five disciples lived during the period in which the change from the Midrashic to the Mishnaic form took place. As long as the Midrashic form was dominant—as long as most laws were followed by a reference to the Bible—there was no need to augment the legislators' authority by invoking the "chain of tradition." The biblical authority of these laws was obvious and explicit. After the change to Mishnaic form, however, there was a need to show that, despite the lack of an explicit biblical connection, the ultimate authority of the Mishnaic laws derived from Moses, who received the Torah from Sinai, in that the rabbis who assembled these laws were Moses' direct successors acting on his behalf.

Thus, the first layer of Aboth serves as an introduction to the Mishnah. Without biblical references in the text itself, the Mishnah had to be hooked on to the Bible externally through the "chain of tradition."[23]

III

The change from Midrashic to Mishnaic form, whenever it took place, was, understandably, not complete. Jews cannot sever their laws from the Lawgiver, whose legacy is incorporated in the Bible. Even Maimonides, who made a conscious attempt in his *Mishneh Torah* to codify only pure law without naming names or recording dissenting opinion, frequently had to resort to biblical references. No law is really binding on the Jew unless it can be shown to have its origin in the Bible.

Midrashic form continued to exist, therefore, even after the change to Mishnaic form. It existed in the laws that are found only in the Midreshei Halakhah (that is, those not found in the Mishnah), and it existed concomitantly in the laws that are found in both the Midreshei Halakhah and the Mishnah. For the latter, Midrash served as the ground, the justification, the life support. Indeed, one may legitimately wonder whether the Mishnah would have survived at all were it not for the parallel existence of Midreshei Halakhah. When a Tanna of the Mishnah was asked for the biblical sources of his Mishnah he could, unlike the Sadducees of yore, point to the Midreshei Halakhah, without which the laws would have seemed arbitrary and nonbinding. Mishnah eventually supplanted Midrash, but it owes its early survival to Midrash—a phenomenon not entirely unknown from elsewhere.

Internally as well, it can be shown that the Mishnah, unlike the Midreshei Halakhah, is not a self-sufficient book; it relies heavily on other and earlier texts (not necessarily written ones), quoting them verbatim. The first line of the Mishnah can serve as an example (although not the best one): "From what time in the evening may the Shema be recited?" On this the Babylonian Talmud (ad loc.) rightly inquires: "On what does the Tanna base himself [that he commences, 'from what time']?" (He should have first stated that there is an obligation to recite the Shema and then defined its time.) The Babylonian Talmud answers: "The Tanna bases himself on Scripture where it is written, 'And thou shalt recite them . . . when thou liest down and when thou risest up' [Deut. 6:7, the scriptural source for the obligation of reciting the Shema, on the basis of which] he [the Tanna of the Mishnah] asks: When does the time of the recital of the Shema lying down begin?" Mishnah, it is clear, must be studied in conjunction with Midrash.

Another example, though of a different nature, of the dependence of Mishnah on Midreshei Halakhah is Mishnah Yebamoth 6:4:

> ארס את האלמנה ונתמנה להיות כהן גדול — יכנוס. ומעשה ביהושע בן גמלא שקדש את מרתה בת בייתוס ומנהו המלך להיות כהן גדול — וכנסה.

> If he [a priest] had betrothed a widow and was afterward appointed High Priest, he may consummate the union. It once happened that Joshua the son of Gamla betrothed Marta the daughter of Boethus, and he consummated the union after the king appointed him High Priest.

The English translation does not show that a different verb for "betrothed" is used in the first clause (where the law is stated) than in the second clause (where the story about Joshua the son of Gamla is related). The first clause uses the biblical verb for betrothal, the second clause the rabbinic verb. The reason for this is that both clauses are taken from the Sifra, Emor 2:6 (ed. Weiss, 95a). The first clause is a drashah on Lev. 21:14, which uses the formula "from where does one know that a priest who betrothed a widow and was appointed High Priest may consummate the marriage?" We know it "because it says [but a virgin of his own people] should he take for a wife." Since it is a drashah based on a biblical verse, it uses the biblical verb for betrothal, whereas the second clause, which relates a story, uses the more common, spoken verb for betrothal. The Mishnah created the first clause by transforming the drashah into a fixed law, in which all biblical references are omitted, but the original biblical verb for betrothal is retained.[24]

A third example of the Mishnah's dependence on Midrash Halakhah is Mishnah Bikkurim 1:1–2. I have chosen this example despite its length and textual complexity because it is an instance in which the Mishnah is literally a continuation of the Sifrei, and such examples are not very frequent. The Mishnah reads:

> יש מביאין ביכורים וקורין; מביאין ולא קורין; ויש שאינן מביאין. אלו שאינן מביאין: הנוטע לתוך שלו והבריך לתוך של יחיד או לתוך של רבים, וכן המבריך מתוך של יחיד או מתוך של רבים לתוך שלו; הנוטע לתוך שלו והבריך לתוך שלו ודרך היחיד ודרך הרבים באמצע, הרי זה אינו מביא. ר׳ יהודה אומר כזה מביא.
> מאיזה טעם אינו מביא? משום שנאמר ״ראשית ביכורי אדמתך״, עד שיהיו כל הגידולין מאדמתך. האריסין והחכרות והסקריקון והגזלן אין מביאין מאותו הטעם משום שנאמר: ראשית ביכורי אדמתך.

> Some there are that may bring the first fruits and make the avowal [the recitation of the required verses; Deut. 26:5ff.]; others that may bring them but not make the avowal; and some there are that may not [even] bring them. These may not bring them: he that plants a tree in his own domain but sinks a shoot of it [so that it grows] in another's domain or in the public domain; so, too, he that sinks a shoot from [a tree planted in] another's domain or the public domain [so that it grows] in his own domain; or he that plants a tree in his own domain and sinks it [so that it still grows] in his own domain but with a private or public road in between. Such a one may not bring the first fruits. R. Judah says: such a one may bring them.

(Here the first Mishnah ends and the second begins):

> For what reason may he not bring them? Because it is written: "The first fruits of your land" [Exod. 23:19] [you may not bring them] unless their growth is wholly from your land. They that lease the land or that hire it, a usurping occupant or a robber may not bring them for the like reason, because it is written: "The first fruits of your land."

The flow of the Mishnah would have been smoother if it had omitted the question "For what reason may he not bring them?" and placed the answer, "Because it is written, etc." before the disagreement between R. Judah and the sages rather than after. The Mishnah would then have read:

> He that plants a tree in his own domain . . . so too he that sinks a shoot from [a tree planted in] another's domain or the public domain [so that it grows] in his own domain. Such a one may not bring the first fruits [because it is written: "The first fruits of your land" (Exod. 23:19)] [you may not bring them] unless their growth is wholly from your land. He that plants a tree in his own domain and sinks it [so that it still grows] in his own domain but with a private or public road in between, such a one may not bring the first fruits. R. Judah says: such a one may bring them.

The advantage in this version would have been twofold: the elimination of the question (which, incidentally, is employing a phrase, "for what reason," that is not found anywhere else in the Mishnah), and the location of the answer immediately after the first two instances, in which everyone (even R. Judah) agrees that he may not bring the first fruits.

Further, the second Mishnah quotes and refers to the drashah of the first Mishnah, saying, "They that lease the land or hire it, a usurper or a robber may not bring them for the like reason [of the first Mishnah], because it is written: 'The first fruits of your land.'" The phrase "for like reason" implies that the drashah in the second Mishnah was first expounded in connection with the contents of the first Mishnah. It further implies that this drashah better fits the instances of the first Mishnah, namely, "he who plants a tree, etc.," than it does those of the second Mishnah, namely, "they that lease the land . . . a robber."

Yet it would have been more logical first to exclude from the biblical phrase "your land" a usurper or a robber who has no legal share in the land whatsoever, than it is to exclude "he who plants a tree in his own domain and sinks a shoot of it in another's," since he has a share in the land. Note that by excluding "he who plants a tree in his own domain" the Mishnah adds to the second half of the drashah the phrase "wholly from your land," for part of the land is his; whereas in excluding "they who lease . . . —the robber" no such addition is necessary, for none of the land is theirs. The Mishnah should have expounded the drashah in connection with the contents of the second Mishnah first, and then pointed to the contents of the first Mishnah as a weaker example of the lack of *admatekha,* "your land."

The Mishnah departs from the logical order here because it is a repetition and continuation of a passage in the Sifrei Deut. (piska 297, p. 317) as it was originally composed. Our present version of the passage is influenced by the Mishnah. In fact, it is identical with the Mishnah, except that it mentions the exclusion of those who lease the land (and so on) before the exclusion of the one who plants a tree in his own domain (and so on). The Sifrei reads as follows: "'The land' [Deut. 26:2] comes to exclude those who lease . . . the robber. They may not bring them for the like reason, because it is written [Exod. 23:19] 'the first fruits of your land.'" It continues: "'That the Lord your God gave you' [Deut. 26:2] comes to exclude the one who plants a tree in his own domain," and so on (verbatim as in the Mishnah). Not all the readings of the Sifrei have the words "for the like reason," although the majority do. Nevertheless, it is clear that these words were not original to the Sifrei and that they were brought there from the Mishnah. For, unlike the Mishnah, the Sifrei starts with exclusion of the one who leases (and so on) and thus could not say "for the same reason" in this context. ("Same" as what?)

Not only were these words brought over from the Mishnah, but the whole drashah was imported from the Mishnah. The Sifrei does not exclude those who lease the land (and so on) from the verse in Exodus (23:19), which reads "your land," but from the verse in Deuteronomy (26:2), which reads "the land." Originally the Sifrei had only one drashah, the one from "the land." The second drashah, from "your land," was added later.

Similarly, the question, "For what reason may they not bring them?" and the answer, "Because it is written [Exod. 23:19], etc." (which are found in all readings of the Sifrei at the end of the piska) are also imported from the Mishnah; they are not original to the Sifrei. For the Sifrei excludes "the one who plants a tree in his own domain, etc." not from the wording in Exodus, "your land," but rather from the verse in Deuteronomy, "the land that the Lord your God gave you." Originally the piska concluded with the disagreement between the sages and R. Judah; the question and answer were added later.

We can now understand why the Mishnah disturbed the natural arrangement and placed the question and answer after the disagreement between the sages and R. Judah rather than before. We can also understand why it reversed the order and expounded the drashah first in connection with "he who plants a tree in his own domain, etc." It did so because it was reacting to the Sifrei, which, in its first exclusion, "those who lease the land, etc.," does not specify whether the exclusion was from bringing the first fruits or only from making the avowal (there is a whole list, both in the Sifrei and the Mishnah, of those who are excluded only from making the avowal, but not from bringing the first fruits). In the second exclusion, "he who plants a tree in his own domain, etc.," the Sifrei states explicitly that he may not bring them. It was the opinion of the author of the Mishnah (not shared by the author of the Sifrei) that the exclusions from verses in Deuteronomy entail only exclusions from avowal, the principal topic of the verses. An additional drashah was necessary to exclude them from bringing first fruits as well. The author of the Mishnah, therefore, added two notes to the quotation from the Sifrei. To the exclusion "he who plants a tree in his own domain, etc.," concerning which the Sifrei states explicitly that he may not bring them, the author of the Mishnah added the question, "For what reason may he not bring them?" (To him, the verse in Deuteronomy, cited by the Sifrei, "that the Lord your God gave you," excludes the former only from making the avowal.) To this question he answered, "Because it is written [in Exodus], 'The first fruits of your land [you should bring to the House of your Lord]' [since the verse explicitly mentions *bringing,* we learn that] you may not bring them unless their growth is wholly from your land." Further, to the exclusion of "those who lease, etc.," concerning which the Sifrei does not specify whether they bring first fruits or not, the author of the Mishnah supplied the law, "They may not bring them for the like reason [which he gave previously to account for the Sifrei's explicit statement that he may not bring them], because it is written [in Exodus] 'the first fruit of your land.'"

Logically the drashah from "your land" should have been expounded first in connection with "those who lease the land . . . the robber," since it fits better there. The author of the Mishnah, however, commented first on the Sifrei's explicit statement that "he who plants a tree in his own domain, etc." cannot bring them. His attachment to Midreshei Halakhah took precedence over the logical sequence.[25]

One of the achievements of modern Mishnaic studies is the awareness that the Mishnah is best understood in light of antecedent texts with which it originally formed a unit. That unit was often broken by incomplete and piecemeal quotations, causing the many difficulties we presently encounter in our study of the Mishnah. The solution is to restore the original text, to view Mishnah as abridged Midrash. By doing so, we also make sense of the ellipticalness, the sudden interruptions, the awkward contextual arrangements that are so common in the Mishnah[26] (though individual sentences or phrases are expressed in delectable Hebrew). The

Mishnah is a composite work rather than an original creation; it was not composed *de novo* but was excerpted from earlier sources, from Midrash. The excerption was sometimes too narrow, giving rise to the feeling that something is missing in our text and that it needs to be completed. This feeling motivated the Gemara to say occasionally: "There is a lacuna in the text and this is how it ought to read." There is indeed a lacuna, for the reason that a unit was broken, and unless it is restored a feeling that something is missing will persist.[27]

The dependence of the Mishnah on Midreshei Halakhah is manifold. The Mishnah quotes Midreshei Halakhah, sometimes verbatim (without, of course, mentioning the authors by their names), paraphrases them, and even abbreviates them in such a manner that at times a given phrase in the Mishnah is unintelligible when read without its source in Midreshei Halakhah. It is difficult to ascertain whether the author of the Mishnah assumed that Mishnah would be studied in conjunction with Midreshei Halakhah or erred in thinking that a given phrase was clear enough; whereas, in fact, it was clear to him only because he had the Midreshei Halakhah before him. All one can say is that a similar situation exists vis-à-vis the dependence of later Mishnah on earlier Mishnah. Here, too, though less frequently, a given phrase in a later Mishnah may be unintelligible without the realization that it was abbreviated from an earlier Mishnah. For a beautiful example of this, see my *Sources and Traditions,* Baba Kama (forthcoming), the comment to the Babylonian Talmud 49a. Here, presumably, it is more certain that the author of the later Mishnah did not intend to have his Mishnah studied in conjunction with the earlier Mishnah. Therefore, the unintelligibility of a given phrase in a later Mishnah could only be due to an error in judgment as to its clarity. Analogously, one may perhaps assume that this was true also with respect to Mishnah and Midreshei Halakhah, where an occasional unintelligible phrase in the Mishnah is due to an unconscious overreliance on Midreshei Halakhah.

On the other hand, the Mishnah is probably responsible for the fact that Midreshei Halakhah—now a separate entity—are concentrating, as it were, on complex Midrash, though not exclusively. With the emergence of Mishnah, complex Midrash further distanced itself from the Mishnah and increasingly took on a dialectical posture, arguing and raising unlikely possibilities using the formulas

יכול ... אתה אומר ... או אינו אלא...

("Perhaps this only means...," "You say...," or "One might think..."), which were immediately rejected. That is not to say that none of these rejected possibilities represented genuinely held opinions of an adversary; some did, and occasionally we can even identify the adversary, who could come either from within (a fellow rabbi) or without (a sectarian). In the majority of instances, however, the possibilities were invented to stimulate the mind and broaden the horizon of learning.

This aspect of complex Midrash reappeared with much greater force, though not necessarily in conjunction with scriptural verses, among the later Amoraim, and particularly, I hope to show, among the Stammaim. This assured Midreshei Halakhah a kind of reincarnation after the Mishnah had almost totally supplanted them (to the extent that substantial parts of Midreshei Halakhah did not survive and were forgotten). The supplantation did not occur because of the intrinsic superiority of the Mishnaic form over the Midrashic form; on the contrary, theologically the Midrashic form is preferable since it preserves the link between the law and the Divine, who is the only one, according to the Jewish apperception, entitled to enact laws. The Mishnah prevailed, rather, for practical reasons: it was easier to remember.

The particular political and social circumstances of the time were undoubtedly factors in the change from the Midrashic to the Mishnaic form. The destruction of the Temple in 70 C.E., with its attendant trauma, no doubt heightened the fear that another tragedy would wipe out learning and cause the law to be forgotten. Simpler means of remembering the law had to be devised. But above all, the impetus for the change to Mishnaic form came from the development of complex Midrash. As long as the prevalent mode of Midrash was simple Midrash, as was the case in the early centuries after the Bible, the attachment of Midrash to the Bible provided the former with a convenient mnemonic handle, making it relatively easy to remember. There was no need to change to Mishnaic form. However, the development by Hillel of complex Midrash[28] with its massive hermeneutical arguments made Midrash increasingly difficult to retain[29] and prompted the change to the Mishnaic form, which was easier to remember. (To this day, when students are assigned portions of Tannaitic literature to memorize, they prefer to memorize Mishnah or Tosefta rather than Midreshei Halakhah.)

Part of the success of the Mishnah undoubtedly reflected the enormous stature of R. Judah Hanassi, at least from the last quarter of the second century until his death (ca. 220 C.E.).[30] R. Judah, known as Rabbi, inherited the Mishnah tradition from his paternal grandfather, Gamaliel the Second, and it became a matter of prestige to him, and probably to the whole patriarchal family, to have that tradition perpetuated. So great was R. Judah's stature that whatever material he did not include when he did his compilation of the Mishnah was later designated in a belittling way as "outside" the normative code, making it vulnerable to being forgotten. After his death the Amoraim partially restored the balance, complementing the Mishnah with formulas like "From where do we know these things" . . . "Scripture says," a variation of "as it says," which is often taken from the Midreshei Halakhah. The Amoraim merely reverted back to Midrash.

IV

Another sign of the incomplete change from Midrashic to Mishnaic form are the numerous drashoth in the Mishnah as we now have it. Since we do not have the original text of the Mishnah, we have no way of knowing how it appeared in its earliest form. One may assume, however, that it changed in the course of time and that the change was in the direction of adding drashoth, old and new, simple and complex. (The Tosefta, which is later than the Mishnah, has proportionately more drashoth than the Mishnah.) The process of adding simple drashoth did not cease even during later Amoraic times, and was certainly prevalent during Tannaitic times. See, for example, B.T. Kiddushin 43a:

> האומר לשלוחו צא הרוג את הנפש הוא חייב ושולחיו פטור. שמאי הזקן אומר משום חגי הנביא שולחיו חייב שנאמר ואותו הרגת בחרב בני עמון.

> If a person tells his agent "go and kill a human being" [and he did so] he [the agent] is guilty, and his sender is absolved. Shammai the Elder says in the name of Chaggai the Prophet, the sender is guilty, as it is written: [God told David] "and him [Uriah the Hittite] you killed with the sword of the Ammonites" [2 Sam. 12:9].

On the surface, it appears as if Shammai, in the name of Chaggai the Prophet, quoted this drashah as support for his opinion that the sender is guilty. Indeed, some scholars have deduced from this quotation that drashoth are old,[31] or that the book of 2 Samuel (from which the Biblical quotation is taken) was already canonized during the time of Chaggai the Prophet.[32] It is clear, however, from the Gemara's question there, "What is the reason of Shammai?" that the anonymous questioner (whose anonymity indicates that the question was late) did not have the portion beginning "as it is written" in the text before him; it entered the text in the wake of one of the Gemara's answers there:

שאני התם דגלי רחמנא ואותו הרגת בחרב בני עמון.

> That is a special case because the Merciful One revealed [in the Bible], "And him you killed with the sword of the Ammonites."

Thus the drashah is the Gemara's; it found its way into the text proper afterward.

That drashoth entered our Mishnah by way of Midreshei Halakhah cannot be denied (even as Mishnah influenced Midreshei Halakhah). The few instances in which the Mishnah does not start as usual, with the law followed by a quotation from Scripture, but, like Midreshei Halakhah, begins with a verse from Scripture,[33] amply attest to the Mishnah's receptivity to Midreshei Halakhah. A particularly striking example of the penetration of Mishnah by Midreshei Halakhah is Sanhedrin 10:5–6. This Mishnah begins with biblical verses (some later readings could not resist the temptation to add "as it says" three times to bring it more in line with Mishnaic terminology).[34] It also uses the expression *mikan omru* ("from here they said"), which occurs only four or five times in the Mishnah but frequently in the Midreshei Halakhah. Moreover, parts of the passage are found almost verbatim in Sifrei Deut. (piska 94–95, pp. 155–156).

I am inclined to view all the instances of complex Midrash in the Mishnah as later additions (after the change from Midrashic to Mishnaic form) coming from Midreshei Halakhah, whether they are contained in the extant Midreshei Halakhah or not. I am not sure about drashoth that are of the simple Midrash variety; they may date from before the change. The practical reasons that brought about the change from Midrashic to Mishnaic form could not completely overcome the natural reluctance of the Jews to detach the laws from the Bible. Some outward connection had to remain, and the expression "as it says" served that purpose.[35]

Be that as it may, the susceptibility of Mishnah to Midrash, whether it was so from the beginning or only sometime after the change from Midrashic to Mishnaic form took place, confirms my contention that there existed among Jews a deep-seated belief that no law ought to be a categorical imperative, without justification, unless it springs forth from the Divine, whose will is recorded in the Bible. Occasionally, even He provides a justification.

It should be added that the degree of susceptibility of Mishnah to Midrash apparently differed among the schools. The Mishnah of R. Judah (bar Ilai) contained a substantial number of drashoth. He, therefore, defined Mishnah as consisting of Midrash (B.T. Kiddushin 49a), whereas R. Meir's Mishnah contained few drashoth and thus he defined Mishnah as consisting of "fixed laws" (ibid.). R. Meir's Midrashic activity seems to have been more limited than that of R. Judah. In contrast to R. Judah (and R. Simon—all mid-second century Palestinian scholars), no Midrashic book is attributed to R. Meir (see B.T. Sanhedrin 86a), and he is mentioned in Midreshei Halakhah far less often than is R. Judah. R. Meir concentrated more on Mishnah, and this may be the reason why Rabbi adopted, among the students of R. Akiba, R. Meir's Mishnah as the base for his Mishnah. Unless it is stated or proved otherwise, the anonymous portions of our Mishnah follow the view of R. Meir.[36]

I believe that initially the Mishnah consisted entirely of fixed laws; the nonapodictic material, including scriptural as well as logical motives, entered the Mishnah later, except, perhaps, for the very simple ones which may be old, having survived the change from Midrashic to Mishnaic form because the main impetus for the change—facilitating memorization—did not apply to them. One good example of a logical motive in the Mishnah is M. Oholoth, 7:6: "If a woman was in hard travail, the child must be cut up while it is in the womb and brought out member by member, since the life of the mother has priority over the life of the child; but if the greater part of it was already born it may not be touched since the claim of one life cannot override the claim of another life". Initially the Mishnah contained few motives. Gradually, impelled by the Jewish preference for the justificatory, some fixed laws acquired motives; most of the laws, however, remained without. Those that received motives display no particular pattern or overall plan. It is quite possible that individual motives surfaced on their own strength as a result of their unique context without being part of an inclusive theme. This would account for the relatively small number of motives in the Mishnah: they were the result of special circumstances that were not often duplicated.

Rarely do we know the full circumstances prevailing at the time when a reason became attached to a fixed law. However, when the Tannaim disagree as to the reason for an earlier law, we assume that the law reached them without a reason; if this were not true, both parties would have accepted the transmitted reason. Allowance should be made for the possibility in such cases that the disagreement reflects an earlier controversy that was contemporaneous with the promulgation of the law. Most often, however, the disagreement reflects the parties' own efforts to find an explanation for a law that reached them without an explanation.

Most disagreements among Tannaim about the reason for a law in the Mishnah are implicit; a few are explicit. M. Parah 3:7 is a most appropriate illustration: it is explicit, and the Tannaim disagree not only regarding what the reason is but also about its nature. One disputant gives a logical reason, while the other claims that he has a better reason, a scriptural one: "If the red heifer refused to go forth they may not send out with her a black heifer [the reason] lest any say 'they slaughtered a black heifer,' nor another red heifer, lest any say, 'they slaughtered two.' R. Yose says it was not for this reason but because it is written, 'And he shall bring her forth' [Num. 19:3]—by herself." The law that if the red heifer refuses to go forth, no other heifer should accompany her is older than the time of R. Yose (mid-second century C.E.) and his adversaries.[37] They received this law in an apodictic form, without justification. They offered their own justification, but disagreed as to its nature. Either R. Yose or his adversaries are right; that is, when the law was promulgated it was done so because of one or the other specified reason. Yet immediately preceding their time this law, like the overwhelming majority of the Mishnah's laws, was transmitted without a reason. Apodicity is the hallmark of the Mishnaic form.

Mention should also be made of the fact that the causes for the change from Midrashic to Mishnaic form affected halakhah more than aggadah (the non-legal part of the Talmud). The fear that the Torah might be forgotten was more realistic with regard to halakhah, which requires greater concentration and attention (ill affordable in times of social turbulence) than does aggadah. The distinction between simple and complex Midrash hardly applies to aggadah, since a successful passage of aggadah is never really complex.[38] Therefore, the impetus that gave rise to the change in halakhah was not operative on aggadah. Its form remained the same throughout the ages, though the intent and style often changed.

It is not surprising, then, that the Mishnah contains relatively little aggadah (although it was flourishing at the time). Indeed, some tractates have no aggadah at all. The Mishnaic form arose to meet a need that was unique to halakhah. Midrashic form, on the other hand, perfectly suited the nature of aggadah and its durability. Aggadic passages entered the Mishnah either as further elucidation of some halakhic points[39] or because originally the halakhah and aggadah were taught together[40] and remained together, even after the halakhah was excerpted from the Midrash to the Mishnah. The Sifra is the closest among the Midreshei Halakhah to the Mishnah, and, like the Mishnah, has little aggadah. Indeed, it is only in the last portion, Bechukotai, that the aggadah comes into its own. One may question whether aggadah could have survived outside of a biblical context. Biblical references bestow authority on halakhah; without them it is less authoritative. On the other hand, they provide aggadah with sustenance; without biblical references it could not subsist.

V

The Mishnah enjoyed a short-lived success. In the course of its more than 100-year history—from the time of Gamaliel the Second to the death of R. Judah Hanassi—it is probable that the Mishnah achieved undisputed supremacy only during the last quarter of the second century and the first quarter of the third (that is, during Rabbi's reign). We do not know how the change from the Midrashic to the Mishnaic form was received initially. Was there opposition to the change, and if so, from which circles? We do not know whether the Tannaim, whose names are hardly mentioned in the Mishnah but appear frequently in Midreshei Halakhah, opposed the very idea of Mishnah or not. Our image of the Mishnah is refracted through the prism of the school of R. Akiba. We do not know how R. Ishmael's school reacted to the Mishnah as an institution—did they embrace it wholeheartedly, or did they have reservations about it? Was there in fact any Mishnah from the school of R. Ishmael?

Reservations about Mishnah on the part of the school of R. Ishmael (and perhaps some others) would explain why Rabbi adopted the Mishnah of the school of R. Akiba as the base of his Mishnah, in spite of the friction that had existed between the household of the Patriarch and the rabbinic establishment: R. Akiba's would have been the only Mishnah of note.[41] This friction is evident in the first textual layer of Aboth, where the chain of tradition after Hillel is continued by R. Yochanan ben Zakkai (Aboth 2:8) and not by Hillel's son, R. Simon. That layer, which concludes with the sayings of the five disciples of R. Yochanan ben Zakkai, was composed during the time of R. Akiba, a disciple of the first two (R. Eliezer and R. Yehoshua) of these five disciples. He wanted to show that the chain of tradition extended all the way from Moses to his day. He omitted the patriarchal family; the chain of the patriarchal family was added later, most likely by Rabbi (1:17–2:3).[42] Thus, the rabbinic establishment did not consider the patriarchal family a link in the chain of tradition. We must conclude that Rabbi nevertheless followed the Mishnah of R. Akiba because there was none other of note. The change to Mishnaic form was sanctioned by Rabbi's grandfather, R. Gamaliel the Second, in Yabneh,[43] and that form was continued and developed principally by the school of R. Akiba.[44] Rabbi had no choice but to rely heavily on the Mishnah of R. Akiba. I would like to add in passing that in this respect R. Akiba's role in the controversy between R. Gamaliel and R. Yehoshua ought to be reexamined; it stands to reason that R. Akiba's role determined the patriarchal family's relation to R. Akiba himself.[45]

This explanation by itself, however, is insufficient to answer the question of whether the school of R. Ishmael had reservations about the Mishnah. Other possible explanations could be offered for Rabbi's choice of R. Akiba's Mishnah. I therefore return to the problem in a different form, referring to the absence of the teachings of the school of R. Ishmael in the Mishnah and Tosefta. R. Ishmael himself is eminently represented in the Mishnah, although the representation is only a third of that of his counterpart, R. Akiba. R. Ishmael's two outstanding students, R. Yoshiyah and R. Jonathan (see B.T. Men. 57b), however, are not mentioned in the Mishnah (except R. Jonathan, once, in M. Aboth 4:9) or in the Tosefta (except once, Shebuoth 1:7), while their counterparts, R. Meir, R. Judah (bar Ilai), and R. Yose are mentioned hundreds of times in both the Mishnah and the Tosefta. R. Judah Hanassi, the editor-anthologizer of the Mishnah, knew the teachings of R. Ishmael's students, and he is quoted in their Midrashim almost as often as he is quoted in the Midrashim that stem from the school of R. Akiba. Even more important, in his Mishnah he quotes statements from the Mekhilta of R. Ishmael verbatim.[46] Why, then, are the students of R. Ishmael not mentioned in the Mishnah? Is it merely an accident that we are not in possession of Mishnah from the school of R. Ishmael (although we do have Midreshei Halakhah from both schools), or was there no Mishnah of the school of R. Ishmael?

The evidence seems to favor the latter solution. The Mishnah as a separate corpus, analogous to Bible and Talmud, is mentioned only in texts that stem from the school of R. Akiba, such as the Mishnah, Sifra, and Sifrei Deut. (after piska 54).[47] It is not found in the non-Akiban sources, such as the Mekhilta of R. Ishmael, Sifrei Num., and Sifrei Deut. prior to piska 54. Moreover, both the school of R. Akiba and the Mekhilta of R. Ishmael sometimes use the root *shamar* to refer to fixed laws. While the school of R. Akiba employs the term *Mishnah* and says:

חקתי תשמרו — זו המשנה or ושמרתם — זו משנה or
תשמרון — זו משנה

(Sifra Acharai, end parshah 9, p. 85d; ibid. 99c, Sifrei Deut., piska 58, p. 124; Sifrei Deut., piska 59, p. 125. See also ibid. piska 79, p. 145 and Sifrei Zuta, p. 292), the Mekhilta of R. Ishmael employs the term *halakhoth* and says

ושמרת כל חוקיו — אלו הלכות

(Beshallach, parshah 1, p. 157; see Horovitz's note ad loc.). All this suggests that the Mishnah as a form of transmission of laws was championed by the school of R. Akiba and was either ignored or opposed by the school of R. Ishmael.

This hypothesis is consistent with what we know of R. Ishmael's conservative use of language: he employs older (biblical) expressions and words more often than his colleague R. Akiba. R. Ishmael may have similarly insisted on adhering to the older mode of learning, that of Midrash, and frowned upon the innovative mode of Mishnah.

It is true that we find references to the Mishnah even in the Midreshei Halakhah that come from the school of R. Ishmael, using the term *mikan omru*. The number, though fewer than the references found in the Midreshei Halakhah that come from the school of R. Akiba, is large enough seemingly to show that the school of R. Ishmael, too, had its own Mishnah. We are not sure, however, that those references were there in the beginning; they may have been added later.[48] Moreover, as the appearance of the names R. Akiba, R. Meir, R. Judah, and R. Yose indicates, much that was taught in the school of R. Akiba found its way into the Midreshei Halakhah that we classify as coming from the school of R. Ishmael. The reverse is much less common; with the exception of R. Ishmael himself, there is very little from his students to be found in the academies of the school of R. Akiba. Elsewhere, I hope to prove that the bulk of the teachings of the school of R. Akiba found in the Midrashim of the school of R. Ishmael were added later and were not a part of the curriculum of the students of R. Ishmael. This should not be surprising; the editors of the extant Midreshei Halakhah of both schools were most likely close to the circle of Rabbi, for of all the sages he alone is quoted profusely in both Midreshei Halakhah. His adherence to the school of R. Akiba would have caused some of that school's teachings to penetrate the Midreshei Halakhah of R. Ishmael, which his circle was editing. It is distinctly possible, therefore, that the *mikan omru* passages that refer to the Mishnah (or Tosefta) may not really be an integral part of the teachings of the school of R. Ishmael.[49]

J. N. Epstein[50] is of a similar opinion, albeit for textual reasons, that the *mikan omru* passages in the Midrashim attributed to the school of R. Ishmael are in the majority later additions taken from the school of R. Akiba through the mediation of Rabbi and his circle. Epstein further claims that this thesis is already implied in the statement of R. Yose ben Avin (a fourth-century Palestinian scholar) in P.T. Shabbath 16:1 (15c) and parallels, where he speaks of the period prior to which Mishnayoth were embedded in the Talmud (Tannaitic Midrash). Since most versions of the Palestinian Talmud contain the word "Rabbi" as the one who did the embedding, this is an explicit assertion that Rabbi and his school were responsible for the additions of the *mikan omru* passages in the Midrashim.

In any case, one may safely assume that there was opposition to the Mishnaic form, at least during its early stage. Mishnaic form represents too great a break with the past to have enjoyed smooth sailing from its outset. The Book of Decrees of the Sadducees was attacked by the Pharisees because it contained fixed laws without biblical motives (which roughly corresponds to Mishnah without Midrash). It is extremely unlikely that when the successors of the Pharisees, the rabbis, introduced a similar mode of transmitting tradition it was fully accepted; it must have encountered opposition that lingered on for generations. Indeed, the statement by R. Natan (a mid-second century scholar) in the B.T. Sanhedrin 99a:

כי דבר ה׳ בזה — כל מי שאינו משגיח על המשנה.

("'For he has spurned the word of God' [Num. 15:31] refers to one who does not honor the Mishnah") suggests exactly that—that there were those who did not honor the Mishnah (indeed, who opposed it),[51] against whom R. Natan invoked this verse. In the parallel source, Sifrei Num. (p. 121), this statement by R. Natan is omitted and another statement is substituted:

זה היכול ללמוד ואינו לומד.

("One could learn and doesn't"), which in B.T. Sanhedrin 99a is attributed to another sage. The difference between the two sources probably reflects the fact that, in the circles from which the Braitha is taken, the mode of Mishnaic study was well entrenched, accepted and hallowed, so much so that not honoring the Mishnah was a sin worthy of comparison to spurning the word of God; whereas in the circles of the authors of the Midreshei Halakhah, especially those that stem from a non-Akiban source, as does Sifrei Numbers, Mishnah learning was not hallowed. To these authors, not to honor the Mishnah was not a blasphemous act. On the contrary, they may well have shared the condemnatory sentiment expressed in a bold Braitha in B.T. Sotah 22a:

התנאים מבלי עולם.

("The Tannaim [those who teach Mishnah] are destroyers of the world"); they deprive students of the proper mode of studying Torah. The Jewish way of learning is to have the laws attached to the Bible (by way of Midrash) rather than to circulate them separately, as does Mishnah. To counteract this sentiment, another source, attributed to the disciples of Elijah, taught:

כל השונה הלכות מובטח לו שהוא בן עולם הבא.

("Whoever studies halakhoth [laws of the Mishnah] is sure to have a share in the world to come"). This timid attempt to extol the study of Mishnah hoped to diminish the opposition of those who see in the mode of Mishnaic study a break with traditional learning, which is that of Midrash.[52]

It should be added that the statement favorable to the Mishnah attributed to R. Natan in B.T. Sanhedrin is probably genuine; the Sifrei undoubtedly omitted it because of ideological reservations about its content. What we know of R. Natan's activities after he arrived in Palestine (his origins are shrouded in darkness) is consistent with this favorable attitude. He was, so to speak, a Mishnah enthusiast. He was (according to the Babylonian Talmud, end of Horayoth) Vice-Patriarch during the patriarchate of R. Simon ben Gamaliel, who was the father of Rabbi, the anthologizer of the present Mishnah. He therefore lived at the center of Mishnaic activity.[53] He is also reported (Ecc. Rabbah 5:7) to have composed additions to the Mishnah along the lines of those composed by the household of Rabbi. These additions, though on occasion they differed in some details from Rabbi's Mishnah,[54] were wholly supportive of the Mishnah as a mode of learning. He was thus well steeped in the Mishnaic tradition and is, therefore, very likely to have expressed the comparison recorded in the Babylonian Talmud, namely, that whoever does not honor the Mishnah is spurning the word of God.

The career of R. Natan was quite remarkable. He most likely was in the company of the disciples of R. Ishmael; he is quoted frequently in their Midreshei Halakhah[55] and is totally absent from the Sifra. Yet he joined the ranks of the Patriarch, collaborating with him in the formation of the Mishnah. Tradition has it that he was the son of the Babylonian Exilarch and, upon his arrival in Palestine, was appointed Vice-Patriarch because of his high nobility.[56] Could it be that he was appointed to that position as a reward for having abandoned his circle's opposition to the Mishnah and having actively engaged in its composition?

VI

Later on, the opposition to the Mishnah subsided and almost disappeared. But in reality it did so only for a relatively short time. The stormy political events that ultimately led to the abortive Bar Kokhba revolt (132–135 C.E.) most likely contributed to the prevalence of the Mishnah over Midreshei Halakhah. During periods of political turbulence, when "the masses flock to hear a word of aggadah,"[57] the elite prefer the simple, easy-to-remember Mishnah over the complex, dialectical Midreshei Halakhah. The effect of these political events reverberated through the remainder of the second century and the beginning of the third century (corresponding to Rabbi's rule), long after the turbulence had ceased.

The Mishnah, with its relatively simple content, came into being as a result of the exigencies of the post-Temple era, and was sustained by the semi-insurrectional state that prevailed in Palestine during the first three and a half decades of the second century and culminated in the Bar Kokhba revolt. When the political conditions improved toward the second half of the century, with the termination of the oppressive Roman regimes, the Mishnah continued to flourish through the activities of the enormously prestigious R. Judah Hanassi, who in this activity probably continued a family tradition of oral law[58] (though containing fewer drashoth) that began with his ancestor, R. Gamaliel the Second, in Yabneh, only to collapse of its own weight soon after R. Judah Hanassi's death.

As a result, relatively few additions entered the Mishnah; it basically remained much the same as it was when compiled by the editor-anthologist. This is why the Mishnah is the only classical rabbinic book about whose editor we are relatively certain. We have no idea who the editors were of any of the other classical rabbinic texts (including the Talmud), but the evidence clearly indicates that R. Judah Hanassi was the editor-anthologist of the Mishnah. This evidence is based on two sources: the occasional reference by R. Yochanan (B.T. Chullin 85a) to R. Judah as editor-anthologizer and, above all, the fact that no one who lived after R. Judah Hanassi is mentioned in the Mishnah.

The Mishnaic form froze, as it were, with the death of R. Judah Hanassi. With it also were preserved the self-identifying traces of his editorial activity, which enabled later generations to recognize him. In contrast, the forms of the other classical rabbinic books continued to evolve long after their editing. Evolution invites additions, and additions ultimately obliterate the self-identifying traces of the editors. The editors became unknown.

The Amoraim abandoned the Mishnaic mode and chose a different one. The incentives that had launched the Mishnaic form 130 years earlier were no longer operative. When not besieged by external factors, Jewish apperception is aversive to the Mishnaic mode of learning. It dissipates by itself. After the effect of external forces evaporated, there began a slow, gradual process (not deliberate at first) of abandoning the Mishnah and returning, with greater vigor, to some salient features of the Midreshei Halakhah, particularly its dialectical mode. The process was initiated by the Amoraim; but it was during the Stammaitic period, roughly between 427 and 501 C.E., that it reached its culmination. This is the story of the following chapters.

Chapter 4

The Amoraic Period

I CONCLUDED the previous chapter by saying that after R. Judah Hanassi's death began the slow, gradual process of abandoning the Mishnah and returning to some salient features of Midreshei Halakhah. This statement requires qualification, however. "Abandoning the Mishnah" is not meant to suggest that the Amoraim stopped studying the Mishnah and it was gradually forgotten;[1] on the contrary, the Amoraim never ceased studying and commenting on the Mishnah. Their erudition in the study of Mishnah was second only to their knowledge of the Bible (that is, total mastery).[2] Nor should the phrase "abandoning the Mishnah" be construed to mean that the Amoraim stopped formulating fixed laws. The surviving statements of Rav and Shmuel, first-generation Amoraim who flourished during the first half of the third century in Babylonia, primarily consist of fixed laws, very much akin to the Mishnaic form. Later generations of Amoraim, however, did move away from apodicity, indeed, dramatically so in some instances.[3] This tendency is clear even in the sayings of a younger colleague of Rab and Shmuel, R. Yochanan, who flourished during the second half of the third century in Palestine.

What is meant by "abandoning the Mishnah" is that the Amoraim discontinued its development, even when they formulated fixed laws. The fixed laws formulated by the Amoraim were not integrated into the Mishnah; they remained loosely strung along the Mishnaic structure but never became a part of the Mishnah. This is evident when one compares, for instance, the relationship of the fixed laws of R. Judah to the Mishnah of his teacher, R. Akiba, with those of Rav and Shmuel to the Mishnah of their teacher, Rabbi. While the fixed laws of R. Judah are integrated into the Mishnah of R. Akiba, flowing smoothly without visible seams, those of Rav and Shmuel are attendant upon Rabbi's Mishnah, hover over it, but do not interlock. The gates of the Mishnah, so to speak, were already closed to them; they could come close but not enter.

The closest approximation to the Mishnah in the time of the Amoraim was *hora'ah,* rendering practical decisions. There is evidence—albeit conjectural—that the Amoraim, like the Tannaim, collected their fixed laws into a separate corpus called the hora'ah. This is probably what R. Chananyah in the name of Shmuel was referring to when he said (P.T. Peah 2:4 [17a] and parallels):

אין למידין מן ההורייה.

("one does not learn [practical behavior] from *horayah* [or *hora'ah*]"). It is indeed so cited by R. Chananel, Chagigah 10b). This is contradicted, however, by R. Zeira, quoted in the Yerushalmi (ibid.) a few lines above. According to R. Zeira, Shmuel did not include hora'ah in his list of the things from which one does not learn practical behavior. Shmuel said only

אין למידין לא מן ההלכות [משנה] ולא מן ההגדות [מדרשי אגדה] ולא מן התוספות.

("One does not learn [practical behavior] from halakhoth [Mishnah], nor from aggadoth [Aggadic Midrashim], nor from additions [toseftoth]"). This process of collecting fixed laws in a separate corpus probably continued throughout the Amoraic period until the death of R. Ashi (427 C.E., in Babylonia), who is called (B.T. Baba Metzia 86a) "the end of hora'ah."

The approximation of hora'ah to Mishnah is, for our purpose, not too instructive. True, both contain fixed laws, and both were collected in separate corpora. But whereas the Mishnah, at the center of Amoraic study, affected every facet of Jewish religious life by systematically reexamining each law in order to ascertain in what category of classification it belonged—anonymous opinion (with maximum authority), majority opinion (relative authority), or individual opinion—hora'ah consisted of a few meager decisions of a few Amoraim, each law bearing the name of the respective Amora without classifications. The Gemara never refers to the Amoraic fixed laws other than by saying "a certain Rabbi gave a practical decision," and even that rarely (in the Babylonian Talmud not more than twenty times). The authority of hora'ah is derived from that of the individual Amora whose name is attached to a particular hora'ah; it bears no collective authority. The inclusion of a particular Amora's hora'ah in the collection of hora'ah, unlike that of the Mishnah, did not endow it with additional authority; in fact, a hora'ah is never explicitly quoted as coming from a collection. Moreover, there are no special terms associated with hora'ah as there are with the Mishnah, such as "we have learned [in the Mishnah]." Indeed, its very existence is only conjectural, a further indication of its insignificance. *Hora'ah* finally disappeared altogether after the death of R. Ashi.

Much the same can be said about collections of sayings by the same Amora, or by the same combination of Amoraim, or any similar collections that we encounter in the Talmud in the form of "said a certain Rabbi . . ." These collections were made in this manner when the sayings were relatively few, and stringing them together made them easier to remember. Their authority, again, is that of the individual name attached; they bear no collective authority, and no special terms are to be found in connection with quoting them.

Neither hora'ah nor these collections were intended to take the place of the Mishnah, to be a successor to Rabbi's collection. Mishnaic form was no longer dominant during the time of the Amoraim. The major task (one could say the major ambition) of the Amoraim, even the very early ones, was not to carry on R. Judah Hanassi's Mishnaic tradition but to interpret it. By that time the Mishnah was almost closed, canonized, if you please, matchless. If one were to ask the Amoraim "Why is the Mishnah matchless?" they would reply: "Because of the greatness of Rabbi and his predecessors." But if there had been a compelling need to have the Mishnah further developed and extended, they would have found ways to overcome their modesty. They did not do so because there was no such need. The time of the Mishnah was over. The Mishnah could not last too long; it was not indigenous to the Jewish apperception.

The success of the Mishnah in the second part of the second century caused the importance of Midreshei Halakhah to recede and withdraw to horizons that were not within everyone's perception. The Mishnah became the major representation of the oral law, eclipsing Midreshei Halakhah. Paradoxically, after the Mishnah won its battle with Midreshei Halakhah and law became detached from the Bible, whose product it was, a natural need arose to have the apodictic laws of the Mishnah re-justified, either biblically or logically. Jews cannot live by apodictic laws alone; sooner or later they demand justification for their laws. Obsessed with the Divine, Whose will, they believe, is manifested in the Bible, they naturally prefer biblical justification but have settled for logical justification[4] when the former was not available. This position is not entirely unmishnaic. Along with the biblical justification, using the formula "as it says," the Mishnah also employs logical justification, using the formula "because."

The Mishnah, however, remained basically apodictic. The formula "as it says" is not used very often in the Mishnah; there are some tractates where it does not occur at all, and sometimes it was undoubtedly added later. Nor is the logical justification a frequent occurrence in the Mishnah. The Amoraim, in contrast, gravitated more and more away from the apodictic toward the justificatory, toward the vindicatory. In the Bible, God is His own justification. In the post-biblical period, the Midrash served as the link to the Bible, to God's word. After the interruption by the apodictic Mishnah, which reached its pinnacle during Rabbi's lifetime, the Amoraim gradually (less noticeably during the first generation, but nevertheless it began then) reverted back to the vindicatory style, providing the Mishnah with either biblical justification, using the Midrashic equivalent of "From where do we know these things . . . Scripture said," or logical justification, using the formula "What is its reason? . . . because."

In this respect the Amoraim were closer to the Tannaim of the school of R. Ishmael, who concentrated mainly on biblical exegesis, than to the Tannaim of the school of R. Akiba. The latter, it appears, were functioning both as formulators of fixed laws in the Mishnah and as biblical exegetes in the Midreshei Halakhah—and one cannot escape the impression that their exegesis served primarily, though not exclusively, as a means of deriving fixed laws. To use R. Judah again as an example, he is mentioned almost twice as often in the Mishnah as he is in the Midreshei Halakhah.[5] The study of Mishnah was his primary concern.

When the Tannaim were interpreting an early Mishnah—not an infrequent activity even among early Tannaim—they generally did not assume the role of interpreters, quoting the old source and expounding it, but rather couched their interpretations in the form of fixed laws, which was their main medium of expression (so much so that scholars only recently[6] have begun to realize that many controversies among Tannaim in the form of fixed law are in fact controversies in the reading and interpretation of earlier sources). With the Amoraim, however, the impression is the reverse: their major function was the interpretation of the Mishnah, not the formulation of fixed laws. Laws are necessary in order to know how to behave—a necessity of life which the Amoraim could not ignore—but interpreting the Mishnah was their vocation.

Despite their divergence from the Mishnah, the Amoraim remained essentially oriented toward the apodictic. Even when they interpreted the

Mishnah, they used a style that combined both the interpretive and the apodictic. Characteristic is the formula "They learned this only [in a case such as] . . . but" employed by all Amoraim but hardly found among Tannaim (perhaps in no more than a few instances).[7] This terminology is not purely apodictic because it does not stand by itself; it is unintelligible without a connection to an earlier source (a Mishnah, sometimes a Braitha, and occasionally even a statement by an Amora).[8] On the other hand, its content is easily transformable into apodictic law. If one drops *lo shanu* and adds the connecting line from the earlier source, the result is a perfect apodictic law.

Even more indicative of the Amoraim's basic apodictic orientation is their indifference, shared with the Tannaim, to recording for posterity the various steps of the discussions, the "give and take," that led them to arrive at the apodictic laws. Only the final decisions were bequeathed by them to posterity. We can assume a priori that these final decisions must have been preceded by intensive discussions that gave rise to disagreements. Occasionally we come across these discussions in Tannaitic literature; the Tosefta or a Braitha in the Talmuds sometimes contain a much more elaborate debate than the one preserved in the Mishnah.[9] Yet very few of these discussions have survived. We have very little discursive material from this entire period. We do have an explicit mention of "the deliberations of Rav and Shmuel," but they were not considered worthy enough to be transmitted to posterity[10]—and did not survive. The terms "he raised an objection" and "he asked" are typical ones for asking in-depth questions, questions that ask for more than the supplying of missing information. Those expressions are almost never found in connection with Rav and Shmuel.[11] The term "he asked" (*iteiveih*) is found, however, in connection with R. Yochanan and R. Shimon ben Lakish, younger contemporaries of Rav and Shmuel. But as already noted by the early medieval commentators,[12] some questions and answers supposedly raised by "he asked" are fictitious, a later construction of what R. Yochanan and R. Shimon ben Lakish could have asked and answered. I have reason to believe that all instances attributed to R. Yochanan and R. Shimon ben Lakish are fictitious.[13] During their time, as during the time of the Tannaim, the argumentational, the "give and take," was not officially transmitted to posterity.

One has to concede that discursive material is more difficult to transmit than apodictic material, since the former lends itself less easily to memorization. But the difficulty is commensurate with the interest. Because the Amoraim had no strong interest in preserving the discursive material, they found the difficulties insurmountable. As a result, we do not have from the Tannaim and early Amoraim *sugyoth,* a woven fabric of sustained discussion centered around, and interspersed with, fixed laws. The link of tradition was maintained exclusively through the preservation of apodictic laws.

II

The observation that the principal medium of transmission during the Amoraic period, particularly among the early Amoraim, was the apodictic form is useful not only to literary historians but also to exegetes. It helps to explain several puzzling passages in the Talmud, such as B.T. Shabbath 75 a–b:

> שוחט משום מאי חייב? רב אמר משום צובע ... אמר רב מילתא דאמרי אימא בה מילתא דלא ליתו דרי בתראי וליחכו עלי. צובע במאי ניחא ליה? ניחא דליתווס בית השחיטה דמא כי היכי דליחזווה אינשי וליתו ליזבנו מיניה.

> He who slaughters an animal on the Sabbath—under which category —[referring to the 39 principal categories of work prohibited on the Sabbath (M. Shabbath 7:2)] is he culpable? Rav said: Under the category of dyeing . . . Rav said: to the statement I made [earlier] let me add a supplement so that later generations will not laugh at me. Wherein is one pleased with the dyeing [one is only culpable if he is pleased with the dyeing]? One is pleased that the throat should be stained with blood, so that people may see it [i.e., the stain, and believe the animal to be freshly killed] and buy meat from him.

Why was Rav more concerned about being laughed at by later generations than he was about being laughed at by his own contemporaries? Was their laughter less troublesome to him? The explanation that first comes to mind is that Rav was confident that his contemporaries would hear the supplement either from him or from his disciples, but expressed concern about the later generations who would not have access to him or to his disciples and would have no way of knowing about the supplement.

This explanation is deficient. If that was Rav's concern, how would merely repeating the supplement guarantee that it be remembered? Moreover, one can assume that Rav must have offered the supplement almost concomitantly with his original statement. The statement by itself is unintelligible (Rashi calls it "astonishing"); the audience would not have understood it without the explanation contained in the supplement. What sense is there, then, to Rav's saying later on "let me add a supplement?" He must have done so already.

The answer is that Rav was addressing the transmitter who formerly heard from Rav both the statement and the supplement, but who, in line with the accepted mode of transmission of his time, transmitted only the apodictic statement and not the discursive supplement. In other instances of a similar nature it is supposed that the later generations, who had no access to the debates that gave rise to the apodictic law, would discover them on their own. The case of the slaughterers was different, however. The law (the statement) was so astonishing that Rav feared that the later generations would not take him seriously, that they would laugh at him and never discover the underlying reason behind his statement. Therefore, he asked the transmitter to make an exception and add the discursive supplement. The need to do so apparently occurred to Rav later, after the statement itself was already committed to the transmitter. Hence the semi-dramatic appeal by him: "To the statement I made [earlier, which is now outside of my domain] let me add a supplement."

Of more general interest is the puzzling phenomenon that, in the Talmud, problems (in the form of questions) preceding Amoraic statements are preponderantly anonymous. Such is the case even when it is certain that an Amora addressed himself to the problem, as when he says: "There is no problem. One source follows Tanna X and one source follows Tanna Y." In such an instance it is clear that the problem the Amora was trying to resolve was a contradiction between two sources which he or another Amora before him had raised. Yet the contradiction is stated anonymously. Why? Because official transmission was responsible, as it were, only for the formulation of the apodictic resolution (or the apodictic statement and the like), not for the formulation of the discursive raising of the question. As a result, the formulation of the former was transmitted as closely as possible to the original, whereas the latter was often improvised. Each academy formulated the discursive as it saw fit. The language of the problem preceding an Amoraic statement is not necessarily that of the Amora; more often than not it is the language of the later redactors, who may have modified or completely changed the original language. Hence the anonymous form of these problems.

A word should be said about who we consider the Amoraim to be. R. Chiya, R. Oshayah, Bar Kaparah (second quarter of the third century), and other contemporary compilers of Braithoth are usually classified as Amoraim even though they did not abandon the Mishnaic form.

They opposed Rabbi's "codificatory system,"[14] his order of arranging the material, but they did not break with his mode of presentation. They continued to employ the Mishnaic form. Nevertheless, since they were Rabbi's younger colleagues, they should be considered as belonging more to the end of the Tannaitic period than to the beginning of the Amoraic period. The standard beginning of the Amoraic period is a few decades later, with Rav, Shmuel, and R. Yochanan. With respect to them, our observations concerning the abandonment of the Mishnaic form are correct. Indeed, it is this characteristic more than anything else that sets the Amoraim apart from their predecessors, both Tannaim and the post-Tannaim like R. Chiyah and R. Oshayah. The Amoraim became interpreters rather than imitators of the Mishnah.

III

The standard definition of the root *drash,* "to inquire," "to seek out" and, derivatively, "to exposite [texts]," which is adequate for biblical, sectarian and Tannaitic literatures, is seemingly not adequate for Amoraic literature. There are numerous instances in both Talmuds where the root *drash* introduces fixed laws accompanied by neither biblical exposition nor logical inquiry. Even if one concedes the possibility (which to me is unlikely) that later editors omitted the supporting evidence for these fixed laws, evidence that initially justified the use of the root *drash,* one would still have to account for the seeming difference between Tannaitic and Amoraic literatures in this regard. Whereas in the Bible *drash* is used more generally, denoting almost any kind of inquiry, in Tannaitic literature (and to some extent also in sectarian literature) its use is limited exclusively to biblical exposition or to hermeneutic principles relevant to biblical exposition.[15] In Amoraic literature, on the other hand, the root *drash* is used in connection with laws that are entirely rabbinic, having no biblical support, such as the first instance of *drash* in the Babylonian Talmud, Berakhoth 38b:

דרש רב חסדא ... שלקות מברכים עליהם בורא פרי האדמה.

> *Darash* Rav Hisda . . . over boiled vegetables one recites the blessing of "he who created the fruit of the ground."

The designation of the blessing "he who created the fruit of the ground" over boiled vegetables is entirely rabbinic; it has no biblical support. Yet the word *darash* is used. Given the specific usage of the word *darash* in Tannaitic literature, how did the Amoraim justify applying it to fixed laws without scriptural proof text?

The answer perhaps lies in the distinction between the more common use of *amar* "he said," and the less common use of *darash* preceding a fixed law. That the two usages are not interchangeable can be seen, for instance, from the statement in the B.T. Chullin 14a:

אמר רב הונא דרש חייא בר רב...

("Said Rav Huna '*darash* Chiyah the son of Rav . . .'"). The same statement contains both usages, *amar* and *darash*. Rav Huna quotes a fixed law in the name of Chiyah, the son of Rav. Rav Huna's statement is introduced with the word *amar,* and Chiyah's fixed law with the word *darash*. The close proximity of the two words precludes the possibility that the two usages may be interchanged. The conventional form of quoting someone else's opinion is

אמר רבי פלוני אמר רבי פלוני

("Said Rabbi X or Rabbi Y") or משום ("in the name of") or משמיה ("in his name"). The use of the word *darash* together with *amar* in the same sentence is significant in that it indicates difference.[16]

It is generally assumed that the word *darash* preceding a fixed law means that the law was promulgated in public.[17] After the phrase

אוקי ר׳ פלוני אמורא עליה

("The lecturer placed an Amora [mouthpiece] by his side")[18]—customary when an "official"[19] law is delivered to a large public audience—the word *darash* is employed. The difference between *amar* and *darash* is that the former represents the formulation given in the academy, whereas the latter refers to the same law being delivered to the public.[20] In the example given above, it means that R. Huna told his colleagues in the Academy that Chiyah, the son of Rav, has publically promulgated the following law; hence the difference in usage.

It is quite plausible, therefore, that the use of the word *darash* preceding fixed laws in Amoraic literature was justified on the basis of its public posture. In Tannaitic times biblical exposition, Midrash, was taught in public either as part of worship in the Synagogue following the reading of the Torah, or in some other manner. In the course of time the root *drash* became attached not only to biblical exposition but to any teaching done in public, so that later on with the emergence of Mishnah, when fixed laws were also taught in public, the use of the root *drash* was transferred to fixed laws announced in public as well. Thus in Amoraic times the root *drash* was employed both for scriptural exposition and for introducing fixed laws. The latter usage was justified on the grounds that, like Midrash of old, it too was public.

Paradoxically, the use of the root *drash* was not extended to the exposition of Tannaitic texts. When it came to exposition, the expression was used exclusively in connection with the Bible. This is true despite the phenomenon, noticed by many, that exegetically the Amoraim did with the Mishnah what the Tannaim did with the Bible:[21] they subjected both texts to detailed hermeneutical analysis. This analysis was called by different names: *darash* in relation to the Bible, *t'na* in relation to Tannaitic texts.[22] The Amoraim did not transfer the use of the root *drash* to the exposition of Tannaitic texts, apparently out of fear that a similar usage would blur the distinction between the two texts. They had to draw a line between the texts, and they chose to draw it with respect to the official terminology employed in the Academy rather than that in the public halls. The latter, they must have thought, would not endow Tannaitic text with the same respect accorded the Bible.

This offers further support to my thesis that the Mishnaic form—that of transmitting fixed laws without scriptural support—was a relatively late mode of Jewish learning. In Tannaitic times the root *drash* was not yet applied to it, and even in Amoraic times the root *drash* was used only as a means of introduction, not as a description of the expository activity of the Mishnah.

Chapter 5

The Stammaitic Period

THE QUASI-APODICTIC APPROACH of the Amoraim was radically altered after the death of R. Ashi (427 C.E.). The gradual process of "de-apodictation" that began with the early Amoraim reached its climax with the Stammaim, who flourished between 427 and 501 or 520.[1] (Stammaim means simply anonymous authors; *stammoth* is the term for anonymous sections.) Some sages, like Mraimar, Rafram, Mar bar Rav Ashi, and Ravina the Second, continued more or less in the old tradition; they remained quasi-apodictic, though not to the same extent as the previous generation of Amoraim. In contrast, however, the overwhelming majority of sages of this period preferred to break completely with the Mishnaic mode of learning: they were almost totally non-apodictic, and very few fixed laws were attributed to them. The few anonymous fixed laws that we encounter in the Gemara in the form of והלכתא ("the law is") were determined by modern scholars[2] to be of Gaonic origin.

The Stammaim were concerned almost exclusively with the "give and take," the discursive (to the extent that one wonders how they coped with practical halakhah that requires the formulation of fixed laws). They offered interpretation in depth for the opinions of the Shammaites, for instance:

משנת ב״ש אינה משנה.

("whose teaching is not teaching [for practical purposes]"),[3] as well as for the opinions of the Hillelites, whose views are generally followed. It is hard to ascertain from their discussions which view they wished to reject, since contrary views are equally justified. They must have drawn practical conclusions from their discussions, but no evident traces of them are left in the text. Page after page is filled with discursive material without any discernible trend to tell us what the final decision ought to be. To the Stammaim, theoretical learning was a main mode of worship, worth pursuing even if it does not lead to practical decision making.[4] Any decision, however, that is the result of honest discussion and an attempt to seek out the truth through discussion is acceptable. When there are conflicts, one must decide and select one point of view. The basis for the selection is a practical one:[5] one simply cannot simultaneously follow contradictory views. But even the rejected view is not false; it is no less justifiable than the view that is being accepted. This explains the enormous effort lavished by these sages on the justification of opinions that would ultimately be rejected. Rejection was more for practical reasons, for religiously, even the rejected view was acceptable.

The concern of the Stammaim with the argumentation was most probably a consequence of their realization that the "give and take," the discursive, is no less—and perhaps even more—important than the apodictic and deserves to be preserved. Therefore, they set out to reclaim what was left of the argumentational material from previous generations and to redact it. Since the Amoraim did not deem it important enough to have the discursive material committed to the transmitters with the same exactitude and polish with which they committed the apodictic material, most of the discursive material did not survive, and what did survive was cryptic and truncated. The task of the Stammaim was to complete what was missing (usually through conjectural restoration) and to integrate the whole into a flowing discourse. They reserved for themselves the right to preface, conclude, and even interpolate the words of the Amoraim;[6] otherwise they could not have integrated and reconstructed them. The state of some of the argumentational material that survived was such that it required the intervention of the Stammaim at almost every turn. As a result, it is often very difficult to distinguish between what belonged to the Amora and what was added by the Stammaim, since the two are often interwoven. I did not exaggerate, therefore, when I said elsewhere that between us and the Amoraim stand the Stammaim.[7] We know the non-apodictic parts of the Amoraim only through the intervention of the Stammaim.

This close interlocking between the Amoraim and the Stammaim is truer of the middle generation of Amoraim than it is of the early generation, particularly Rav and Shmuel (mid-third century, Babylonia). From these two sages hardly any argumentational material survived, despite the explicit testimony that speaks of "the deliberations of Rav and Shmuel."[8] The deliberations must have been lost by the time the Stammaim appeared on the scene. The situation is different, however, in relation to the middle generation of Amoraim, particularly Abaye and Rava (first half of the fourth century, Babylonia). Here too we have testimony that speaks of "the deliberations of Abaye and Rava,"[9] but, in contrast to Rav and Shmuel, the Babylonian Talmud is replete with their discussions on all aspects of rabbinic learning—so much so that "Abaye and Rava" became in later jargon a synonym for the Talmud itself.

We attribute the preservation of the argumentational material from Abaye and Rava more to the short amount of time that elapsed between them and the Stammaim than to a special awareness by Abaye and Rava of the need to transmit the discursive as well. In other words, it was the Stammaim who preserved for posterity the non-apodictic material of Abaye and Rava, and not Abaye and Rava themselves. Because the Stammaim lived closer to the time of Abaye and Rava, for example, than to the time of Rav and Shmuel, the non-apodictic literary remains of the former survived better. This is also true of the non-apodictic literary remains of Abaye and Rava's teachers Rabba and R. Joseph, and of their respective students R. Papa and R. Ashi, among others.

Of course, one has to take into consideration also the quantity of production. R. Papa, for instance, produced less than Abaye and Rava, and therefore less of his productivity remained even though he lived closer to the time of the Stammaim. All things being equal, of those who lived closer to the time of the Stammaitic redactors, less was lost in the interval and more was reclaimed. Since it is unlikely that the realization of the importance of the non-apodictic material came suddenly to the Stammaim without any antecedents, one may assume that an awakening interest in, a burgeoning appreciation of, the non-apodictic existed even prior to the Stammaim.

In this respect, the middle generation of Amoraim may have served as a transition between the Tannaim and early Amoraim, who did not transmit formally and carefully the discursive, and the Stammaim, who concentrated on the discursive. But even though the middle generation of Amoraim may have evinced an interest in preserving the discursive, the actual preservation (that is, the collecting, completing, and integrating) was done principally by the Stammaim. The evidence is overwhelming that the redaction of the discursive material (and occasionally even the apodictic) was not contemporaneous with the composition of the material; the redaction was done later. We know, through critical analysis of the forced reconstructions and explanations of the redactors, that they did not always have an exact and accurate text before them; they often had to complement and correct it.[10] This would not have happened if the redactors had been living at the same time as the authors, for then the redactors would have had a more accurate text, straight from the authors or from their school. The absence of an accurate text of the Talmud—the lack of faithful reproduction, as it were, of the sayings and statements of the sages as early as prior to the closing of the Talmudic period—is definite proof that the redactors of the Talmud were not contemporaries of the authors, that the redactors lived later (sometimes much later), at a time when first-hand information was difficult to obtain. They had to rely on conjecture (which gives the right to a later scholar to try his own hand at an alternate conjecture, to "re-redact," as it were, the Talmud).

The notion of non-contemporaneity is the foundation of modern higher textual criticism of the Talmud. Much of the discursive material that was circulating for a while in a non-redactive state was forgotten during the interval; what remained was in a precarious state. The Stammaim reclaimed it, complementing and integrating it. The luxurious and flowing texture of the Talmud is the achievement of the Stammaim; prior to them there were only short dialogues and comments strung along the Mishnah and Braithoth. The Stammaim created the *sugya,* a semi-independent, sustained, multi-tiered "give and take." They redacted the Gemara from incomplete and truncated traditions. This explains the many almost incomprehensible instances where the argumentational proceeds along lines that seem to us totally unnecessary, and seems to make assumptions that are not warranted by the material at hand. This material could have been organized in a much simpler, more poignant way than the one proposed by the redactors. The redactors apparently had bits of tradition whose original context they did not quite know. They drafted these bits onto the material at hand, organizing their material not in accordance with its natural inclination but in a manner that would make it more assimilative of the stranded bits of tradition. A striking example is B.T. Baba Kama 14b–15a:

ע״פ עדים — פרט למודה בקנס ואח״כ באו עדים שהוא פטור. הניחא למ״ד וכו׳ פטור אלא למ״ד וכו׳ חייב מאי איכא למימר? סיפא אצטריך ליה בני חורין ובני ברית בני חורין למעוטי עבדים, בני ברית למעוטי נכרים.

On the evidence of witnesses [he pays the fine]—thus excepting a confession of a [wrongful act for which a] fine [is imposed] and subsequently there appeared witnesses. That would accord with the view that in the case of a confession of a fine for which subsequently there

> appeared witnesses, there is exemption, but according to the opposite view . . . What is the import of the Mishnah? The important point comes in the concluding clause—that free men and persons are under the jurisdiction of the law. Free men excludes slaves. Persons under the jurisdiction of the law excludes heathens.

There is absolutely no necessity to say that the phrase "on the evidence of witnesses" in the Mishnah is meant to exclude confession where there subsequently appeared witnesses. It is amply sufficient to say—as is indeed stated in the Tosefta Baba Kama 1:2, followed by the P.T. Baba Kama 1:3 (2c)—that the phrase excludes confession without witnesses subsequently appearing. Had the Gemara so stated, it would not have had the problem of explaining the Mishnah according to the opinion which holds that if witnesses appear after the confession, the confession is not valid. Why did the Gemara complicate the meaning of the Mishnah, adding that subsequently there appeared witnesses, which in turn forced it to say, according to the view that witnesses cancel confession, that the phrase "on the evidence of witnesses" is in apposition to what follows and should be read accordingly, namely, on the evidence of witnesses (that are) "free men and under the jurisdiction of the laws?"[11]

The Gemara did so because it had a tradition that there is such an interpretation that the phrase is in apposition, but it did not quite know what prompted that slightly unusual interpretation of making the phrase technically dispensable. The best explanation it could come up with was that the usual interpretation, that the phrase excludes confession, requires the addition of having witnesses appearing after the confession, which makes this interpretation unacceptable according to the view that the witnesses cancel the confession. In fact, however, we have a better explanation as to why there existed two interpretations of this phrase of the Mishnah—one of the oldest Mishnayoth—without adding the coming of witnesses. There is an old debate among Tannaim[12] concerning whether money damages paid for tort liability are considered fines, so that if the perpetrator confesses he is exempt from paying the fine, or whether they are considered compensation, so that even if he confesses he is liable for payment. The two different interpretations of the phrase "on the evidence of a witness" reflect these two divergent opinions. The opinion that holds that all indemnities are fines interprets the phrase to exclude confession without a witness; if the perpetrator confesses, he is exempt. The opinion that holds that the indemnities are compensation, on the other hand, is compelled to interpret the phrase to be in apposition with what follows. The Gemara (that is, the Stammaim, the redactors) knew only of the opinion that indemnities for damages with a few exceptions are considered compensation. In order to explain the motives behind the two divergent interpretations of the phrase "on the evidence of witnesses," the Gemara had to add artificially the coming of witnesses after confession, involving it with another controversy, which in turn is made to account for the divergence of interpretations.

I consider it improbable that the Talmud's redaction took place piecemeal, that every second or third generation redacted the works of the forebears of their forebears. Rather, I assume, using Occam's razor, that the redaction of the Talmud was done at one time. And since I discern no difference in redactional treatment between the sayings belonging to R. Ashi and those belonging to Abaye and Rava, I conclude, in conjunction with other evidence, that the redaction of the whole Talmud was done after R. Ashi's death, reaching its greatest intensity in the last quarter of the fifth century.[13]

A brief argument should be made here concerning why I consider the beginning of the sixth century the period when the redaction of the Talmud (the composition of the anonymous parts) was completed, rather than extending the redaction into the era of the Saboraim (the middle or end of the sixth century, or even later). I do so because of two reasons, one impressionistic and one factual. The Geonim (from the seventh to the tenth century) and the Rishonim (tenth to fourteenth centuries), our sole sources for identifying Saboraic materials, speak of the Saboraim as having added texts to the Talmud, which creates the impression that the Talmud was more or less complete during the time of the Saboraim. Without the anonymous parts, the Talmud would not have been even half completed. Second, Amoraic quotations in the materials generally attributed to the Saboraim can be traced to other places in the Talmud and were undoubtedly taken from there, whereas Amoraic quotations in the anonymous parts of the Talmud often have no parallel anywhere else in the Talmud. The authors of the anonymous parts of the Talmud had access to original collections of Amoraic statements, while the Saboraim —like the Geonim and Rishonim after them—depended solely on the existing Talmud for Amoraic information (Braithoth circulated independently and were always better known in some circles than in others. A knowledge of Braitha or a lack of it is no indication of a particular age). The Saboraim, therefore, were not the authors of the anonymous parts, were not the redactors of the Talmud, and lived at a time when the anonymous parts were already integrated into the Talmud proper.

It should also be added that apodictic material has no distinct literary style other than being apodictic—that is, responding to the concern at hand in minimal, concise language. In contrast, the Stammaitic Gemara possesses a rich and varied literary style (I am referring to those places where it does more than merely comment on early sources or fill in textual lacunae—where it composes a flowing discussion of its own). At the time of the Stammaim, the Gemara, because of its vast accumulated material and qualitative difference from Mishnah and Braitha, was rapidly becoming a separate book, and in the process acquired a literary style of its own. A notable example is its attraction to symmetry, to the extent that it will sometimes pad the discussion artificially in order to provide literary balance to the respective points of view.[14]

It has often been pointed out that the Babylonian Talmud differs from the Palestinian Talmud in that the argumentational material of the former is more complex, more dialectical, richer and more variegated in content, more removed from the *peshat* (the simple meaning) of the texts it discusses.[15] This is true even when the same opinion of the same sage is discussed in both Talmuds. Indeed, the discussions are qualitatively different. Z. Frankel[16] has already noted that the argumentational, the "give and take" of the Palestinian Talmud is qualitatively not unlike that of the early generations of Amoraim (I would add also that of the middle-generation Amoraim) in the Babylonian Talmud, in those instances where we can ascertain with a high degree of certainty that the "give and take" is actually from the Amoraim. Both are simple, narrow in focus, responding to the question at hand, and without a unique style, whereas the argumentational in the Gemara of the Babylonian Talmud is colorful, pulsating, outreaching, often presenting an interwoven and continuous discourse with a distinct, identifiable style of its own. For the purpose of tracing the various modes of Jewish learning, the Babylonian Talmud is more pivotal than the Palestinian Talmud; hence the heavy representation of examples in this book from the Gemara of the Babylonian Talmud.

The thesis bears restating. Even a cursory examination will show that the apodictic parts of the Talmud were better preserved than the "give and take," the argumentational, the discursive. Sometimes it is difficult to determine the exact extent of the apodictic material, to differentiate between substance and accretion. Nevertheless, the apodictic kernel frequently stands out. One has only to compare parallel sources to realize that the apodictic remained more or less the same throughout the literature,[17] whereas the argumentational material is almost always radically different in the parallel sources. It is my contention that the difference between the apodictic and the argumentational in this regard is due to the fact that until after the death of R. Ashi (427), the Amoraim did not deem the argumentational important enough to be transmitted. When it was deemed important enough to be transmitted, there was no longer any access to the original statements, and it was necessary to be content with conjectured reconstruction. I concede that the inherent difficulty in transmitting discursive material was a factor; but I maintain that it was not the major factor. These difficulties could have been overcome. In fact, they were overcome later; otherwise we would not have today a Gemara with its variegated "give and take."

To the best of our knowledge, the present Gemara was compiled and transmitted while still in an oral state. (Our first reliable record of a written Talmud dates no earlier than the eighth century.)[18] Transmission of discursive material did not present insurmountable problems then, and indeed the problems did not have to be insurmountable at an earlier period. What did change was the interest in and the attitude toward the "give and take."

As already noted, very little argumentational material survived from the period of the Tannaim and early Amoraim; so little, in fact, that it is clear that this lack of survival cannot be attributed to the inherent difficulty of transmitting non-apodictic material. It can only be attributed to the disregard of the Tannaim and early Amoraim for perpetuating the "give and take." Our Gemara is the result of a new interest in the argumentational. The question is, when did this interest arise—during the period of the middle generation of Amoraim, from whom much "give and take" survived, or during the period of the Stammaim, after the Amoraic period? Since the argumentational material stemming from the middle-generation Amoraim and from the Amoraim that followed them (like R. Ashi and his colleagues) is basically not different with respect to reliability from the argumentational material of the Amoraim that preceded them, neither of which were redacted contemporaneously with the enunciation of the sayings, and since to the best of our knowledge during the time of the Saboraim (sixth century) the Gemara looked not unlike the way it looks today (minus, perhaps, terminological expressions and a few additions that the Saboraim added to the Gemara), we must conclude that the interest in the "give and take" arose after the Amoraic period, and that the redaction was done between the period of the Amoraim and that of the Saboraim.[19] This corresponds roughly to the period between 427 and 501 (or 520). Since we do not know exactly who these redactors were, I call them the Stammaim, the anonymous.

II

I have been arguing, on the basis of textual evidence, that the anonymous redactors of the Talmud did not live at the same time as the Amoraim. Further evidence can be seen in their different modes of thinking. If the Stammaim were contemporaneous with the Amoraim, they would have shared similar thought patterns. The fact that they do not is best accounted for by positing that they did not live at the same time—that they were the product of different periods, and that each period has its own thought patterns.

I will mention one intriguing example from the Talmud that is relevant to our discussion. It deals with the question

ואי מכללא מאי?

("What if it is by deduction?"). This question comes after a statement to the effect that a previous opinion of an Amora "was not stated explicitly by him but was rather implicitly deduced." Sometimes the stam (an anonymous statement) will proceed to show that there is something wrong with the deduction. The Amoraim too occasionally observed that a given opinion by an earlier Amora was implicitly deduced, but they were apparently content with this observation and did not seek to find fault with the deduction. They asked no further questions. To the Amoraim, the observation that an opinion attributed to a sage was not stated by him explicitly was in itself worthy of transmission, requiring no further elaboration. To the Stammaim, however, such an observation was not worthy of transmission, and they therefore assumed that the observation must carry the additional negative purport that something was wrong with the deduction. By the time of the Stammaim, attributing a statement of an Amora on the basis of an inference was quite common; it was of no special significance to point this out unless it implied that the deduction was wrong. Such differences between the Amoraim and the Stammaim are evidence that the Stammaim lived after the Amoraim; they could not have been contemporaneous.

There is further support for a post-Amoraic dating of the anonymous redactors in passages in which they have added Amoraic statements to their own. The anonymous material of the Talmud is made up of passages that contain no names at all and passages that contain names attached to statements imported from elsewhere. These statements were imported from Amoraic material because they were thought to be relevant to the new subject as well. Their relevance, however, was determined not by the Amoraim themselves but by the anonymous importer. They are, therefore, no less stammoth than when no name is mentioned. The imported Amora often lived after (sometimes much after) the Amora whose statement initiated the anonymous discussion. That type of stam was certainly not composed by contemporaries of the Amora whose statement opened the discussion. It is not likely that there were two groups of Stammaim—that the stammoth containing no names were composed contemporaneously with the Amora who opened the discussion, whereas the stammoth with imported names were composed not earlier than the time of the latest Amora mentioned in the discussion.

One must, however, differentiate between various kinds of anonymous commentary in any discussion of dating. I make a distinction between simple, concise explanatory comments, which can be as old as the text itself, and complicated discursive explanations, which are late, after the time of R. Ashi. For instance, B.T. Ketuboth 47a comments on the Mishnah's saying (4,4) that the father has control over his minor daughter's findings "in order to avert ill feeling between father and daughter." The comment is anonymous, but it is quite old, as old as the Mishnah itself, and probably accompanied the text from the very beginning. The Mishnah and the comment were always studied together. Brief comments may appear anonymously in one place and in the name of a given sage in another place (both B.T. and P.T.).[20] Because they are taken for granted, such comments may appear with or without a name; the absence of a name does not in itself indicate age. It is the presence or absence of a name in a complicated argumentational passage that is a likely indicator of age.

Any discussion of the anonymous sections of the Talmud must look at the question of why they are there. Why would a society that proclaimed, among other sayings, "He that tells a thing in the name of him that said it brings deliverance into the world" (Braitha Aboth 6,6) transmit more than half of its oral literature anonymously? More specifically, why would an Amora (say of the mid-third century, a contemporary of Rav) who, breaking with the exclusive apodictic form of the Mishnah, was interested in preserving argumentational material insist that the "give and take" be anonymous to the extent that he would set a rigid pattern for future Amoraim to follow? What is the cause-and-effect relationship between "give and take" and anonymity? If we believed that the Stammaim were contemporaries of the Amoraim, we would presumably answer that the break with the Mishnaic form was not as complete as one assumes and that, apodicity remained dominant even in Amoraic times. As in Tannaitic days, only the apodictic material was transmitted attributionally, associated with names, whereas the "give and take," the argumentational, though by now considered worthy of preservation, was nevertheless thought of as being of lesser importance. To set the argumentation apart from the more important fixed law, it was transmitted anonymously, indicating its inferior status.

I find this answer unpersuasive, however. The half-break with the past does not seem logical. Once the early Amoraim decided to preserve the "give and take" they really had no reason to do so halfheartedly, especially since an ample precedent existed in the Midreshei Halakhah for the preservation of attributionally discursive material. More serious is the fact that bits of attributed argumentational material survive from almost every generation of Amoraim (and Tannaim); we come across them frequently in the Talmud. If there was a conscious decision by the early Amoraim not to break fully with the Mishnaic form, to transmit the "give and take" anonymously only, why was the policy so frequently flaunted?

One certainly cannot consider all stammoth to be contemporaneous with the authors of the text they are expositing. In that case, to what period would the many anonymous discussions around Mishnah and Braitha belong? Not to the Tannaim, because the discussions are in Aramaic. If these passages were earlier than those commenting on Amoraic passages, there would be some signs in the text of an early origin. But no such signs exist. Whether a stam explains a Mishnah or a very late Amora, like R. Ashi, the stam is qualitatively the same.

Clearly the stammoth around the Mishnah and Braitha came from the same period as those around the Amora; they are all from the post-Amoraic period. This late dating helps to explain why there are stammoth. I am arguing that the interest to preserve the "give and take" arose only in the post-Amoraic period, after R. Ashi. Prior to that period, as in the time of the Tannaim, only the apodictic was deemed worthy of being preserved. The argumentational, of course, was necessary; without it there would have been no fixed and determined law. But once the law was arrived at, the argumentational that gave rise to it was neglected, left to each succeeding academy to formulate as its members saw fit. There was no official version of the argumentational. As a result, in the course of time most of the argumentational was forgotten, especially that of the Tannaim. Bits of it, however, survived. Some survived with names attached, albeit haphazardly. But the overwhelming majority of the arguments did not survive and were reconstructed by the Stammaim in the Post-Amoraic period.

When the Stammaim added their discursive additions to the Talmud of the Amoraim, they added them anonymously in order to distinguish their additions (which they considered of lesser worth) from the teachings of the Amoraim. In the ancient world, anonymous additions signified subordinate activity, an acknowledgment of the supremacy of the main text. By being anonymous, the Stammaim acknowledged the supremacy of the Amoraic text. That recognition was consistent with their view of themselves as rebuilders of the old rather than creators of the new, as explicators and not originators. They considered their work as an explicit restatement of what to earlier generations was self-evident, and sincerely believed that they were adding nothing new. Paradoxically, this distorted image was shared by future generations, who failed to appreciate the Stammaim's activity. The two classical historians of the Talmud, the author of *Seder Tannaim ve Amoraim* and R. Sherira Gaon in his famous *Epistle,* do not mention them. The notion that the Tannaim and Amoraim did not show interest in preserving the "give and take," whereas the post-Amoraic sages did, does not sit well with those whose perception of Jewish spiritual history is that of constant decline. According to R. Sherira Gaon (*Epistle,* pp. 31, 62–64), both the Mishnah and the Talmud arose because "with each succeeding generation the hearts were weakened" and "many things that were simple to the earlier generations . . . were now in this [later] generation a matter of doubt [in need of recording and clarification]". Following such a general view of history, the post-Amoraic sages were perforce inferior to the Tannaim and Amoraim. Their interest in argumentational material was not a burst of intuition lacking in previous generations but rather a sign of weakness, part of a general intellectual decline marked by difficulties in figuring out things that had seemed self-evident to earlier generations. The work of the Stammaim was a concession to those who, so to speak, needed to be coached. To the learned they offered little. The Stammaim therefore did not attach their names to their additions, and future generations did not bother to attribute them.

III

The zealousness of the Stammaim to preserve the "give and take" led them sometimes to pursue the discursive as an end in itself. A characteristic feature of the Stammaim is their indulgence in the rhetorical and in pseudo-dialogue. Among the Amoraim, it is rare to find rhetorical questions or transparently false answers. But such questions and answers, along with their refutation, are frequent in the anonymous sections of the Talmud. They are there as literary devices. A striking example is found in B.T. Erubin 76b. The Mishnah states:

> If a wall that is ten handbreadths high and four handbreadths thick was placed between two courtyards, the inhabitants of the two courtyards require two *erubim* [allotments of food]. One joint *erub* is not enough [a wall of that size makes them into two distinct dwellings and family members from one courtyard cannot carry objects during the Sabbath into the courtyard of the other]. If the wall was not four handbreadths wide, it is the opinion of R. Yochanan that the area is considered one courtyard and the people can carry objects over the wall from one courtyard to the other.

The anonymous Gemara raises the question of whether R. Yochanan's opinion contradicts the Mishnah or not, and notes that the Mishnah states that they are considered two separate courtyards, whereas R. Yochanan says they are one. The answer to the anonymous Gemara is that the Mishnah is talking about a wall that is four handbreadths wide, while R. Yochanan is dealing with a wall that is not four handbreadths wide. The answer that the anonymous Gemara gives to its question is obvious: the text explicitly stipulates that R. Yochanan refers to a case where the wall is not four handbreadths wide. The early medieval commentators were hard put to explain the Gemara's question. The question does not need an explanation, however; it is there merely as a rhetorical device to emphasize clearly, though verbosely (another characteristic of the Stammaim), the difference between the cases of the Mishnah and of R. Yochanan.

A typical example of an answer that is not seriously intended is found in B.T. Rosh Hashanah 16a. The Gemara there quotes R. Yitzchak "asking": "Why do we blow a *shofar* on the New Year?" (that is, why do we blow a *tekiah*?). The anonymous Gemara interrupts him and expresses wonderment: "Why do we blow [*tokin*] the *tekiah*—because God said so" (in the Bible), and continues: "R. Yitzchak must be asking: 'Why do we blow the *teruah*?' [but this is no question either]? Why do we blow the *teruah*—because God said *sichron teruah*" (Lev. 23:24). Therefore, the question of R. Yitzchak must be: "Why do we blow the *tekiah* and the *teruah* when we are sitting and again when we are standing?"[21] The first answer, that the meaning of R. Yitzchak's question was "Why do we blow the *teruah*," was not intended to be a serious answer because the same objection that exists in connection with the *tekiah* exists in connection with the *teruah.* This is a rhetorical device, expressing in question and answer form the idea that even though R. Yitzchak uses the word *tokin,* he is not referring to the *tekiah* alone.

Another kind of rhetorical device appears when the entire discussion is unnecessary, as when the sage whose saying is being discussed has already explained himself, putting to rest the questions now needlessly raised. An example is found in B.T. Baba Kama 11b. Ulla says there, in the name of R. Eleazar (an early fourth-century scholar): "The law is that distraint may be made of slaves." R. Nachman says to Ulla: "Did R. Eleazar apply this statement even in the case of heirs [of the debtor]?" "No [replies Ulla], only to the debtor himself." "From the debtor himself [the Gemara, the stam, asks], could not a debt be collected even from the cloak upon his shoulders? [The Gemara answers]: We are dealing here with a case in which a slave was mortgaged [by the debtor who had meanwhile died] as in the case stated by Rava [who lived a generation after Ulla and R. Nachman], for Rava said . . ." The Talmud continues: "After R. Nachman went out, Ulla said to the audience: the statement made by R. Eleazar refers even to the case of heirs. R. Nachman said: Ulla escaped my criticism." As it turned out, as Ulla finally divulged, R. Eleazar intended the law to apply to heirs too (otherwise there is no significance to the law). R. Nachman apparently surmised that and understood Ulla to be saying the opposite in order to divert his (R. Nachman's) criticism. There is no historical or legal sense in defending the position that R. Eleazar meant to have the law apply only to the debtor himself. This, however, did not prevent the Gemara from positing that position (and connecting the rule of R. Eleazar with the saying of Rava, a later scholar), not out of historical necessity but out of love for logical discourse.

This is reminiscent of later *pilpul,* which also sometimes ignored the sages' explanations. A case in point is Maimonides' statement that whatever is not explicitly written in the Bible is termed "from the words of the scribes." This statement of Maimonides generated much discussion, and various explanations were offered as to its source and meaning. Fortunately, we have a responsum by Maimonides in which he explains what he meant and what the source was. But publication of this responsum did not put an end to all discussion, which continues to this day, often ignoring Maimonides' own explanation.[22] Maimonides' name in this context, after the publication of his responsum, is merely a holdover from earlier times; it bears no historical reality.

More important than the rhetorical quality of Stammaitic literature is its dialogical quality, the tendency to stylize simple statements in question and answer form, as if there were a debate. This proclivity for discussion on the part of the Stammaim often transforms even a simple statement into a discussion. The anonymous Gemara may interrupt a statement that contains a law and a reason, and add before the reason the words "What is its reason? because:"[23] as if indeed someone had interrupted the author of the statement asking him what his reason was, which he revealed only because of the prompting of the interlocutor. This, of course, was not the case; the author gave the reason without prompting. Nor did the Stammaim intend to convey that it was the case. It is merely an expression of their love for the dialectical.

Another example is that of B.T. Baba Metzia 21a (already noticed by the early medieval commentators, who, however, did not see it as a part of the overall style of the Stammaim). The Mishnah there states: "One who finds fruits scattered about may retain them [since they are lacking any specially identifiable characteristic, it may be assumed that the owner has abandoned them]." The Gemara inquires: "What is the proportion of the fruit to the space, before abandonment of the fruit is performed? Said R. Yitzchak: One *kav* [spread over] four cubits." The question "What is the proportion of the fruit to the space?" assumes that there is a proportion, whereas in fact, this does not have to be so. Fruit that does not have any specially identifiable characteristic, spread over any territory, large or small, could conceivably belong to the finder. The question raised here requires an unjustified assumption. It is the opinion of R. Yitzchak that there is such a proportion, and this anonymous question was added after he expressed his opinion in order to endow R. Yitzchak's statement with a dialogical quality. In their zeal for the discursive, the Stammaim occasionally overstepped and included also the rhetorical and the pseudo-dialogical.

One should also note that discursive material lends itself more to fictionalization than does fixed law. It is rare (though not unknown)[24] to have someone attribute a fixed law to a sage who did not say it, although it is generally frowned upon on moral grounds; whereas to attach a reason to a fixed law enunciated by a sage and pass them both on in the sage's name is common and acceptable. This is the case only as long as the reason carries logical force. The Stammaim, being more involved with the discursive material, were more given to fictionalization than the Amoraim or the Tannaim before them.

We have now come full circle. The very late Stammaim, through their complete break with the apodictic, have in a sense followed the very early

Midrash. Though not as scripturally oriented as the Midrash (Stammaitic material contains, however, plenty of scriptural references), the Stammaim share—against the Mishnah—the vindicatory quality of the Midrash and the biblical motive clauses. This vindicatory quality appeared to take the position that Jewish law must be justified, if not biblically at least logically. It is not surprising that the Midrash and the Gemara (the Stammaitic Talmud) share some common terminology. For instance, instead of the Midrashic

אתה אומר (כן) ... או אינו אלא ...

("You interpret it to mean . . . perhaps this is not so . . ."), the Stammaim say

ממאי ... דלמא ... וכו׳

("How do you know it is so . . . perhaps this is not so . . .").

I have already noted that the Midrashic formulas, which may have had their origin in polemical discussion, with real adversaries later on had only rhetorical value. Their content could have been equally well expressed categorically. It might not be incorrect, therefore, to say that the Gemara is the successor of the Midrash, both having important features in common. During Rabbi's time, it seemed as if Mishnaic form was superseding Midrashic form; that Jewish law, like the laws of other peoples, would be mainly apodictic, not accompanied by justification, biblical or logical. But this did not happen. The Amoraim abandoned the Mishnaic form but remained apodictically oriented. It was the Stammaim, flourishing during most of the fifth century, particularly the last quarter, who broke radically with apodicity and concentrated almost exclusively on the discursive,[25] restoring to Jewish law its original justificatory nature. Like Midrash and like some parts of the Bible, the Gemara reaffirmed the principle that Jewish law cannot be categorical. Making law categorical leads to autocracy, which Jewish apperception instinctively rejects. It must be accompanied by justification, either biblically like the Midrash, or logically like the Gemara.

So pervasive was the influence of the Stammaitic proclivity for the "give and take" that post-Stammaitic codes (with the exception of Maimonides' code, to which we shall return later) consisted of abridged Gemara, a mixture of fixed law with "give and take," including occasionally even the rhetorical and the pseudo-dialogical. The classical post-Talmudic codes like the *Sheiltoth* (eighth century), *Halakhoth Gedoloth* (ninth century), *Rif* (eleventh century), and *Rosh* (thirteenth century) all display the complete break with the Mishnaic form stimulated by the Stammaim. Their laws, whether they follow the order of the Gemara (like the last two) or another order (like the first two), are embedded in a matrix of discursive material,[26] which is now indispensable for any book of Jewish learning. (Of a slightly different genre is the work of M. Hameiri, 1249–1316, who actually composed two different tracts, one dealing with the "give and take," *Chidushim,* and one summarizing the fixed laws of the Talmud, *Beth Habchirah.* As one would expect, the tracts intermingled.)

The Stammaim captured the Jewish imagination, which was prepared all along to become captive to them by its natural reluctance to accept categorical law. Jewish imagination insists on having a reason, a justification, even if this can be obtained only through dubious discursive means. This was especially true during and following late antiquity, when the law was vast and its origin was difficult to track down. Law by its nature had to be fixed; it could not go on for long following the model of the Stammaim of almost total concentration on the discursive. But neither could it, after the Stammaim, discard the discursive, the "give and take." The justificatory nature of Jewish law remains, to this day, the most unique characteristic of Jewish learning.[27]

Chapter 6

The Gemara as Successor of Midrash

I HAVE SPOKEN of the affinity between Midreshei Halakhah and the discursive parts of the Talmud, the Gemara. Indeed, the Gemara may be viewed as a successor to Midreshei Halakhah.[1] Both are dialectical, tending toward the rhetorical. Particularly striking are the many long passages in the Midreshei Halakhah where the hypothetical alternatives offered are clearly untenable from the very start.[2] These alternatives were never intended to be presented as viable options; their purpose is rhetorical, and only rhetorical.[3]

Midreshei Halakhah often ask "Why is this said?" without implying that the words or verse under discussion are superfluous. They have either been adequately explained before or they need no explanation. The question "Why is this said?" is asked rhetorically, designed to strengthen what follows, as if the content of what follows is necessitated by the superfluity of the word, words, or verse, while in fact the support for what follows lies elsewhere. A disposition for the rhetorical is among the characteristics common to both Midreshei Halakhah and Gemara and is found, though in different forms, in the Bible, particularly in Deuteronomy.[4] In the Mishnah, the rhetorical is rare.

Another shared characteristic is the tendency for prolixity. In the Gemara, it is easy to edit out words without disturbing the flow of the argument. They are often there more for stylistic purposes than to enhance the substance. One can edit out words in Midreshei Halakhah as well, although there it is necessary first to examine thoroughly the content of the constituent parts of the argument—a laborious process. Editing out is therefore less common (but not uncommon) in Midreshei Halakhah. In the Mishnah, on the other hand, every word is an integral part of the statement. One can hardly remove a word or change an expression without changing the meaning as well. The Mishnah seems to place a premium on brevity, cutting corners of expression,[5] as it were, wherever possible. Sometimes the brevity in the Mishnah is so extreme that one has to provide orally the missing words to ensure understanding. In such instances, the Babylonian Talmud usually, although not always,[6] says: "There is a lacuna in the text. This is how it ought to read . . ." This idea is often conveyed by the Palestinian Talmud as well, even though it is not explicitly stated.[7]

When brevity is that extreme, it is probably a result of overexcerption. The Mishnah as we have it was excerpted from Midreshei Halakhah and early Mishnaic sources. The editor, who had the early sources in full before him, did not always assess correctly the amount of text needed to convey the full meaning to those who did not have the early sources. Perhaps he intended to quote more, but, without being consciously aware, he underquoted. When the brevity is not extreme, however, it is probably the result of a conscious decision to be as brief as possible. Laws that can be inferred from the context need not be stated explicitly. The third chapter of Moed Katan, for instance, begins: "These may cut their hair during mid-festival . . . ," without having first stated that one is not allowed to cut one's hair during mid-festival. This fact must be understood from the context.[8] Midreshei Halakhah rely less on contextual understanding, and the Gemara is even more explicit. In this respect, too, Midreshei Halakhah have an affinity with the discursive material in the Gemara.

Perhaps more important is an affinity between Midreshei Halakhah and the apodictic statements in the Talmud with respect to the way in which these statements were subject to a fixed terminology, an accepted form of expression of later origin. The editor (or more correctly, the anthologizer) of the Mishnah subjected his early sources to little or no change, quoting sources as he received them. Indeed, it can be shown that many of the difficulties in individual pericopes of the Mishnah are the result of his occasionally juxtaposing contradictory clauses. If he could not transform the respective traditions into regular controversy and record them as such without changing their language, he sometimes quoted them in their entirety despite contradiction, relying on external indications for the determination of the final law.[9] He did so out of consideration for the continuity of tradition which to him, in contrast to Maimonides a thousand years later, also included the preservation of the original language. It was important to him how the teacher said something, not only what he said.

Provided it did not lead to misunderstanding of the actual halakhah, the editor-anthologizer of the Mishnah, in combining different sources, often—though not always (far from it!)—ignored stylistic niceties and preferred quoting the sources as they were, even in those instances where doing so made for awkward reading.[10] He abided by the maxim attributed to Hillel (in some readings of Mishnah Eduyoth 1:3): "A man must use the language of his teacher." This was probably a religious commitment from which few deviated. Certainly the editor-anthologizer of the Mishnah did not make his sources comply with a preconceived structure or construct of his own. This is not to say, however, that the editor-anthologizer did not exercise any influence on the Mishnah. His influence was primarily through omissions and codificatory classification.[11] Many laws were excluded from his compendium altogether; they remained Braitha, "outside." When a law that the editor-anthologizer did include originally contained elements that halakhically contradicted his opinion, he occasionally preserved the form and substituted other elements that were more or less of the same scale.[12]

I should add that this description of the "editorial policy" of the editor-anthologizer applies more to the way in which the opinion of the first Tanna, *Tanna kamma,* is quoted than it does to the opinion of the second Tanna, the opposing opinion. After stating the case in the language of the first Tanna, the editor-anthologizer does not repeat the case again in the language of the second Tanna, even when their formulations differ. He summarizes the opposing opinion in the briefest of terms, often using a single word, with no pretense of having given a verbatim reproduction of the latter's view. To have done otherwise, to have repeated the case with each opinion, would have been intolerably redundant, and the editor naturally refrained from doing so.

Unlike the Mishnah, the statements in the Talmud—even the apodictic ones—do seem to have been made to comply with a unique fixed terminology. Statements by Palestinian scholars quoted in the Babylonian Talmud follow the general terminology of the Babylonian Talmud. An example is found in B.T. Baba Kama 20a, where R. Yochanan's statement begins with *lo shanu* and Resh Lakish disagrees with him, saying *akholho* (a Babylonian Aramaic construct). This disagreement is quoted in the P.T. Baba Kama 2:3 (3a) in a manner consistent with the style of the Palestinian Talmud:

ריש לקיש אמר על כולה הושבה, ר׳ יוחנן אמר, על הראשונה הושבה.

Resh Lakish said: It [the phrase under discussion] refers to all [the clauses of the Mishnah]. R. Yochanan said: It refers only to the first [clause of the Mishnah].

Similarly, statements by Babylonian scholars quoted in the Palestinian Talmud follow the general terminology of the Palestinian Talmud. An example is P.T. Erubin 8:4 (25a), where Rav (the founder of Babylonian learning) begins a statement with the term *hada deteimar, hada de'ittamar* (equivalent to *lo shanu*), which is not found in the Babylonian Talmud. It is clear that these statements are not recorded in the manner in which they were enunciated by their respective authors, but in the style of the compilation.

The situation with regard to Midreshei Halakhah is less certain. On the one hand, we encounter a faithful reproduction of a statement by R. Akiba in the Mekhilta of R. Ishmael, Mishpatim, parshah 20 (p. 336), that includes the term *perat,* which is not found anywhere else in the Mekhilta of R. Ishmael and which is a distinct terminological characteristic of the school of R. Akiba. (The school of R. Ishmael uses the equivalent of *lehozi et.*) Similarly, the phrase *umah ra'ita* is part of the linguistic usage of the school of R. Akiba. It is found nowhere in the Mekhilta of R. Ishmael except once in Bo, parshah 9 (p. 32), and this time, too, it is in the name of R. Akiba. On the other hand, many a statement reflecting the opinion of R. Akiba or his students is recorded in the Mekhilta with the strictest adherence to the terminology and linguistic usage of the school of R. Ishmael (and vice versa).

A beautiful example of this phenomenon, where the school of R. Akiba quotes a statement of R. Ishmael in the terminology of the school and not that of R. Ishmael, can be found in the Sifra Bechukotai, parshah 8:2 (p. 114c). The text there reads:

ר׳ ישמעאל אומר מניין לא יקדיש אדם בכור? ת״ל בכור לא יקדיש איש אותו. יכול לא יקדישנו הקדש עילוי? ת״ל כל זכר תקדיש. מה ראית להביאו להקדש עילוי ולהוציאו מהקדש מזבח? אחר שריבה הכתוב מיעט. מפני מה אני מביאו להקדש עילוי שהוא חל על הכל ומוציאו מהקדש מזבח שאינו חל על הכל.

R. Ishmael says: whence do we learn that a man shall not sanctify a firstling? Scripture [Lev. 27:26] says: a firstling—no man shall sanctify it. You may infer from that that he may not sanctify it as something whose estimated value falls to the Temple, Scripture [Deut. 15:19] says: All the male firstlings . . . sanctify (unto the Lord, your God). What makes you include sanctification as something, the estimated value of which falls to the Temple, and exclude sanctifica-

> tion as an offering that falls to the altar? [Because] after Scripture included it excludes [implying that there is a case of inclusion and a case of exclusion]. I include sanctification as something, the estimated value of which falls to the Temple because it is applicable to all and exclude sanctification as an offering that falls to the Altar because it does not apply to all [only to animals eligible to be offered on the altar].

This statement of R. Ishmael uses the expressions *lehavi, mah ra'ita,* and *ulehozio,* linguistic usages hardly found outside of the Sifra, the most Akiban Midrash of all. These expressions are the Sifra's, not R. Ishmael's; he uses different expressions. Indeed, the Mishnah, which is generally more faithful to the original sources than any other classical rabbinic text, quotes the second part of R. Ishmael's statement in quite a different language. It says (M. Arakhin 8:7) in the name of R. Ishmael:

> One verse of Scripture says: [all the firstling males] you shall sanctify; and another verse says: no man shall sanctify. It is not possible to say: you shall sanctify, since it is written, no man shall sanctify; and it is not possible to say: you shall not sanctify, since it is also written: you shall sanctify. Say, rather, you may sanctify it as something, the estimated value of which falls to the Temple, but you may not sanctify it as an offering that falls to the Altar.

The original wording of R. Ishmael was undoubtedly closer to the formulation of the Mishnah than to that of the Sifra. The Sifra changed the formulation to comply with its own terminology.

Despite the conflicting evidence, I believe that adherence to their own terminology is more representative of the styles of the schools of R. Akiba and R. Ishmael than any contrary assumption one may make. Examples to the contrary may be just exceptions. Otherwise we have to assume that R. Simon, for instance, used both terminologies, *perat le* in Sifra 73a and in Sifrei Deut. piska 299 (p. 318), and *lehozi et* in Sifrei Num. piska 70 (p. 67).[13] It is also possible that the contrary examples were added later, at a time when those who added them were either not sensitive to the differences in terminology or did not dare to change the statement's terminology. (The statement of R. Akiba where the term *perat le* is used is also found in Sifrei Deut. piska 104 and may have been imported from there.)

In brief, it is my contention that, with respect to subjecting earlier material to a fixed terminology developed later, the Midreshei Halakhah are closer to the Talmud than they are to the Mishnah. Both the Talmud and the Midreshei Halakhah (of both schools, though probably the school of

R. Akiba more so than the school of R. Ishmael; the latter, being more conservative in its exegesis, was probably less prone to tamper with given texts) superimposed their imprint on received material. In this regard there is an affinity between the two.

Unfortunately, we do not know precisely who is responsible for the particular terminological styles of the Talmud, and when these distinctive styles developed. Were these formulators contemporaneous with the authors of the statements, or did they live later? If later, were the styles developed by the Amoraim, the Stammaim, or even later by the Saboraim? If the terminological styles are indeed the work of Stammaim, then the Talmud could be viewed as a successor to Midreshei Halakhah, not only in its discursive parts but also in its apodictic statements with respect to style. This suggestion seems likely in view of the overall plan of the Stammaim to make the Gemara into a separate and independent book from the Mishnah, possessing a distinct character of its own. The Saboraim, on the other hand, would appear to be too late to have initiated such an essential aspect of composition.

I distinguish here between the Talmud's "terminological style" and its "terms." The style I attribute to the Stammaim; the terms, to the Saboraim. Terminological style such as "with what case are we dealing here"[14] transforms a saying or part of a saying attributed to a particular sage into a fixed formula that will be repeated whenever a similar saying, or part of a saying, is quoted. It has a routinizing effect, relieving the original author of his unique expressions and imposing a collective sameness on the saying. It also makes the author stylistically unrecognizable. On the other hand, words of terminology such as *vehatanya,* "has it not been learned [in a Braitha]," and *veraminhu,* "is this not in contradiction [with another Tannaitic source]," have little routinizing effect. They function as single-word abbreviations for longer expressions, and they facilitate transitions. Since they are most often applied to anonymous material (primarily discursive), they rarely interfere with the unique style of an author. While the aim of terminological style is uniformity, the aim of words of terminology is brevity; they are not interchangeable.

The Stammaim are responsible for the terminological style of the Talmud, because, as I have already posited, the Amoraim were not as yet interested in making the Gemara a separate book requiring a distinct style of its own. The Amoraim followed the contours of the Mishnah and Braitha closely, and would not have allowed themselves to be distracted by a new and different terminology. In contrast, the Saboraim—based on the references by Geonim and Rishonim, the sole evidence for their existence—already had the Gemara as a separate book. Their Talmud closely resembled our present Talmud, which would not have been the case if they had given it new terminological style and thus radically altered its face. Both chronologically and functionally, the Stammaim were best suited to be the initiators of the new and distinct terminology. It constituted a part of their function as redactors.

This function did not necessarily extend, however, to standardizing of terms. Standardized terms could come after the book was almost completed and accepted, as added refinements for the sake of clarity and smoothness. They would act as compact explanatory notes needed for the many audiences that would flock to study the Gemara. This function accords well with the period of the Saboraim.

We have firm evidence that the term *veraminhu,* "a contradiction was raised," stems from the time of the Saboraim. The evidence is found in B.T. Gittin 61b:

> ורמינהו המוליך חיטין וכו׳ לאו אוקימנא בפירות שלא הוכשרו? ודקארי לה מאי קארי לה? משום דקא בעי למירמא אחריתא עלה הרי אלו בחזקתן למעשר ולשביעית. ולחלופי לא חיישינן ורמינהו הנותן לחמותו מעשר וכו׳.
>
> A further contradiction was raised, if a man takes wheat . . . Have you not just explained . . . [according to which there is no contradiction]. What, then, was the point of the question? Because the questioner wanted to deduce another contradiction. If one gives his mother-in-law . . ."

If the questioner wanted to deduce another contradiction relative to "if one gives his mother-in-law . . . ," there could not have been the term *veraminhu* signifying contradiction before "if a man takes wheat . . . ?" The term must have been added later by someone who mistakenly thought that "If a man takes wheat . . ." introduces a contradiction. But how could he have thought this when the term *veraminhu* appears later on, before "If one gives his mother-in-law . . . ?" He probably did not have the term *veraminhu* there either. Yet the Gemara concludes that "If one gives his mother-in-law . . ." introduces another contradiction. Hence a contradiction could be raised without using the term *veraminhu.* It is a later term.

Tradition[15] had it that questions in the Talmud of the nature of "What then was the point of the question?" are of Saboraic origin. The question and answer just quoted from Gittin 61b are Saboraic. According to my analysis, the Saboraim assumed that previously contradictions were raised without the term *veraminhu.* This leads to the conclusion that the present ubiquitous appearance of the term *Veraminhu* before a contradiction is raised is Saboraic or even later.[16]

II

Paradoxically, despite the lesser involvement of the editor-anthologizer of the Mishnah, it retained a greater degree of uniformity than the Talmud. There is some variety among the tractates, even among the chapters of the same tractate (chapter 5 of Tractate Menachoth, for instance, contains no controversies). Basically, however, the style of the Mishnah is relatively similar throughout. Proceeding from one Mishnah to another, one does not generally sense that one is moving from genre to genre, from mode to mode, from taciturnity to loquacity or vice versa. It is a strikingly homogeneous work.

The Talmud is more kaleidoscopic in nature, a mosaic of different shapes and colors, with no two pages alike. Sometimes the same page may display disparate sources.[17] One rarely progresses in the study of the Talmud without realizing that one has moved from halakhah to aggadah or vice versa (there is little aggadah in the Mishnah), from the apodictic to the discursive mode, from prolixity to brevity or vice versa, all conducted in dual languages, Hebrew and Aramaic. Multiformity is part of the very fabric of the Talmud.

From its very inception (ca. 90 C.E.), the Mishnah had a definite goal —to facilitate memorization. That goal created the Mishnaic form and standardized all subsequent Mishnaic compositions. Material (like Midrash) that did not easily lend itself to memorization was not initially included in the repertoire of the Mishnah. (In the course of time, however, Midrash proved to be irresistible, and portions of it entered the Mishnah.) The Mishnah was, and remains, *bachranit,* "highly selective"[18] (despite Midrashic inroads), conforming to rigid standards upheld by all Mishnaic sages. Rabbi, the editor-anthologizer of our Mishnah, innovative as he undoubtedly was, did not and could not alter the uniformity of the Mishnah mandated by the original goal.

The Talmud at its inception had no definite goal other than collecting data. No single genre or form was designated as being particularly suitable for that purpose; multiple genres and forms operated simultaneously. Halakhah and aggadah commanded equal interest. The Amoraim steadfastly followed the contours of the Mishnah and Braitha by having their additions take on the coloring of the Mishnah and Braitha (apodicity, for instance), and whenever comments were necessary to explain the source of the Mishnah or Braitha, they offered Midrashic comments such as: "From where do we know these things . . . Scripture says . . ." Apodicity and Midrashic comments of all varieties are the characteristics of Amoraic Talmud.

In the course of time, multiformity was further increased. Much of it can be attributed to the functions of the Stammaim. Their first function was to reclaim the "give and take," the discursive, which previous generations did not deem worthy enough to perpetuate. They thus introduced a new type of Talmud (when anonymous, we call it Gemara) of enormous richness and variety. When this was combined with their second major function, the redaction of the surviving material into a separate corpus, it would have been impossible for the Stammaim to contain the argumentational material to a few limited forms. Many forms had to be employed to record this astonishing literature, with its propensity for constant expansion and continuous development. The Talmud could not be other than multiform.

The Mishnah did have the benefit of having been edited (or anthologized) by a single hand (or hands belonging to the same group, that of Rabbi and his school), whereas different sections of the Gemara were redacted by different Stammaitic schools. (Sura and Pumbedita are the most outstanding of these schools, but not the only ones.) I deduce this from the many contradictions found in the Gemara (there are contradictions in the Mishnah, too, but for other reasons), from the occasions when one source does not know the literature quoted in the other source,[19] and from the differences in the quality of redaction and literary style among the respective sections. Unlike the Mishnah, the Gemara was too vast to be redacted by one school. Multiple schools with different forms of redaction shared in the composition of the Gemara, and multiple redactorship leads to multiple form.

Probably because of the vast quantity of Amoraic statements available to them, the Stammaim did not have an opportunity to redact all of the Amoraic statements worthy of preservation. We often encounter in the Talmud single apodictic statements without any comment at all, followed or preceded by a lengthy discussion of another apodictic statement. There are instances where the same statement that is transmitted without comment in the Babylonian Talmud is profusely commented on in the Palestinian Talmud, and vice versa. The lack of comment in the Babylonian Talmud does not stem from the inability of the Stammaim to comment on a particular statement, but rather from their lack of opportunity to do so.[20] This is another factor that indirectly contributed to the multiformity of the Talmudic texture.

At the same time, some sections are so well redacted that one does not notice at first that the sayings come from different schools. Intermingling of sources is more frequent in the Talmud than in any other book. Along with unredacted single apodictic sayings and sections redacted by different schools, there are also sections that transcend schools, forming a woven continuum of "give and take" that utilizes sayings of different origin. This combination heightens the multiform effect of the Talmud, and indeed makes it appear as if multiformity is the essence of the Talmud.

Midreshei Halakhah are more multiform than the Mishnah, less so than the Talmud. They intermingle materials of different schools (materials from the school of R. Akiba are more prominent in the Midrashim assigned to the school of R. Ishmael than vice versa) and contain a large number of both complex and simple Midrash. Unlike the Mishnah, Midreshei Halakhah contain a fair portion of aggadah (with the exception of the Sifra, which in our editions does not contain aggadah until the last portion of Bechukotai). What makes them uniform is that they almost always begin with a verse of the Bible; this beginning restrains experimentation with multiple forms and restricts the form to what could broadly be called Midrash. Even stories of later periods have to show their relevance to biblical verses or words in order to be included. There is an insistence that the contents of Midrash be Midrash. The word "Talmud" carries no such restrictions; almost anything could be included as material of the Gemara.

III

It is important to add that the affinity between Midreshei Halakhah and the apodictic material in the Talmud does not extend to the authenticity of their content. As far as authenticity is concerned, Midreshei Halakhah —or any Braitha for that matter, whether of Midrashic or Mishnaic variety (like the Tosefta), coming from the school of R. Chiya or of R. Oshayah—have an advantage over the apodictic statements of the Talmud. The traditions of the Midreshei Halakhah are more faithful to the original enunciations of the respective authors.

In twenty instances, the Babylonian Talmud declares an apodictic statement not to have been stated in that form originally but rather to be the result of an implicit deduction ("It was not taught so explicitly, only implicitly") which someone later put in an explicit form. In a few cases the Babylonian Talmud even challenges the deduction, saying, "It is not so!" The statements so declared or challenged are all Amoraic statements; we do not have a single declaration or challenge related to a Tannaitic statement. This is not a matter of chronological distance of the Amoraim from the Tannaim, for R. Papa (ca. 375) was further removed chronologically from Rav (ca. 247) than, say, Rav was from R. Judah (second half of the second century). Yet R. Papa says of Rav, "It was not taught so explicitly," while Rav does not say this of R. Judah. Tannaitic statements were transmitted with greater fidelity.

The fidelity of Tannaitic transmission is also confirmed when one compares parallel sources. Braithoth retain a higher degree of sameness throughout their parallel appearances than do apodictic statements when they are quoted, for instance, both in the Babylonian Talmud and the Palestinian Talmud; apodictic statements were transmitted in the Talmud with less scrupulous exactitude (that is, relative to the Braithoth, not to speak of the Mishnah). The Mishnah, as we have seen, is the most reliable ancient rabbinic text.[21] It was generally transmitted "in the language of the teacher"—in the original form—and is almost always the same, despite minor variations in the different quotations. In contrast, the lowest level of reliability was maintained by the discursive portions of the Talmud, which are rarely the same in the parallel sources.

Arranged hierarchically, the order of reliability is as follows. The Mishnah displays the greatest fidelity to the actual statements enunciated by the respective authors. On occasion the Mishnah retains the author's first version despite his subsequent change of mind. R. Judah Hanassi, according to his disciple R. Yochanan, once let stand an old opinion of R. Akiba quoted in his name even though R. Akiba changed his mind.[22] It is especially notable that nowhere in the Mishnah is there any sign that the law follows the opinion of the Hillelites. Yet R. Judah Hanassi was a descendant of Hillel, and his patriarchical family a few decades before the composition of the Mishnah[23] undoubtedly played a role in the decision that the law should follow the opinion of the Hillelites. Nevertheless, in compiling our Mishnah, he let the old text stand.

After the Mishnah the most reliable texts are the Braithoth. It is possible that the Braithoth that are arranged in the Mishnaic form, like the Tosefta (provided they stem from the schools of R. Chiya and R. Oshayah), are more reliable than those arranged in the Midrashic form of the Midreshei Halakhah, which are of the complex Midrash variety. Complex Midrash is difficult to remember and, therefore, more prone to inaccuracies in transmission. After Braithoth in reliability come the apodictic statements in the Talmud. They are not difficult to remember—on the contrary, their apodicity serves as a mnemonic device—but they were subject to editorial workings, to fixed terminology, and, when the scholar lived in Palestine and was quoted in Babylonia or vice versa, also to translations from one Aramaic dialect to another (translations that were not always verbatim). Finally, the discursive passages in the Gemara are least faithful to the original, for the Amoraim, like the Tannaim before them, did not deem it necessary to preserve the argumentational, at least not with the same exactitude as they did the apodictic material. With the Stammaim arose the interest in carefully preserving the discursive material as well, but by then much of the original sources were gone and they had to rely on their reconstruction or conjecture.[24]

Chapter 7

The Legacy of the Stammaim

THE MEDIEVAL EXEGETES were heirs to the traditions and modes of thinking of the Stammaim and give expression to this heritage in their exegesis. One of the marvels of medieval Jewish biblical exegesis is the type of exegesis expounded by the Rashbam (died in 1174), R. Joseph Bechor Shor (twelfth century), to some extent also by R. Abraham Ibn Ezra (died in 1164), and a few more.[1] These exegetes systematically and unrestrainedly maintained the freedom to explain the Bible differently from, and in opposition to, accepted halakhah. They did so in peripheral matters as well as in matters of great religious sensitivity, such as when to begin the Sabbath and festivals, putting on phylacteries, or the laws of bastardy. There is no doubt that their exegesis bore no relevance whatsoever to halakhic practices. Yet in practice, the Rashbam, one of the great religious authorities of the Middle Ages, did not deviate an iota from the accepted halakhah. This was true also of the other exegetes. What value, then, did these exegetes attach to an exegesis that not only did not have any practical implication but was, from the standpoint of practical halakhah, false?

Practical halakhah, for instance, sees the difference between Exod. 22:6–8 (which absolves the one who took it upon himself to watch over an object if the object is stolen) and Exod. 22:9–12 (which makes one responsible if the object is stolen) that in the former case the one who took it upon himself to watch over the object was a "gratuitous bailee" (that is, he did not get paid), while in the latter case he was a "bailee for hire" (he was paid). The Rashbam, on the other hand (and his explanation is found also among the nonrabbinic, early Jewish Greek commentators),[2] interprets the difference between these two passages in Exodus more in accordance with the wording of the text. In the former case, the wording is: "If a man gives another silver or chattels for safekeeping"; in the latter case it is: "If a man gives another an ass, an ox, a sheep or any beast unto his neighbor's keeping." The difference, according to the Rashbam, is in the nature of the object being given for safekeeping. If the object that was stolen was inanimate, he is absolved; if it was animate, he is responsible. This distinction between animate and inanimate objects is totally rejected by normative halakhah (demonstrably so, since it was aware of the distinction's existence). The Mishnah at the beginning of the third chapter of Baba Metzia says:

המפקיד אצל חברו בהמה או כלים ונגנבו או שאבדו

("If a man left an animal or chattels in his fellow's keeping and they were stolen or lost . . ."). The Gemara raises the question: Why does the Mishnah have to specify both animal and chattels? The answer (not given by the Gemara) is that the Mishnah was aware[3] that there are those who make a distinction between animal and chattels, between animate and inanimate objects. To preclude such a distinction, the Mishnah explicitly states that there is no difference between them and that the same law applies to both. But even such an explicit statement of the Mishnah did not deter the Rashbam from following the literal wording of the text in his commentary.

Civil laws are primarily designed for practical purposes; there is little in them that is edificatory. The question therefore is: If in practice the Rashbam did not follow the distinction between animate and inanimate objects with regard to the laws of safekeeping, why, then, did he make such a distinction in commenting on the text? What value does one derive from writing down and disseminating rejected opinions in matters of civil law? I can think of only one answer:[4] The value one derives from an exegesis that is opposed to practical halakhah is that through that exegesis he fulfills the commandment to study Torah. The *mitzvah,* divine commandment, of studying Torah does not require that the Torah being studied be capable of practical application. What these exegetes introduced—though nowhere do they say so explicitly—is that to fulfill the mitzvah of *talmud torah,* of studying Torah, one does not have to study in a manner consistent with practical halakhah. As long as what is studied is contained within the wording of the text, is in line with its spirit, or accords with its context, it is Torah, and he who studies it is fulfilling a divine commandment. The realm of the mitzvah of *talmud torah* and the realm of practical halakhah need not coincide.

This added dimension of studying Torah introduced by these exegetes might not have come into being were it not for the Stammaim. They prepared the ground for the independence of the study of Torah from practical halakhah through their concentration on the "give and take" of all views (including those that will be ultimately rejected) instead of on the practical applications. Following in the footsteps of the Midreshei Halakhah, the Stammaim added the rhetorical and the pseudo-dialogical to Torah study (one who is studying them has to recite the benediction that is recited before the study of the Torah). The medieval exegetes added *peshat* (the common meaning) to Torah even when it contradicts practical halakhah; yet surely they recited the Torah benediction before they studied and wrote down their exegesis. The affinity between these two groups is unchallengeable.

Medieval exegesis is thus another manifestation of an abiding concern for explaining and justifying the law. Without a predilection for justified law the Stammaim would not have concentrated so strongly on the reasoning and the argumentational, and the medieval exegetes would not have dared to be so innovative, pursuing exegesis almost for its own sake.

The Stammaim, too, were continuing a process that started very early in the history of rabbinics. In the Bible proper (without rabbinic interpretation), studying Torah is not a mitzvah by itself but rather a means or an instrument for observance. Without study one does not know how to observe. The verses in the Bible that one usually quotes to show that studying Torah is a mitzvah are the following: "Repeat them to your sons and converse in them" (Deut. 6:7) and "Teach them to your children and speak of them" (Deut. 11:19). But "them" refers to the commandments, the observance of which is being exhorted in the previous verses there—that is, transmit the observance to your children, talk about the commandments, so that they and you will know how to behave. Learning as an independent activity is not implied. The parallel in Joshua 1:8 to "You must keep it in mind day and night" is "so that you may diligently observe all that is written in it." Study in order to know how to observe. Study by itself is not a mitzvah.

The rabbis, however, understood the relevant biblical verses differently. (Psalm 119 is perhaps in this respect a transition between the Bible and the rabbis).[5] In rabbinic literature, study is a separate mitzvah. It is often regarded as distinct from, or even in opposition to, deeds (observance).[6] Only in rabbinic literature could there have arisen the question (Sifrei Deut., piska 41, [p. 85 and parallels]):

תלמוד גדול מעשה גדול

("What is more important, study or deeds?"). Legend has it that even God is studying Torah every day[7] for its own sake; God is beyond action.

The many exhortations[8] found in Talmudic literature against those who study Torah and do not observe attest to the temptation of Torah study without observance. This would not have been so attractive had there not been a mitzvah of pure studying; the urge for intellectual pleasures could have been satisfied elsewhere. During the biblical period there was no need to exhort against learning without observance, any more than there was a need to exhort against toil without harvesting. The phrase "you must keep it in mind day and night" is no more of an independent mitzvah than is the phrase "six days you shall toil and do all your work" (Deut. 5:13). Toiling for its own sake is no mitzvah,[9] any more than learning for its own sake is. Each phrase is subordinated to what follows immediately afterward: the former to "so that you may diligently observe" and the latter to "but the Seventh day is Sabbath unto the Lord, thy God, in it thou shall not do any manner of work." It was the rabbinic ethos that made learning a part of worship, which, in turn, stimulated the desire to study Torah independent of mitzvoth, against which the literature is warning.

This ethos is partially a result of the initial biblical insistence on giving a reason or justification, on arguing something out, thereby encouraging study which eventually became an independent mitzvah. It is impossible to argue meaningfully without posing counterarguments and refuting them. These counterarguments and their rebuttal became, in the course of time, Torah—no less than when one is studying the final conclusions. The seed for learning as an independent mitzvah was thus being sown. If even the refuted sections constitute Torah, the mitzvah of *talmud torah* cannot be subordinate to action; it must be independent. If the Bible had initially followed the pattern of ancient Near Eastern law, that of apodicity, the trend would have been more in the direction of practical halakhah, diminishing the importance of study and impeding it from eventually assuming independent importance. Thus the ethos is rabbinic, while its roots are biblical.

The notion of study as an independent mitzvah was further developed as time went on. Five subsequent stages of development in the relationship of Torah study to practical halakhah can be discerned. Very early the study of even those laws that had no practical application was accepted as Torah. (We should remember that there were always some laws that ceased to have practical application.) After the Torah was given at Sinai, for example, the laws pertaining to entering the mountain (Exod. 19:10–15) were no longer applicable.[10] The study of even those laws fulfilled the (by now universally accepted) mitzvah of *talmud torah.* Early sources took up the study of those laws, and they did so not only out of historical curiosity but also as a religious act.

The second stage involved the analysis of rejected opinions, of dissenting views. We know of hardly any halakhic disagreements prior to the Shammaites and Hillelites.[11] The number of disagreements between Shammai and Hillel themselves is given in the Babylonian Talmud (Shabbath 14b) as three and in the Palestinian Talmud (Chagigah 3:2 [76d]) as four. Yet there must have been halakhic disagreements in all periods; they are a part of human nature. Prior to the Shammaites and Hillelites, however, the disagreements were not preserved for posterity. The rejected views undoubtedly were not considered worthy of being preserved because they had no practical value; they were not considered Torah. Why, then, preserve them? Apparently the change from simple Midrash to complex Midrash also brought in its wake an awareness of the importance of recording a rejected opinion, a dissenting view—the conviction that such an opinion too is Torah, and whoever studies it is fulfilling the commandment of studying Torah. (If a Jew should study all his life only the views of the Shammaites, "whose teachings are no teachings," he would still have to recite the benedictions for Torah study.) Our Mishnah is replete with dissenting views, which is, indeed, one of its great hallmarks.

I am assuming here that the decision to preserve the dissenting view was made during the time of the Shammaites and Hillelites (around the first half of the first century). The chronological proximity to Hillel suggests that the change from simple to complex Midrash pioneered by Hillel had something to do with this decision. The connection is not clear, however, other than that complex Midrash by its very nature engenders a greater degree of skepticism in the finality of the conclusion than does simple Midrash, and thus there is more room for dissent.

On the other hand, if the decision to preserve the dissenting view was made later in Yabneh—and this is implied in the statement of the Tosefta at the beginning of Tractate Eduyoth, "let us begin [recording controversies] with Hillel and Shammai"—then the connection ought to be made with the change from Midrashic to Mishnaic form. This overarching event must have had an impact on the subsequent formulation of the Mishnah. Again the connection is not clear, other than perhaps that the presence of a scriptural support inhibits dissension.

The Mishnah in Eduyoth 1:4–5 (see also Tosefta, ad loc.) gives two reasons why the dissenting view was recorded. The first reason is to provide the possibility for a future court to reopen the case. Without a dissenting view, a future court will not be able to reopen the case even if it feels that it has sufficient cause to do so. Second, if someone questions the conclusion, saying that he has a different tradition, "another may answer: you heard it only as the opinion of such a one." Neither of these reasons, however, explains why the recording of the dissenting view happened when it did and not earlier. One is forced to conclude that at that time a sense of uncertainty prevailed which eroded confidence in the conclusions and induced scholars to give a fairer representation to the opposing view. This is in line with the Mishnah's first reason, which envisions the possibility of a future court reopening the case and reversing its conclusion. Prior to that time, no such possibility was contemplated; certainty reigned supreme.

The third stage of development is the study of laws that were *never* applicable, nor were they so intended by the Lawgiver, according to the rabbis. In biblical times there was no sense in studying laws that never had any practical application; it would have been considered a futile intellectual exercise. In rabbinic times, however, this was considered a mitzvah for which one would receive a reward. We are told (B.T. Sanhedrin 71a and parallels) that the laws pertaining to the rebellious son and the condemned city[12] were never applied.[13] "Why, then, were they written? In order to study them and receive reward."[14] We also come across in the B.T. Chullin 66b the expression יגדיל תורה ויאדיר (based on Isa. 42:21) in connection with unnecessary phrasing, whose content we know from elsewhere. Why then this unnecessary phrasing? "To make the Torah greater and more glorious." I have no doubts that one who studies only those phrases has to recite the benediction over Torah study. They, too, are Torah.

This kind of study may have been the precursor for the fourth stage in the development of Torah study relative to practical halakhah. "To make the Torah greater and more glorious" must also have been the justification for the Stammaim to include the rhetorical and the pseudo-dialogical as Torah.

Finally, the fifth stage of development was that of the Rashbam and his fellow exegetes. They considered whatever could be elicited from the text as Torah, even if it conflicts with established halakhah.[15] Indeed, it may even be contended that when it contradicts established halakhah, it is more Torah. The sovereignty of a mitzvah entails that it be performed for its own sake, not for the sake of something else. Observing one mitzvah for the sake of another is to deprecate the former. Studying for the sake of observing deprecates the mitzvah of *talmud torah.* True *lishmah* (without expectation of reward), as the word indicates, must be for its own sake.[16]

At the opposite pole to the Rashbam's exegesis stands the *Mishneh Torah* of Maimonides (died 1204). Judging by his introduction and from hints culled from his letters, it appears that he wanted to reduce all of the Torah to practical halakhah,[17] leaving the rest of his time for the study of other disciplines, principally philosophy, which to him was an integral part of Jewish learning and worship (not for its own sake, but as an instrument for the cultivation of proper belief).[18] No wonder Maimonides' attitude toward the anonymous sections of the Talmud, which consist primarily of the argumentational, was less than benign;[19] indeed, he often ignored them. Many a so-called "difficult Rambam" would be less puzzling if one realized that Maimonides did not always reckon with the stam.

Maimonides modeled his *Mishneh Torah* after Rabbi's Mishnah, but he left out all dissenting views, which are, as we have seen, a hallmark of Rabbi's Mishnah. Maimonides explains in one of his letters[20] that he did so because of the Karaites, lest they see in disagreement a proof that the Rabbinites had no reliable continuous tradition. Maimonides, however, in contrast to the Mishnah, quotes an extensive array of justifications, often stemming from basic principles that he states at the outset. He also quotes a number of drashoth, some presumably of his own composition.[21] His *Mishneh Torah* is less apodictic than Rabbi's Mishnah. After the Stammaim (whose formulations Maimonides often quotes in a beautiful reworded Hebrew), it is difficult to be purely apodictic.[22] Even if Maimonides intended his *Mishneh Torah* to be essentially apodictic, the many books that were composed about it, most of them in a highly pilpulistic and Stammaitic style, rendered the study of *Mishneh Torah* far from being apodictic.

Most significantly, both R. Akiba and Rabbi, the fathers of our Mishnah, never abandoned Midrashic activity. Concomitantly with the composition of the Mishnah, they continued expositing Midrash. Perhaps they even intensified the exposition in order to provide a basis for the Mishnah. In contrast, if one is to follow the suggestion of Maimonides in the preface to *Mishneh Torah* to proceed from the study of the Bible straight to the study of his book, Maimonides would not have continued the study of Midrash simultaneously with the study of Mishnah. The study of Mishnah would have been exclusive, and very little Midrash would have survived.[23]

II

The exegetical approach of the Rashbam and his colleagues was not followed by the biblical scholars of subsequent generations. Later biblical scholars insisted on a close agreement between learning and observance, between exegesis and practical halakhah.[24] In the centuries after the Rashbam and his colleagues it was rare indeed[25] for a Jewish exegete to interpret a biblical text in contradiction to accepted halakhah. Torah study became subordinated to halakhic norms.

In a parallel development in the area of Talmud exegesis, the Geonim, who followed the Saboraim (from the seventh to the tenth century), and the Rishonim, who followed the Geonim (from the eleventh to the fifteenth century), were relatively free of the rhetorical devices, pseudo-dialogical style, and special dialectic that appear so often in the anonymous portions of the Talmud, the Gemara. Their works do contain forced interpretation, but only, on the whole, when no better alternative is available. The Geonim and Rishonim did not indulge in discussion for its own sake, or in the refutation of obviously false positions or positions without historical reality. In halakhic matters, they generally adhered to what they considered to reflect the intentions of the respective authors. Little was written by them for the sole purpose of "making the Torah greater and more glorious."

In the sixteenth century, however (and to some extent already in the fifteenth), a new genre of the argumentational arose with such force that it threatened to become the dominant mode of Jewish learning. I am referring to *pilpul.* It is difficult to define pilpul, both because there are many varieties and because there seems to be no clear agreement as to its exact nature. Many of those who decried pilpul seem to have fallen victim to it themselves.[26] My interest here is with that type of pilpul (which, while not completely dominant, was quite widespread) that allows for a deduction to be made when the practitioner knows that what he is suggesting as interpretation does not convey the original intention of the authors.[27] This type of pilpul is akin to the rhetoricity of the Stammaim, and, as such, belongs to this survey.

Again, the legacy of the Stammaim asserted itself. The legacy lost out in biblical studies but won in its home territory—Talmudic studies. Paradoxically, however, the same Rashbam who in biblical exegesis was so devoted to the peshat, the wording and simple meaning of the text, that he followed it (intellectually, not in practice) even when it collided with accepted halakhah was not such a devotee of the peshat in his Talmudic exegesis. In his commentary on the Talmud, the Rashbam did not hesitate to accept, for instance, the Gemara's emendation of a Mishnaic text (or of a Braitha) that is introduced with the statement "There is a lacuna in the text. This is how it ought to read" and other similar forced interpretations.[28] While the Rashbam is much more critical (devoted to peshat) than his grandfather Rashi in his commentary on the Bible, he is less critical than Rashi in his commentary on the Talmud. There he seems to have accepted the Gemara's forced interpretations even when a simpler alternative was available. That he did so indicates that the Gemara's authority prevailed over his natural inclination.

Apparently, the closer the Rashbam came to the source of practical halakhah, the more submissive he was to authority, and the more restrained became his exegesis. By the time of the Rashbam, hardly anyone deduced a practical law from the Bible alone. The source of authority for practical halakhah, the final decision maker at that time, was not the Bible but the Talmud. The Rashbam apparently believed that an interpretation of a biblical text different from accepted halakhah will not necessarily encourage change in practical halakhah; whereas an interpretation of a Mishnah or a Braitha (or a statement by an Amora) different from a later Amora, or from the Gemara, may lead to an undermining of accepted halakhah. In fact, even his language is different in the two commentaries. In his commentary on the Bible he is quite concise; every word is weighed and measured, his style is polished, and it is written in pure Hebrew. In his commentary on the Talmud, on the other hand, he is rather verbose; his style is loose and unadorned, and it is written in rabbinic jargon, a mixture of Hebrew and Aramaic.[29] The Rashbam apparently intended his two commentaries for two different audiences, with each one written in the style of the audience it was intended for: the biblical commentary for the *maskil,* the enlightened (real or fictional), and the Talmud commentary for the *talmud chacham,* the rabbinic scholar.

The subtlety of this distinction adhered to by the Rashbam, between the Bible and the Talmud, escaped R. Yom Tov Heller (1579–1654) when he argued in his commentary on the Mishnah Nazir 5:5, on behalf of Maimonides, for the permissibility of interpreting a Mishnah differently from the Amoraim. He offered in support the example of the medieval biblical commentators who explained the Bible differently from the Gemara:

שאין אני רואה הפרש בין פירוש המשנה לפירוש המקרא

> For I see no difference [in this regard] between the commentary to the Mishnah and the commentary to the Bible [in both instances, one is permitted to follow his natural inclination] as long as he is not deciding a practical halakhah against the authors of the Gemara.[30]

The author of the *Tosafoth Yom Tov* should have wondered why, if his analogy holds true, we do not have from the Rashbam, one of the greatest Talmudic commentators of medieval Jewry, interpretations of the Mishnah or the Talmud that differ from those offered in the Gemara, similar to the interpretations of Maimonides and others. In his defense of Maimonides' right to interpret a Mishnah according to one's sense of peshat, R. Yom Tov Heller resorted to Rashbam's commentary on the Bible but ignored his commentary on the Talmud. Had he consulted the Rashbam's commentary on the Talmud, he would have realized that the Rashbam drew a distinction between interpreting the Bible nontraditionally and interpreting the Mishnah (and other Talmudic texts) nontraditionally. The former he embraced wholeheartedly; the latter he shunned completely.

Rashbam's distinction is more psychological than logical, however, more a fear of deviation than an actual justification. Logically, the author of the *Tosafoth Yom Tov* is right. The principle is the same in both the Bible and the Talmud: the natural integrity of the text—and peshat preserves that integrity—should not be sacrificed on the altar of tradition. Tradition's realm is behavior, not intellect. The intellect must remain free. We are allowed—R. Yom Tov Heller tells us elsewhere, in M. Nedarim 9:1—to explain a Mishnah as Abaye did even though the law follows Rava's view. This is consistent with Maimonides' thesis[31] that in matters of belief (intellect) one does not necessarily follow the decision-making rules (like majority opinion) of practical halakhah. Nor does one necessarily follow the decision-making rules of practical halakhah in matters pertaining to interpretation of texts.[32] Interpretation of a text is no less a matter of intellect than is belief; neither should be subordinated to behavior. Their independence must be upheld.

Study should not be "exploited" for either promoting or reforming observance; it must be its own purpose. This is undoubtedly part of the secret of the enormous success that pilpul enjoyed and is enjoying still.[33] It is being nurtured precisely because it is not applicable to practical halakhah. In places where there was an attempt to combine the study of pilpul with the study of practical halakhah, neither subject fared well. So also with genuine Torah study: it must be pursued for the sole sake of fulfilling the mitzvah of studying Torah. It suffers no partners.

Reviewing the book as a whole, one can see that the road leading from motive clauses in the Bible to insistence on study as an end in itself was long and tortuous. It covered different periods, different continents, and different modes of expression. What seems to have remained constant, however, was the relentless drive of Jewish law toward becoming ever more justificatory—even if the justification is merely pro forma. Justification entails argumentation, and argumentation leads toward a higher esteem of study. Not all participants were aware of the historical trend they were setting; some would even have opposed it had they known. But the trend inexorably moved on with or without their knowledge, with or without their consent, into our own times. It has not yet run its course.

Appendix: On the Lack of Uniformity in the Use of the Word "Halakhoth"

A THOUGHTFUL READER might accuse me of inconsistency. On the one hand, I have continuously identified halakhoth with Mishnah, and on the other hand, I have claimed that the school of R. Ishmael either ignored or opposed Mishnah, even though the Mekhilta of R. Ishmael mentions the word "halakhoth" twice (in its comments on the verse Exod. 16:26, pp. 157–158). By mentioning halakhoth, the Mekhilta has confirmed Mishnah.

My answer is that the accusation incorrectly assumes that there was a uniform use of the word "halakhoth" in both schools. This was not so. The word "halakhoth" most likely predates the schools of R. Ishmael and R. Akiba, and referred to rules and regulations needed to conduct a religious life. The learned and the unlearned alike had to know the rudiments of their religion, which was comprised primarily of behavioral patterns. The instructions were called halakhoth. A father instructed his wise son in "the laws of Passover," but he did not necessarily teach him Mishnah.[1] And R. Simon ben Gamaliel (T. Shabbath, end of chapter 2 and parallels) laments the fact that

רשבג״א: הלכות הקדש וחטאות ומעשרות הן הן גופי תורה ומסורין הן לעם הארץ.

("laws pertaining to holy things, sin offerings and tithes, all of which are essentials of the Torah, are entrusted to the ignorant [that is, we believe them and eat in their homes]").[2]

These laws were not organized as a corpus; they were handed down from father to son, from mother to daughter, as a guide to personal observance.[3] Their natural abode was not so much the school as it was the home. Of course, they were discussed in the schools as well. The Mekhilta, at the end of Bo, speaks of a

חבורה של חכמים או של תלמידים שצריכים לעסוק בהלכות פסח

("company of teachers or disciples of the wise, sitting and discussing the laws of the Passover"). But these laws were less organized, less formal, less academically oriented than the later Mishnah. They were the product of a practical need, and must be very early, whereas the Mishnah was motivated by abstract intellectual stimulation as well.

When the Mekhilta mentions "halakhoth," it is referring to these practical laws. When the school of R. Akiba mentions "*halakhoth,*" it may also be referring to the Mishnah. Whether "halakhoth" is Mishnah or these laws depends on the context. When the word appears referring to a genre, together with Midrash and aggadoth without Mishnah (as a noun), as it does in the beginning of chapter five of P.T. Shekalim:

ר״ע התקין מדרש הלכות והגדות

("R. Akiba established [redacted] Midrash, halakhoth, and aggadoth"), it most certainly means Mishnah; when it appears with the word "Mishnah" (as, for instance, in Sifrei Deut., piska 344, p. 401), it of course refers to these practical laws. However, when the word "halakhoth" appears by itself it may refer to either Mishnah or practical laws, requiring outside criteria to determine its exact reference. For instance, the statement "whosoever studies laws [halakhoth] is sure to have a share in the world to come"[4] probably refers to Mishnah, given the verb *shanah* "to study," "to learn," whereas, for instance, the statement

כותבי הלכות כשורף התורה

("One who writes *halakhoth* is like one who burns the Torah"; B.T. Temurah 14b) most likely refers to single halakhoth.

In short, when the word "halakhoth" appears in texts that are generally attributed to the school of R. Ishmael, its reference is to practical laws that were taught to everyone as part of religious instruction.[5] The same word appearing in the texts generally attributed to the school of R. Akiba may already refer to Mishnah, depending on the context. The word "halakhoth" has no uniform meaning in the texts attributed to the school of R. Akiba.[6]

A slightly different shade of meaning for the word "halakhoth" is implied in R. Meir's definition of Mishnah (B.T. Kiddushin 49a). The Talmud there is presumably citing a Braitha when it quotes: "What is Mishnah? R. Meir says: halakhoth; R. Judah says: Midrash." The definition of R. Judah was misconstrued by those who understood it as it reads on the surface, namely, that R. Judah equates Mishnah with Midrash and that he blurs all distinctions between them—an unlikely opinion for a Tanna of the middle of the second century. Instead, R. Judah was defining not Mishnah in general, but rather Mishnah as it pertains to a particular situation in which a man tells a woman:

הרי את מקודשת לי על מנת שאני שונה [משנה]

("You are betrothed to me on the condition that I study Mishnah"). R. Meir and R. Judah disagree as to what kind of Mishnah the man had in mind. According to R. Meir he had in mind halakhoth, the fixed laws of the Mishnah (the original Mishnah), and these only; whereas, according to R. Judah, he had in mind all portions of the Mishnah, including the drashoth that occasionally accompany them.[7]

This Braitha is a follow-up of a similar Amoraic disagreement quoted immediately before. This Amoraic disagreement states explicitly that the disagreement is about a man who was betrothed to a woman on the condition that he study, using the verb *shoneh,* which generally applies to Mishnah. The Braitha is not explicit. It may have spelled out the word "Mishnah," or it may have used the word *shoneh* and it was taken for granted that "Mishnah" was meant. Either way, the inquiry "What is Mishnah?" is not a historical inquiry. One cannot deduce from it that during the time of R. Meir and R. Judah (mid-second-century Palestine) there was no clear idea yet of what Mishnah was. There *was* a clear idea of what Mishnah was as a corpus, but not what the average man meant when he said that he was studying Mishnah. This also explains why this Braitha is found in tractate Kiddushin (which deal with the laws of betrothal); it pertains to a subject connected with betrothal.

"Halakhoth" in the definition of R. Meir of course means Mishnah, but it also means fixed laws, the fixed laws of the Mishnah (to the exclusion of its Midrashic portions). This is why I said earlier that the word "halakhoth" in the definition of R. Meir carries a slightly different shade of meaning.

Notes

Introduction

1. A. S. Diamond, *Primitive Law, Past and Present,* Methuen, London 1971, p. 15. See his notes to p. 14 for bibliographical literature.

2. "The famous laws of Hammurabi are in the words of the prologue and epilogue to the laws the work of the King himself. They are *not* received from Shamash the god of justice. This god is conceived as approving and demanding just action on earth, but he does not reveal the law itself as the law of Israel is revealed by Yahweh himself." J. J. Finklestein, in *Commentary,* vol. 26, 1958, p. 442. See also *Biblical Encyclopedia* (Hebrew), Mossad Bialik, Jerusalem 1968, vol. 5, pp. 609–610, s.v. "mishpat."

3. A. Alt, *Die Ursprunge des Israelitischen Recht,* Leipzig 1934, *Kleine Schriften zur Geschichte des Volkes Israel,* vol. 1, C. H. Beck, Munich 1953, pp. 278–332.

4. For the latest treatment of the subject, see M. Weinfeld in *Tarbiz,* vol. 41, no. 4., 1972, pp. 349–360.

5. See H. F. Jolowicz, *Historical Introduction to the Study of Roman Law,* Cambridge University Press, Cambridge 1967, pp. 106ff.

6. Cf. S. Paul, *Studies in the Book of the Covenant . . . ,* E. J. Brill, Leiden 1970, pp. 27ff.

1. The Biblical Period

1. It was popularized by Rashi, who opened his *Commentary on the Pentateuch* with this question. For the source, see *Tanchuma,* ed. S. Buber, Lemberg 1883, Genesis, p. 7, n. 59.

2. An interesting parallel is that of R. Ishmael ben Hachmon

ר׳ ישמעאל בן חכמון

a late fourteenth-century scholar (Egypt?) who wrote in his *Commentary on Tractate Erubin,* ed. M. Steinberg, Bnei-Braq 1974, p. 152b:

ואל תבקש לה טעם אלא אמור שהיא הלכה ואל תצטרך לדבר אחר.

("Seek no reason. Say that it is a *halakhah* [a law] and you do not need anything else [any justification]").

3. *Sifra,* ed. I. H. Weiss, 86a, Acharai, Chapter 13:10; Babylonian Talmud (hereafter cited as B.T.), Yoma 67b. This distinction, however, was not accepted by all sages. The author of the statement (ibid., at the end of *parshah* 9, p. 85d) disagreed. For additional references, see L. Finklestein's notes to his edition of the *Sifrei Deut.*, p. 124, line 11, and his article in F. Baer's *Jubilee Volume,* Historical Society of Israel, Jerusalem 1960, pp. 33–41.

4. See E. Jenni and C. Westerman, *Theologisches Handwörterbuch zum Alten Testament,* Chr. Kaiser Verlag, Munich 1971, pp. 626–633, s.v. חקק (*chakak*); and pp. 999–1009, s.v. שפט (*shafat*).

5. I owe this reference to my colleague Professor Shaye Cohen.

6. *Galen on Jews and Christians,* Oxford University Press, London 1949, p. 11.

7. See *Midrash Rabbah, Song of Songs,* chap. 1:4 and M. Kasher, *Torah Shleimah,* vol. 1, p. 13, note 53.

8. B. Gemser, "The Importance of the Motive Clause in Old Testament Law," supplement to *Vetus Testamentum,* Vol. 1, 1953, p. 50.

9. This possibility is even more plausible in the second Decalogue, Deut. 5:6–18, where, if we count the first commandment, we have not ten but eleven commandments. Being a motive clause, the first commandment is not here counted among the commandments. As to which of the ten commandments constitute the Decalogue, see G. Beer, *Handbuch zum Alten Testament,* J. C. B. Mohr, Tuebingen 1939, p. 99, which lists them according to the different religious traditions. See also M. D. Koster, "The Numbering of the Ten Commandments in Some Peshita Manuscripts," *Vetus Testamentum,* vol. 30, no. 4, 1980, pp. 468–473.

10. Two are dissertations: R. W. Uitti, "The Motive Clause in Old Testament Law," Lutheran School of Theology, Chicago 1973, and R. V. Sonsino, *Motive Clauses in Hebrew Law: Biblical Forms and Near Eastern Parallels,* Society of Biblical Literature, Dissertation series, no. 45, Scholars Press, Chico, Calif. 1980.

11. On the whole, because there are among them some that are not wholly particular. In context they are given as justification for particular commandments, but their content is suitable to commandments in general. Take, for example, Deut. 11:8: "Therefore you shall keep all my commandments which I command you this day, that you may be strong and go in and possess the land." The justification to be holy because God is holy (Lev. 19:2, 20:7, 26) is quite inclusive.

12. Gemser, "Importance of the Motive Clause," p. 52. Sonsino has found a few motive clauses in Cuneiform Laws. However, he too concedes ("Motive Clauses in Hebrew Law," p. 173) that "legal motivation is not characteristic of Cuneiform laws and its appearance is rather unusual."

13. See *God's Search for Man: Sermons by Karl Barth and Edward Thurneysen,* T. and T. Clark, Edinburgh 1953; A. J. Heschel, *God in Search of Man,* Jewish Publication Society, Philadelphia 1956.

14. Without necessarily agreeing with all the major points developed by M. Gertner in his article "The Masorah and the Levites" (*Vetus Testamentum,* vol. 10, 1960, pp. 241ff.), I do subscribe to what he says on p. 249 concerning the post-Ezra period: "No more could a priestly decree be accepted as an undisputed law. The fixed text of the Torah and an adequate exposition of its sayings and stipulations became the early source of religion and law. The authority of the personality

—priest or prophet—was replaced by the authority of the Book." Gertner believes this change took place soon after Ezra. However, I think that this is too early.

15. See K. G. Kuhn, *Konkordanz zu den Qumrantexten,* Vandenhock and Ruprecht, Goettingen 1960, pp. 17–18. A study entitled "Explicit Old Testament Quotations in Qumran Literature and in the New Testament" was made by J. A. Fitzmeyer, in *Essays on the Semitic Background of the N. T.*, G. Chapman, London 1971, pp. 3–58. I find puzzling what he says on p. 53: "The introductory formulae which are found in the Qumran text appear to be without parallel in the Mishnah despite the common use of the verbs 'to say' and 'to write.'" Why, for example, is "as it is written" in Mishnah Taanith 3:3 less of an introductory formulae than "for it is written" mentioned in the article on p. 8, or "as it says" less than "as it said," ibid. p. 10? See *Hebrew Union College Annual,* vol. 53, 1982, p. 133, n. 66.

16. Mishnah Makkoth 2:4 constitutes no exception. Despite saying twice "as it says," it is one long *drashah.* Cf., however, *Tanchuma* at the beginning of the portion of Vayeitzai. The Mishnah in Aboth 3:2 is to be understood with Maimonides as a reference to the end of the verse, "His delight is in the Torah of the Lord," which indicates that those who sit and do not delight in the Torah are sitting in "the seat of the scornful" (Psalms 1:1). That connection is not explicit; hence the expression "as it says."

17. A. Geiger's attack on rabbinic exegesis, "Verhaeltnis des natürlichen Schriftsinnes zur Talmudischen Schriftdeutung," *Wissenschaft. Zeitschrift für Judische Theologie,* vol. 5, 1844, pp. 53–81, did not go unchallenged. For a good summary of the literature, particularly in German, and some sensible comments, see J. Neubauer, *HaRambam al Divrei Sofrim,* Mossad Harav Kook, Jerusalem 1957, pp. 163–173. For a limited attempt at a phenomenology of halakhic exegesis based on two examples, see my article in *Conservative Judaism,* vol. 10, Spring 1956, pp. 52–58.

18. For the dates of the canonization of the Pentateuch and the other two sections of the Bible, see H. E. Ryle, *The Canon of the Old Testament,* Macmillan, London 1904. See also infra, Chapter 3, note 32.

19. See T. W. E. Nickelsburg, *Jewish Literature between the Bible and the Mishnah,* Fortress Press, Philadelphia 1981, for current theories concerning the dating of the respective books.

20. The possible outcome of that activity is plausibly summarized by Y. Kaufmann, *History of the Jewish Religion* (Hebrew), Mossad Bialik, Jerusalem and Dvir, Tel Aviv 1960, vol. 4, pp. 485–486.

21. I. Heineman, *Leshoneinu,* Jerusalem 1946, vol. 14, pp. 182–189.

22. Avi Hurvitz, *The Transition Period in Biblical Hebrew* (Hebrew), Mossad Bialik, Jerusalem 1972, pp. 131–134. For a more extended analysis of the root *drash* see M. Gertner, "Terms of Scriptural Interpretation," *Bulletin of the School of Oriental and African Studies,* vol. 25, 1962, pp. 4–12. For a discussion and summary relevant to the Qumran literature see L. H. Schiffman, *The Halakhah at Qumran,* E. J. Brill, Leiden 1975, pp. 54–60.

23. See Y. Yadin's comments to the *Temple Scroll* (Hebrew), Israel Exploration Society, Jerusalem 1977, vol. 1, pp. 60ff., 298–300.

24. See Nickelsburg, *Jewish Literature between Bible and Mishnah,* pp. 73–80.

25. For a different view of Midrash, see R. Bloch, "Midrash," *Dictionnaire de la Bible,* suppl. 5, Librairie Letouzey et Ané, Paris 1957, pp. 1263–80; followed and brought up to date by R. L. Ecaut, "Apropos a definition of Midrash," *Interpretation,* vol. 25, 1971, pp. 259–282. For a detailed study of the different definitions of Midrash, see G. Porton, *Ancient Judaism* I, ed. J. Neusner, Ktav Publishing House, New York 1981, pp. 55ff.

26. See M. Fishbane, "Revelation and Tradition, Aspects of Inner Biblical Exegesis, *Journal of Biblical Literature,* vol. 99, 1980, pp. 343–361.

27. I. L. Seeligman's definition of Midrash is certainly too broad. See his "Voraussetzungen der Midrash Exegesis," supplement to *Vetus Testamentum,* vol. 1, 1953, pp. 150ff., in particular p. 152, n. 2. J. Kugel's insight in "Two Introductions to Midrash," *Prooftexts,* Johns Hopkins University Press, Baltimore 1983, vol. 3, no. 2, p. 145, "that Midrash is an exegesis of Biblical verses, not of books," should strengthen our limited definition of Midrash. For a Midrash "which finds expression in all manner of contexts [is] alas, not particularly helpful," ibid. p. 144. Raphael I. Panitz in his unpublished dissertation "Textual Exegesis and Other Kinds of Interpretation in Scripture" (University of Pennsylvania, 1983) reviews the literature and definition of "inner biblical exegesis." He defines such exegesis as "a citation of a text of scripture accompanied by the interpretation of that text"; he thus makes inner-biblical exegesis closer to rabbinic Midrash.

28. H. L. Ginsberg has proposed, in a review in *Theological Studies,* September 1967, p. 574, to call this type of literature "parabiblical." He writes, "I should like to contribute a proposal for a term to cover works like Genesis Appocryphon, Pseudo-Philo, and the Book of Jubilees, which paraphrase and/or supplement the canonical Scriptures: Parabiblical literature . . . differs from Midrashic literature by not directly quoting and (with more or less arbitrariness) interpreting canonical Scripture."

2. The Post-Biblical Period

1. I. Halevy, *Dorot Ha-Rishonim,* B. Harz, Berlin and Vienna 1923, vol. 1, book 3, pp. 292ff. He repeats this idea in a few other places; see, in particular, vol. 1, book 5, pp. 467ff. Cf. Saadya, *L. Ginzberg Jubilee Vol.* (Hebrew), p. 152.

2. Halevy considers the antiquity of the Mishnah to be not only a fundamental principle in the formulation of halakhah, but a basic religious belief as well. See ibid., vol. 5, p. 470.

3. *The Writings of Nachman Krochmal* (Hebrew), 2nd ed., S. Rawidowicz, Ararat Publishing Society, London 1961, pp. 194–204.

4. "Midrash and Mishnah: A Study in the Early History of the Halakha," *Jewish Quarterly Review,* vol. 5, 1914–15, pp. 503–527; vol. 6, 1915–16, pp. 23–95, 303–323, reproduced in his collection of *Rabbinic Essays,* ed. S. B. Freehof, Hebrew Union College, Cincinnati 1951, pp. 163–256. (All page references cited hereafter are to Rabbinic Essays.) He states his reason for attributing the change to

Mishnaic form to the time of Yose ben Yoezer on pp. 186ff.

5. *Die Erste Mischna und die Controversen der Tannaim,* Jahresbericht Rabbiner Seminar, Berlin 1881-82, pp. 5-26.

6. See his popular edition of the Mishnah, Dvir, Jerusalem, and Tel Aviv 1953, vol. 4, pp. 275-277 (introduction to Tractate Eduyoth) for his view on the subject.

7. *The History of the Jewish Religion* (Hebrew), Mossad Bialik-Dvir, Jerusalem and Tel Aviv 1960, vol. 4, book 1, pp. 481-485.

8. As an extension, the name *sofer* is also used for a sage or one who teaches the Bible. See J. N. Epstein, *Introduction to Tannaitic Literature* (Hebrew), Magnes Press, Jerusalem 1957, p. 503, nn. 17, 18.

9. E. E. Urbach, "The Derasha as a Basis of the Halakhah and the Problem of the Soferim" (Hebrew), *Tarbiz,* vol. 27, 1958, pp. 166-182. He also refers there to S. Zeitlin, *Jewish Quarterly Review,* vol. 44, 1953, pp. 21-36.

10. See, however, H. F. Jolowicz, *Historical Introduction to the Study of Roman Law,* Cambridge University Press, Cambridge 1967, p. 79: "The part played by custom as a source of law in historical times is comparatively small."

11. *Geschichte der Juden,* 2nd ed., vol. 3, O. Leiner, Leipzig 1863, p. 176.

12. See M. Fishbane, "Revelation and Tradition," *Journal of Biblical Literature,* vol. 99, 1980, pp. 343-361.

13. This may not be quite correct. It is possible that the Mishnah.is not quoting Yehoiada verbatim. It begins by saying: "Yehoiada, the High Priest gave the following exposition." What follows, however, is not the words of Yehoiada but those of the author of the Mishnah, based on the verse in 2 Kings 12:17 with which the Mishnah concludes the chapter and which is attributed to Yehoiada.

14. This Mishnah is also found in Sifra Vayikra, 21:6 (27c), which is the most Akiban Midrash of all. In the Midrashim stemming from the school of R. Ishmael, the expression

כיצד יתקיימו שני כתובים — מקראות — הללו

("How can these two verses be reconciled?") is more frequent.

15. Cf. D. S. Margoliouth, "The Use of the Apocrypha by Moslem Writers," *International Journal of Apocrypha,* Jan. 1916, no. 44, series 12, p. 12, "who pointed out that statements of Ben Sira and the New Testament are ascribed to Jahiz [ninth-century author] by late Moslem writers because the passages were first cited by him." This quote is taken from B. Cohen, *Mishnah and Tosefta,* Jewish Theological Seminary, New York 1935, p. 32, n. 46.

16. D. Z. Hoffmann begins the second chapter of his *Die Erste Mischna,* p. 5, with the statement, "R. Sherira Gaon speaks with such certainty that he must have had a reliable tradition."

17. See, for instance, *Rabbinic Essays,* ed. S. B. Freehof, p. 219: "That Yose had scriptural proofs for his decisions, is evidenced by the fact that the Amoraim in the Talmud endeavor to find these proofs or reasons." What about the many later scriptural *asmachtoth* that we encounter in the Talmud?

18. Ibid., p. 165; see also note 3 there. The right reading is ועד תורה as it is in the Leiden manuscript, in the first edition of the P.T., Venice 1523, and it is quoted thus by a host of Rishonim as reported by D. Ratner, *Ahavath Zion VeYe-*

rusalem, Moed Katan, Jerusalem 1967 reprint, p. 126.

19. The word *ve'od* in P.T. sometimes means *vegam,* "and also," as already noted by Z. Frankel, *Introduction to the Palestinian Talmud* (Hebrew), Schletter, Breslau 1870, p. 16a–b. The phrase in the beginning of P.T. Berakhoth, chap. 5: "*Od* he concluded with words of consolation" is quoted in the *Pesikta,* ed. S. Buber, p. 116a as "*Gam* he concluded with words of consolation." If we follow the reading *ve'od,* the full purport of the statement of Hezekiah is: "Who is a sage? He who studies halakhoth, fixed laws, and also Torah (written and oral)." According to the reading of *ve'ad,* the purport is: "He who studies [the whole gamut of learning] from simple laws to Torah." The Ramban, *Torat Ha'adam,* 17b, reads: halakhoth and Torah. Perhaps *ve'ad* should also be understood in the sense of *ve'od.*

20. Which he did not. He merely defined who is a *talmid chacham,* a sage. The *Barishonah* in early times that R. Yose is speaking of most likely does not refer back as early as the pre-Yose ben Yoezer times, before 190 B.C.E., but rather to events closer to his own time, events that Hezekiah still shared.

21. The meaning is that they studied with the same exactness ("*bedikduk,*" says R. Gershon in his commentary printed in the Vilna edition of the Talmud) with which Moses our teacher did. In the parallel source, in B.T. Yebamoth 72b:

ראיתי לבן פדת שיושב ודורש כמשה מפי הגבורה

the meaning is: "I saw the son of Pedoth holding forth like Moses in the name of the Lord." Incidentally, R. Sherira Gaon, in his *Epistle,* ed. B. M. Lewin, p. 42, (the French version) does not have the word *Kemosheh.* Accordingly, the meaning is "He is holding forth as if he heard it from God." See also Epstein, *Introduction to Tannaitic Literature* (Hebrew), p. 505, n. 47.

22. See, in particular, Mishnah Kelim 1:8.

23. See Mishnah Shekalim 1:3. See also Matt. 21:23; Mark 11:15–17; Luke 2:46, 20:1.

24. *Shenoth Eiliyahu,* Bikkurim ad loc.

25. For a detailed history of the Temple Mount, see *Sepher Yerushalayim,* ed. M. Avi-Yonah, Mossad Bialik-Dvir, Jerusalem 1956, pp. 394–396, 414–416. Cf. also B. Z. Lurie, *Beth Mikra,* vol. 26, 1981, pp. 206–216.

26. *The Temple Scroll,* ed. Y. Yadin, Israel Exploration Society, Jerusalem 1983, 3 vols. See the Concordance, s.v. *ir.*

27. For a contrary view, see B. Levine, *Bulletin of the American Schools of Oriental Research,* no. 232, Fall 1978, pp. 5–23. See also the response in the same issue by J. Milgrom, pp. 25–27 or the article by the latter in *Journal of Biblical Literature,* vol. 97, 1978, pp. 512–518.

28. P.T. Chagigah 1:1 (76a):

בעזרה היו מראים פנים.

("In the Temple Court, they appeared before the Lord"). This Yerushalmi is also quoted by the author of the *Tosafoth Yom Tov,* ad loc. He, however, is giving a nonhistorical reason why the Mishnah mentions Temple Mount instead of Temple Court.

29. I am grateful to Rabbi I. Haut for having drawn my attention to the problem in the Mishnah Chagigah.

30. A useful introduction to the Aramaic Targums is J. Bowker's *The Targums and Rabbinical Literature,* Cambridge University Press, Cambridge 1969, pp. 3–35.

31. For a fuller treatment of the subject see my article "The Location of the Beth Din in the early Tannaitic Period," *Proceedings of the American Academy for Jewish Research,* vol. 29, 1960–61, pp. 181–191. Unfortunately, a number of typographical errors made their way into the article, and several lines were omitted on pp. 183 and 185. Nevertheless, I trust that the major thrust of the article is clear.

32. A. Schalit, *The World History of the Jewish People,* vol. 6, "The Hellenistic Age," ed. A. Schalit, W. H. Allen, London 1972, pp. 255–297.

33. First stated by J. Lewy, as quoted by C. S. Horovitz, *Monatschrift für die Geschichte und Wissenschaft des Judenthums,* vol. 50, 1906, p. 74, n. 5.

34. In Freehof, ed., *Rabbinic Essays,* pp. 221ff.

35. *Introduction to Tannaitic Literature* (Hebrew), p. 506.

36. The "early elders" are mentioned in four more places: Sifra at the end of Metzora (79c) (R. Akiba disagrees with them); Mekhilta, Beshallach, p. 181; Tosefta Oholoth 4:6 (their law was later changed); and in the B.T. Nazir 53a (where disagreements among the "early elders" themselves are reported). All this and much more was noted by Epstein, yet he persists in saying, despite the controversies, that they all date back to considerably before the Hasmonean period.

37. Such as whosoever touches a man who touched a corpse (or whosoever touches an object that came in contact with a corpse) "and entered the Temple has not committed a capital sin." See J. Lewy, as quoted by C. S. Horovitz, *Monatschrift für die Geschichte und Wissenschaft des Judenthums,* vol. 50, p. 74, and C. Albeck's edition of the Mishnah.

38. For a fuller understanding of the Hillelites' opinion, see my *Sources and Traditions* (Hebrew), Jewish Theological Seminary, Jerusalem 1982, Pesachim, p. 535.

39. According to A. Büchler, *Jubilee Volume in Honor of M. Bloch* (Hebrew), S. Markus, Budapest 1905, pp. 21–30, up to the last quarter of the first century the law was generally in agreement with the Shammaites. Relevant to our case, see Tosefta Pesachim 7, 14.

40. As is well known, the first layer of Tractate Aboth, which is also the oldest, consists entirely of triadic statements. Triadicy is a factor not only in aggadah but also in halakhah, as attested by the frequent appearances in the Babylonian Talmud of the expression "Three things can be learned from here" (sometimes when there are not three things, an artificial one may be added in order to make it triadic; see my *Sources and Traditions,* Nedarim, pp. 271–272). For a more general treatment of triple structure in rabbinic literature, see S. Friedman in *Mechkarim U Mekorot,* Jewish Theological Seminary, Jerusalem and New York 1978, pp. 316–319.

41. Perhaps the order of the parts is an additional indication that something is missing in the third part. In good Hebraic style, the longest part of a statement usually comes at the end. See S. Friedman, *Leshoneinu,* Jerusalem 1971, vol. 35, pp. 123–129, 192–202. Here the second part is longer than the first. The third part,

however, is shorter than the second. With a supplement (whatever it may be), the last part would become the longest.

42. Yadin translates the word *orasah* as a passive participle, "who is not betrothed." I have shown elsewhere, *Journal of Biblical Literature,* vol. 81.1, 1962, pp. 67–69, that the proper translation is "who had not been betrothed."

43. Yadin, *Temple Scroll,* pp. 368–371.

44. See my *Sources and Traditions,* Ketuboth, p. 179, n. 12.

45. See, for instance, *Midrash Haggadol* (Hebrew), ed. M. Margolies, Mossad Harav Kook, Jerusalem 1956, Exodus, p. 519.

46. *Temple Scroll,* vol. 1, p. 369. For the omission of the letter alef, see vol. 2, p. 298, n. 9.

47. Another remarkable similarity between the Kaufmann manuscript and the Temple Scroll is the spelling of the word *lo.* The Kaufmann manuscript spells the word *velo* (Deut. 22:28) with an alef; the Temple Scroll with a vav and alef; while the spelling in our Bible version is with a vav only. See Maimonides' commentary to Mishnah Sotah 5:5.

48. It is used hundreds of times, always in the sense of eligibility, except perhaps in P.T. Betzah 2:5 (61c), where according to S. Lieberman, *Tosefta Kifshutah,* Jewish Theological Seminary, New York 1962, p. 952, n. 22, the first version understood the words of the Shammaites in the Mishnah

אלא אם כן ראוין לשתיה

to mean that the water was intentionally prepared for drinking. Being drinking water is not enough; it has to be designated for drinking. Such an understanding would make the meaning of the word *re'uyin* closer to the meaning of the Septuagint, that of "destined." However, I have serious reservations about Lieberman's interpretation. The words *re'uyin lishtiyah* are attributed in the first version to the Hillelites, whereas the Shammaites say *vehu sheshatah mehen,* which prompts me to think that the first version had a different reading in the Mishnah.

49. There is evidence to prove that the Septuagint was influenced by what is called today "rabbinic Hebrew." This, however, is a separate study which I hope to take up elsewhere.

50. When the Rabbis wanted to point to a prohibition about which there was no doubt, they would point to the prohibition of marrying a sister. Its certainty is uncontested:

אמור לחכמה אחותי את — אם ברור לך הדבר כאחותך שהיא אסורה לך,
אמרהו ואם לאו, לא תאמרהו.

("Say to Wisdom you are my sister [Proverbs 7:4]—if the matter is as clear to you as that your sister is forbidden to you, say it: But if not, do not say it"). B.T. Shabbath 145b and parallels.

51. Note the identical word *re'uyah* ("eligible") in the preface to the drashah and the drashah proper. This is characteristic of drashoth; what is a bit unusual here is the lack of symmetry between "eligible to enter the community of Israel" in the preface and "eligible to [marry] him" in the drashah proper. We would also have expected in the drashah proper the words "to enter the community of Israel." The lack of symmetry is due to the fact that the verse on which the drashah is based contains the word *lo,* and this word disturbs the symmetry. The

word *re'uyah* takes on the meaning of *tih'yeh* and the combination of *re'uyah* with *lo* gives us the phrase שהיא ראויה לו, even though our concern is with ראויה לבוא בישראל. The nature of the drashah dictates the lack of symmetry. In a similar drashah in the Sifrei Numbers, piska 7 (p. 11), based on the verse in Num. 5:12 which does not contain the word *lo,* the drashah does not have *lo.* The Sifrei says

כי תשטה אשתו — בראויה לאישות הכתוב מדבר.

(If any man's wife has gone astray—the verse speaks of a woman who is eligible for marriage) without *lo,* without specifying that she is eligible to marry *him.*

52. See Yadin, vol. 1, pp. 386ff.

53. A similar distinction with regard to the Sifra is made by J. Neusner, *A History of Mishnaic Law of Purities,* vol. 7, E. J. Brill, Leiden 1975, pp. 187–209. See the summary on p. 209.

54. Following Avi Hurvitz, *The Transition Period in Biblical Hebrew* (Hebrew), Mossad Bialik, Jerusalem 1972, pp. 131–134.

55. In the Talmudic report of the discussion between Hillel and the Benei Bateyra (B.T. Pesachim 66a and P.T. Pesachim 6:1 [33a]), the Benei Bateyra challenged the drashoth of Hillel. They offered counterarguments, thus implying that in principle they too accepted drashoth and objected only to the particular drashoth advanced by Hillel. We, however, do not consider these challenges historical; they are absent in the Tosefta Pesachim 4:13 (Lieberman's edition) and are recorded in contradictory ways in the Talmuds. See L. Ginzberg, *Studies in Memory of Moses Schorr* (Hebrew), Professor M. Schorr Memorial Committee, New York 1944, pp. 85–89. I. Halevy, *Dorot Ha-Rishonim,* vol. 1, book 3, B. Harz Verlag, Berlin and Vienna 1923, pp. 78ff., followed by J. N. Epstein, *Introduction to Tannaitic Literature* (Hebrew), Magnes Press, Jerusalem 1957, p. 511, accept the Benei Bateyra's challenges as historical. They naturally arrive at different conclusions.

56. The formula "it comes to teach" appears more often in the school of R. Akiba, whereas "it declares" appears more often in the school of R. Ishmael. See W. Bacher, *Exegetische Terminologie,* J. C. Hinrichs, Leipzig 1905, pp. 7, 30–33. For non-halakhic drashoth, even the school of R. Ishmael uses the formula "it comes to teach."

57. 7:8, 14; 8:9, 39; 9:2, 8–9; 10:16; 16:6. I am using A. A. Haberman's edition, Jerusalem 1959.

58. Incidentally, in Mishnah Oholoth 7:4 the womb is called *kever,* "tomb." This should not be construed as a carry-over from the time when the law was like that of the Temple Scroll, namely, that a womb carrying a dead child is likened to a tomb and therefore, like one who touches a tomb, the mother is unclean for seven days. The comparison comes, rather, from the physical similarity between a womb and a tomb: both encase a human being, alive or dead. The parallel has no halakhic implications.

3. *The Mishnaic Period*

1. See G. Vermes, "Bible and Midrash," *Cambridge History of the Bible,* Cambridge University Press, Cambridge 1970, pp. 221ff.

2. *Hebrew Union College Annual,* vols. 8–9, 1931–32, p. 331 (offprint, p. 75). For the historical background and literature, see ibid., pp. 39–41 or 295–297.

3. The accusation that the Sadducees do not know the sources in the Torah for their laws is repeated twice more in the Fast Scroll, in the section on the twenty-seventh of Cheshvan (ibid., p. 82 or p. 338) and in that concerning the twenty-eighth of Teveth (ibid., p. 86 or p. 342). There too the meaning is: only he who can produce scriptural proof (Midrash) and does not rely on Mishnah-like tradition should be a member of the Sanhedrin.

4. This is implied even in the reading that does not have

אמרו להם חכמים וכו'.

5. Laws similar to what were later called *takkanoth* or *gezeiroth* may have been transmitted in the earlier period in connection with a biblical verse. Before lighting the Chanukkah candle, for instance, a benediction is recited which contains the phrase "(Blessed be Thou O God . . .) that had sanctified us with your commandments." Even these commandments were sanctified by God. See B.T. Shabbath 23a and parallels. The distinction between a prohibition that is scriptural and one that is from the sages is a later one. See B. De Vries, *Toledot ha-Halakhah ha-Talmudit,* A. Zioni, Tel Aviv 1962, chap. 6, pp. 69–95. Cf. G. Allon, *Studies in Jewish History* (Hebrew), Hakibutz Hameuchad, Tel Aviv 1957, p. 104, n. 64: "The old law did not distinguish with respect to punishment between that which is prohibited scripturally and that which is prohibited from the sages."

6. See B.T. Temurah 14b:

כותבי הלכות כשורף התורה

("Those who write fixed laws are like one who burns the Torah").

7. Did the glossator interpret the phrase "according to the law which they shall teach you" to mean "teach you orally"?

8. See B.T. Gittin 60a and parallels.

9. "And it is written 'it is time to work for the Lord'; They have made void your law (Psalms 119:125). R. Natan says: They have made void your law because it was a time to work for the Lord." Mishnah Berakhoth 9:5 (at the end).

10. See S. J. Rapoport, *Divrei Shalom Ve'emet,* Prague 1861, p. 15. Halevy's dismissal of Rapoport, *Dorot Ha-Rishonim,* B. Harz, Berlin and Vienna 1923, vol. 1, book 3, pp. 415–416, is not entirely warranted.

11. *Die Sadduzäer,* Mayer and Müller, Berlin 1912, pp. 78ff.

12. Josephus gives this date in *Antiquities,* 20:267. See Shaye J. D. Cohen, *Josephus in Galilee and Rome,* E. J. Brill, Leiden 1979, p. 32, n. 29.

13. Sectarians who claimed direct contact with the Divine (see end of Chapter 2) occasionally deviated from the biblical order. I have already mentioned that the Temple Scroll combines two distinct categories, that of rape and that of enticement; see also the Scroll's formulation of the laws of "Vows," vol. 2, pp. 168–171.

14. See Tosafoth, Sotah 14a, s.v. *Mevi.* Maimonides in his *Mishneh Torah* follows a third order. See also *Tosafoth Yom Tov,* Tractate Sotah, beginning of chapter 2.

15. C. Albeck, in contrast, argues that the Mishnah was arranged at Yabneh and bases his theory on the Tosefta at the beginning of Tractate Eduyoth. He gives his theory in several places; see in particular his introduction to Tractate

Eduyoth in his edition of the Mishnah, Mossad Bialik, Jerusalem 1953, vol. 4, pp. 275–276.

16. See *Seder Tannaim ve Amoraim,* ed. K. Kahana, Herman Verlag, Frankfurt 1935, p. 29, par. 65.

17. As I have noted elsewhere; see my *Sources and Traditions,* Chagigah, p. 613.

18. Epstein's rejection (*Introduction to Tannaitic Literature* [Hebrew], pp. 422–423) of this tradition seems to me to be unfounded. He has two objections: first, that the Tractate Eduyoth contains testimonies that are earlier than the School of Yabneh (as already noted by L. Ginzberg in his *Commentary on the Yerushalmi,* Jewish Theological Seminary, New York 1941, vol. 3, p. 199). This circumstance, however, does not preclude the possibility that the foundation was laid at Yabneh after which it was supplemented by earlier and later testimonies. Indeed, it would be quite surprising were it otherwise. His second objection is that none of the contents that are quoted elsewhere as having been "on that day" are found in Tractate Eduyoth. This is a more serious objection, though it too is not conclusive. Undoubtedly many a Mishnah that was once a part of Tractate Eduyoth was later transferred to its topically appropriate place. It is also quite possible that some of the Mishnayoth that were originally omitted from Tractate Eduyoth were later added elsewhere with the designation "on that day." Either way, it is not a sufficient argument to reject an explicit tradition. Moreover, Epstein's rejection applies only to the dating of the composition of Tractate Eduyoth, not to the existence of apodictic law. That the Mishnaic form existed already at that time (our major concern here) seems to be borne out even by Epstein's reconstruction of the events.

19. The meaning of "Let us begin [with Hillel and Shammai]" is that before we enumerate the disagreements between the Shammaites and Hillelites, let us also mention the few known disagreements between their teachers, Hillel and Shammai. This reading assumes that the original intention of Tractate Eduyoth was to enumerate disagreements between the Shammaites and Hillelites. If, however, the intention was to collect "testimonies," another substantial component of Tractate Eduyoth, then "let us begin" means let us begin the testimonies with three disagreements between Hillel and Shammai, the third of which contains a testimony while the other two were included because they share with the third one the phrase "The Sages say: It is not according to the opinion of either [Hillel or Shammai]." Either way, "let us begin" means let us begin Tractate Eduyoth, and not let us begin a new order of learning to stave off Amos' gloomy prophecy.

20. The "seventy books" mentioned at the end of 4 Ezra 14:46 do not refer (as L. Ginzberg claims, "Mishnah Tamid," *Journal of Jewish Lore and Philosophy,* Hebrew Union College, Cincinnati 1919, p. 37) to the fifty-eight tractates of the Mishnah, the nine books of the Midrash on Leviticus, and the Midrashim on Exodus, Numbers, and Deuteronomy. Soon after the destruction of the Temple in 70 C.E., the date generally assigned to 4 Ezra, the Mishnah certainly was not written yet. Ginzberg's division of Midreshei Halakhah into twelve books is unwarranted. It still makes the best sense (despite Epstein's counterargument, in *Introduction to Tannaitic Literature,* pp. 15–16) to say that these seventy books

were some kind of Apocryphal works. If they were halakhic, they were most likely Midrashic.

21. See my *Sources and Traditions,* Beitzah, pp. 354–355; Shabbath, p. 222.

22. See D. Z. Hoffmann, *Die Erste Mischna und die Controversen der Tannaim,* Jahresbericht Rabbiner Seminar, Berlin 1881–82, pp. 26–27.

23. For a different dating and for an "external" reason for the "chain of tradition," see Elie Bikerman (Elias Bickerman), "La Chaîne de la Tradition Pharisienne," *Revue Biblique,* vol. 59, 1952, pp. 44–54. However, see also W. Sibley Towner, *Hebrew Union College Annual,* vol. 53, 1982, pp. 101ff.

24. Sometimes, however, the drashah contains a rabbinic equivalent to the biblical word. To quote again the Sifra Emor, it says in Chapter 3:6 (p. 95b):

עיור — בין סומא בשתי עיניו, בין סומא אפילו בעינו אחת.

"*Iver* (the biblical word for a blind man [which is mentioned in Lev. 21:18: For whatsoever man he be, that has a blemish, he shall not approach (the altar) a blind man . . .] means) Whether he is blind in both eyes or only in one." The drashah does not use the biblical word *iver,* but the rabbinic equivalent *soma.* In classical rabbinic texts (to the exclusion of late Midrashim and subsequent literature), the word *iver* appears only as a part of a quotation from the Bible, with the exception of the proverb in B.T. Baba Kama 85a:

אסיא רחיקא, עינא עווירא

("The physician from afar has a blind [*iver*] eye"). (The right reading in ibid. 84a is not בהדי דעויר ליה [While he blinds (*iver*) his eye] as our versions have it, but בהדי דעקר לעיניה [But while he takes out his eye] as some manuscripts have it. See R. N. Rabbinovicz, *Dikdukei Sofrim,* ad loc.). Otherwise the verb *soma* is used. R. Yose could have perhaps said it in B.T. Megilah 24b:

וכי מה איכפת ליה לסומא בין אפילה לאורה

("What difference does it make to a blind man [*soma*] whether it is dark or light?") instead of

וכי מה איכפת ליה לעיור בין אפילה לאורה

("What difference does it make to a blind man [*iver*] whether it is dark or light?"). He was following closely the quotation from Deut. 28:29 with which he begins his statement and which has *iver.*

I do not know what criteria, if any, the rabbis employed in deciding when to use a biblical word and when a rabbinic equivalent in the drashah. It stands to reason that their decision had something to do with whether the use of the biblical word was completely abandoned during rabbinic times or merely superseded by a rabbinic equivalent. That would explain why, for instance, the Sifra retained the biblical verb *aras* but not the biblical verb *iver* in the drashah: the use of the verb *iver* was totally abandoned during rabbinic times, whereas the use of *aras* remained along with the use of the verb *kideish.* Compare, however, E. Löw's note in J. Theodor's edition of *Genesis Rabbah,* p. 275. Cf. also the drashah in the Haggadah of Passover:

ואת לחצנו זה הדחק

lachatz is a biblical verb; *dachak* is a rabbinic one. The author is translating the biblical idiom of *lachatz* into the rabbinic idiom of *dachak*. However, other factors, such as symmetry, should also be taken into consideration there. See my article in *Hadoar,* vol. 48, New York 1969, pp. 345–346.

25. For a more detailed exposition of this Mishnah and its relationship to the Sifrei, see my article in the *Annual of Bar Ilan University,* Ramat Gan 1970, vols. 7–8, pp. 73–79.

26. For an interesting example, see my *Sources and Traditions,* Nazir, pp. 402–403.

27. One may not feel, however, that something is missing or sense a quality of awkwardness if one concentrates primarily on discovering the underlying principles of a tractate or even a chapter as a whole. One can discover the underlying principles of a tractate or a chapter without recourse to earlier sources, not even to the Bible which the tractate or chapter may only quote perfunctorily (see Jacob Neusner, *History of Mishnaic Law of Purities,* vol. 7, Negaim Sifra, E. J. Brill, Leiden 1975, particularly pp. 209–210; and *Judaism: The Evidence of the Mishnah,* University of Chicago Press, Chicago 1982, pp. xiv, 217–219). Principles are usually self-contained; it is the individual pericope that needs the supplements of early materials. Their constituent parts are often not well integrated, the transition from one part to another is often rough, and the overall effect is uneven. The only solution is to posit that our Mishnah is a composite of excerpted earlier materials that would regain its natural smoothness if it were combined with its original sources.

28. Jerome 340–420 (on Isa. 8:11–15; Corpus Christianorum series Latina 73:116): "Hillel is the defiler because he defiled the law with his tradition."

29. This is the answer to the objection raised by Lauterbach (in Freehof, ed., *Rabbinic Essays,* pp. 173–179) followed by Epstein (*Introduction to Tannaitic Literature* [Hebrew], p. 508) to the standard explanation that the Mishnah came to facilitate memorization. They asked: are not laws arranged according to Scripture easier to remember than random laws, even when the latter are topically arranged? Their observation is true of simple Midrash, where the connection with the text is smooth and felicitous. Indeed, that was the actual historical situation up to the time of Hillel. With the emergence of complex Midrash, where the connection is often tortuous and far-flung, retention became extremely difficult and new arrangements were needed, either according to names (as in Tractate Eduyoth), around a phrase, or according to topic.

30. Concerning the date of Rabbi's death, see E. Kleinman, *Zion,* Historical Society of Israel, Jerusalem 1973, vol. 38, pp. 59–60.

31. That is, that Chaggai, the Prophet, already engaged in drashoth; see Epstein, *Introduction to Tannaitic Literature* (Hebrew), p. 512. But whatever the meaning of Chaggai 2:11–13, it is not a conventional rabbinic drashah.

32. See S. Zeitlin, "An Historical Study of the Canonization of the Hebrew Scripture," *Proceedings of the American Academy for Jewish Research,* vol. 3, 1931–32, p. 122: "[Uncanonized books] were not authoritative and no new laws could have their validity based on such non-authoritative works."

33. Found most frequently in the order of Nezikin. (See Baba Kama 6:4; Baba Bathra 8:2; Sanhedrin 2:4; Makkoth 1:7; Shebuoth 2:5.)

34. See the variants to the Mishnah published in the Rom-Vilna edition, pp. 249–250. See also my *Sources and Traditions,* Sotah, p. 450.

35. Some drashoth, however, entered the Mishnah for individual reasons. A beautiful example is Mishnah Terumoth 6:6. It first quotes a disagreement between R. Eliezer and R. Akiba without scriptural support, and then adds: "From the same scripture whence R. Eliezer derives the more lenient ruling, R. Akiba derives the more stringent ruling," followed by their respective drashoth. The disagreement was first codified in typical Mishnaic pattern, without drashoth. It was excerpted from the Sifra Emor, chapter 6 (97d), where R. Akiba's view is quoted along with his drashah. (R. Eliezer, in this case being more lenient, is quoted in the Sifra without a drashah. Because only R. Akiba cites a drashah, his opinion is mentioned first, against the standard procedure of having the opinion of R. Eliezer, his teacher, come first. On the other hand, the Mishnah that quotes both drashoth mentions, as usual, R. Eliezer's opinion first). Clearly at a later period someone perceived that these two drashoth are unique, since they constitute one of the few instances where both adversaries use the same scriptural word for opposite conclusions, and thus are worthy of being recorded. He, therefore, added them to the Mishnah with the preface: "From the same scripture whence R. Eliezer derives the more lenient ruling, R. Akiba derives the more stringent ruling."

36. Cf. A. Spanier, *Die Tosefta Periode in der Tannaitischen Literatur,* Shocken Verlag, Berlin 1936, pp. 152–153.

37. How much older? Presumably that law dates back to a time when a red heifer was still used as a means of purification. We have references to Hillel and to R. Yochanan ben Zakkai (see Sifrei Num., at the beginning of Chukath, p. 151 in C. S. Horovitz's edition and Tosefta Parah 4:7) as having been present at a burning of a red heifer. This law dates back at least to their times. Yet the possibility exists that this law does not reflect early reality, that R. Yose and his adversaries were merely conjecturing what the law was at an earlier time and what the reasons might have been.

In a similar case at the end of Mishnah Chagigah, the Babylonian Talmud (Chagigah 27a) interprets the disagreement there between R. Eliezer and the sages as one of substance, that is, in the nature of the law and not merely in the reason thereof. Accordingly, at the time of R. Eliezer and his adversaries, there was no fixed tradition as to whether or not the altar of gold and the altar of bronze required immersion. The interpretation of the Babylonian Talmud may not be the correct one; indeed, some Mishnah commentators, including Maimonides, abandoned it (see my *Sources and Traditions,* Chagigah, p. 615, n. 6). Nevertheless, it indicated that to the author (or authors) of this interpretation, the Tannaim disagreed in matters pertaining to basic ritual procedures in the Temple. There was no reliable, continuous tradition even during the time of the Tannaim informing them exactly what took place in the Temple, and much of the Tannaim's reconstruction may well have been conjectural.

38. In the sense that it is rarely wholly incomprehensible. On the other hand, the aggadah, because of its symbolism and richness in nuances, could never be fully comprehensible to anyone but a contemporary, to whom both content and form would be familiar.

39. See, for example, Mishnah Rosh Hashanah 3:8.

40. See, for example, Mishnah Sotah 1:7–9.

41. See A. Baumgarten, "The Akiba Opposition," *Hebrew Union College Annual,* vol. 50, 1979, pp. 179–197.

42. For detailed analysis and supporting proofs, see D. Z. Hoffmann, *Die Erste Mischna und die Controversen der Tannaim,* Jahresbericht Rabbiner Seminar, Berlin 1881–82, pp. 26ff.

43. See Sifrei Deut., piska 344, p. 401, and the references in L. Finklestein's edition, note 2.

44. R. Gamaliel is mentioned approximately seventy times in the Mishnah and almost that many times in the Tosefta, whereas in the Midrashim that stem from the school of R. Ishmael he is mentioned only a few times. Is that a sign of estrangement between the Patriarch and the school of R. Ishmael?

45. See B.T. Berakhoth 28a: R. Akiba told R. Yehoshua: "Tomorrow, I and you will greet him at his door." See also L. Ginzberg's *Commentary on the Palestinian Talmud,* Jewish Theological Seminary, New York 1941, vol. 3, p. 206: "greet him at his door" means that we should honor him with the honor due a head of an Academy. R. Akiba emerges from the controversy between R. Gamaliel and R. Yehoshua as closer to the former. See also A. Hyman, *Toldoth Tannaim VeAmoraim,* London 1910, p. 994: "R. Akiba constantly sided with R. Gamaliel."

46. Like the first Mishnah of Tractate Baba Kama. See my article in *Studies in Rabbinic Literature, Bible and Jewish History: A Jubilee Volume in Honor of E. Z. Melamed* (Hebrew), Bar Ilan University, Ramat Gan 1982, pp. 108–114. See also E. Z. Melamed, *The Relationship between the Halakhic Midrashim and the Mishnah and Tosefta* (Hebrew), Da'ath, Jerusalem 1964, pp. 105–113.

As far as I can ascertain, the first to raise the question of why the students of R. Ishmael are not mentioned in the Mishnah and in the Tosefta was the pioneering scholar Z. Frankel in *Darkhei HaMishnah,* Tel Aviv 1959 edition, p. 156. However, his explanation of geographic inaccessibility (that Rabbi had no access to the teachings of the students of R. Ishmael) can be safely disregarded. Rabbi knew their teachings and often quoted them anonymously. For the same reason, one should not say along with A. Geiger (*Urschrift und Uebersetzungen der Bibel. . . ,* Verlag Madda, Frankfurt on Main 1928, especially the first excursus, pp. 434–450) that Rabbi intentionally omitted the teachings of the school of R. Ishmael beause they contained the residues of Sadducean elements. He did not omit them, and they did not contain Sadducean elements. The best critical review of Geiger's theory is that of Z. M. Pineles, *Darkhah Shel Torah,* Wien 1861, pp. 168–201.

47. Mishnah as a corpus of law is also mentioned in Sifrei Deut., piska 306 (p. 339), 317 (p. 359), 344 (p. 401), and 355 (p. 418), all of which are attributed by Hoffmann (*Jahrbuch,* vol. 6, p. 307) to the school of R. Ishmael. Epstein (*Introduction to Tannaitic Literature,* p. 628), however, has observed that the terminology of the Piskaoth starting with piska 304 "is mixed because the compiler took them from different sources." The quotations that contain the term *Mishnah* as a corpus of law were taken from sources close to the school of R. Akiba. The general observation should also be made that we lack reliable criteria for determining whether an anonymous aggadic passage comes from the school of R. Ishmael or that of R. Akiba.

48. There is no doubt that some *mikan omru* passages were added later. This is attested to by the differences in the manuscripts concerning the presence of such passages and by the few instances where there is evidence that the *mikan omru* passages are late. It cannot be said a priori, however, that whenever there is such a difference, the *mikan omru* passage was originally absent and only later was it added to the text. Nevertheless, it stands to reason that in the majority of instances that is exactly what happened. Changes through additions are more likely to occur than changes through omissions, especially when the addition comes from such an authoritative book as the Mishnah. Few scribes would dare to omit a passage in the Midreshei Halakhah that has its parallel in the Mishnah, whereas many would do the reverse (that is, add passages to the Midreshei Halakhah that are found in the Mishnah). The similarity between the *mikan omru* in Midreshei Halakhah and *mena hannei millei* in the Babylonian Talmud—following a Mishnah and preceding a Midrashic Braitha—is striking.

The *mikan omru* formula is a convenient way to connect the fixed laws of the Mishnah with their scriptural sources as expounded in the Midreshei Halakhah. It is therefore quite likely that circles close to Rabbi the Patriarch, who had a hand in the editing of Midreshei Halakhah, occasionally attached quotations from their Mishnah to the Mekhilta of R. Ishmael. This was not the doing of the disciples of R. Ishmael; they either ignored or opposed the Mishnah.

49. Nor should the fact that a quotation attributed to R. Ishmael in Tosefta Shabbath 1:13 (and parallels) and actually found in Mishnah Shabbath 1:3 be construed as evidence that R. Ishmael knew Mishnah. All that this indicates is that R. Ishmael knew that particular law, which happens also to be quoted in the Mishnah; it does not prove that he knew Mishnah as a corpus. Similarly, the quote from Mishnah Chagigah 3:2 that is put in the mouth of R. Ishmael in the Palestinian Talmud (ibid. 3:2 [79a]) indicates only that R. Ishmael knew that particular halakhah of the sages. It does not prove that he knew Mishnah as a source book of law.

It is also possible that the quotes put in the mouth of R. Ishmael are not from him but were added later. In the two examples just given, this supposition seems unlikely despite the fact that in the parallel source of the second example, in the Tosefta Kelim Baba Bathra 1:2,3 and B.T. Chagigah 20a, another quotation is given, one that is not found in the Mishnah. However, they all contain a quotation formula

גדולים דברי חכמים שאמרו

("great are the words of the sages who said . . ."). While the nature of the quotation is in doubt in the second example, the parallel sources confirm each other that there was a quotation.

Not so in a similar case in Tosefta Yebamoth 14:5 and parallels. There R. Akiba is quoting a law which the Tosefta earlier attributes to contemporary sages of R. Meir against the view of the latter. R. Akiba would not and could not have quoted the sages of R. Meir (who was his disciple) as authorities, and therefore the quote cannot be from R. Akiba.

R. Zvi Hirsch Chajes, who made the claim in his gloss to B.T. Shabath 12b for the antiquity of the Mishnah on the basis of the quote of R. Ishmael, made a similar claim in his gloss to B.T. Yoma 53b. There it seems the claim is even stronger, for the quote is preceded by "we have learned [presumably in the Mishnah]." However, deeper reflection will show that the quote there could not have been referring to Mishnah as a corpus. The quote is put in the mouth of a High Priest. Chajes accordingly deduces that the Mishnah as a book existed already at the time of the Second Temple—not an impossible position. However, that High Priest is identified in P.T. Yoma 5:3 (42c) as Simon the Just (third century B.C.E.), who is by all accounts too early to have known Mishnah. Moreover, the formula of the quote is missing in the parallel sources, both in the Palestinian Talmud and Tosefta (ibid. 2:13). Clearly, a later writer added the formula on the basis of Mishnah Yoma 5:1.

Another artificial quote is the one attributed to R. Shimon ben Shetach in B.T. Chagigah 16b and B.T. Makkoth 5b. He purportedly told his colleague R. Yehudah ben Tabbai that the sages said: "False witnesses are not put to death unless they both are proved false witnesses." This law is found verbatim in the Tosefta Sanhedrin at the end of chapter 6, and it is implied in Mishnah Makkoth 1:7. According to Chajes' reasoning, this would show that R. Shimon ben Shetach (mid-second century B.C.E.) already knew Mishnah. However, in the Tosefta Sanhedrin 6:6, R. Shimon ben Shetach is not quoting the sages but is expounding a drashah on which the above Mishnah and Braitha of the Tosefta is based. This is more in line with my general thesis that during the second century B.C.E., the Midrashic form was the dominant mode of transmitting law. In the Babylonian Talmud version, someone converted the drashah into a quote from his Mishnah (not necessarily our Mishnah).

50. J. N. Epstein, *Introduction to the Text of the Mishnah,* Magnes Press, Jerusalem 1948, pp. 747–748.

51. According to the Maharal of Prague, *Derech Hachaim* on Mishnah (Braitha) Aboth 6:5, reproduced in his selected writings (ed. A. Kariv, Mossad Harav Kook, Jerusalem 1960), vol. 2, p. 324, the opposition to the Mishnah came from intellectuals who were more interested in learning than in observance, which is the prime purpose of the Mishnah.

52. An attempt to reconcile those two opposing attitudes is made by R. Joshua ben Levi, who concludes: "Studying Mishnah (at the neglect of Talmud) is laudatory. People who do so are assured a share in the world to come. Only those who follow the Mishnah in practical decisions—knowing only the conclusions and not the reasons that prompted them—are destroyers of the world." But the conflict between the two opposing attitudes is not that easily obliterated; see my article "Whosoever Studies Laws," *Rabbinical Assembly, Proceedings of the 1979 Convention,* p. 299. In early Amoraic times, the debate was: Which is more important, Mishnah or Talmud? See the Palestinian Talmud at the end of Tractate Horayoth: "R. Samuel Son of Nachman said Mishnah is more important than Talmud, whereas R. Yochanan said Talmud is more important than Mishnah." This reference to P.T. Horayoth was omitted mistakenly in my *Sources and Traditions,* both in the introduction to Tractate Shabbath, p. 23, n. 67, and in Tractate Erubin, p. 94.

53. R. Natan is grouped together with Rabbi as *sof Mishnah,* with whom the period of the Mishnah concluded (B.T. Baba Metzia 86a, at the top). The Mishnah of R. Natan is also singled out in B.T. Temurah 16a. Yet he is not mentioned

in the Mishnah of R. Judah Hanassi. Our editions of the Mishnah quote him twice at the end of Tractate Berakoth and at the end of the second chapter of Tractate Shekalim; both are later additions. See J. N. Epstein, *Introduction to the Text of the Mishnah* (Hebrew), Magnes Press, Jerusalem 1948, p. 975.

54. See Epstein's masterful discussion (ibid., pp. 51–74).

55. They had high praise for him. "When R. Natan died"—says the Mekhilta, Amalek, Yitro, parshah 2, p. 200—"his wisdom was lost with him." That is, none after him compared to him in wisdom. L. Ginzberg, *Commentary on the Palestinian Talmud,* vol. 4, p. 27, considers the praise of R. Natan excessive and suggests a different meaning for the words "his wisdom."

56. R. Natan ben Yechiel, *Aruch* s.v. *kamar* (3) in the name of R. Sherira Gaon.

57. אמר ר' יצחק: לשעבר כשהיתה הפרוטה מצויה היה אדם מתאוה לשמוע דבר משנה ודבר תלמוד. ועכשיו שאין הפרוטה מצויה וביותר שאנו חולים מן המלכות, אדם מתאוה לשמוע דבר מקרא ודבר אגדה.
"R. Yitzchak said, formerly when money was available, people were eager to learn something of Mishnah or Talmud; but now money is not available, and still more, now that we are worn out by oppression from the kingdoms, they want to hear only lessons of Scripture and Aggadah" (Tractate Sofrim 16:4, ed. M. Higger, New York, 1937, p. 286; Pesikta of Rav Kahana, piska 12, ed. B. Mandelbaum, Jewish Theological Seminary, New York 1962, p. 205). According to R. Levi (quoted in *Midrash Rabbah,* Song of Songs, parshah 2:5.1), "They want to hear only words of blessing and comfort."

58. B.T. Chagigah 14a calls R. Yehudah ben Teima and his colleagues "Masters of the Mishnah." We know very little about this sage, not even when he lived. He is mentioned only a few times in the literature. A. Hyman, *Toldoth Tannaim ve Amoraim,* London 1910, p. 573, infers from a prayer in Mishnah Aboth 5:20: "May it be your will, O Lord our God and the God of our Fathers, that the Temple be built speedily in our days" that R. Yehudah ben Teima (whose statements are quoted immediately before the prayer) lived after the destruction of the Temple. This inference is based on the assumption that the prayer too is from R. Yehudah. Most probably, however, the prayer is from the editor who wanted to conclude the tractate (the rest is a later addition) with a prayer for the rebuilding of the Temple. See Epstein, *Introduction to the Mishnah* (Hebrew), p. 978. Yet Hyman is right that R. Yehudah ben Teima lived after the destruction of the Temple. If he had something to do with the Mishnah, he could not have lived prior to 90 C.E. when the change from Midrashic to Mishnaic form took place.

4. The Amoraic Period

1. "The Braitha was not known to me," (B.T. Sabbath 19b and parallels) applies to both types of Braithoth, those found in the Tosefta and those found in the Midreshei Halakhah. Cf. B.T. Yebamoth 72b. R. Yochanan apparently did not know the contents of the Sifra until he was advanced in age, when an exchange with R. Shimon ben Lakish, his colleague and student, made him memorize and study the book.

2. J. N. Epstein, in his monumental book *Introduction to the Text of the*

Mishnah (Hebrew), Magnes Press, Jerusalem 1948, has devoted a chapter (pp. 771–776) to the question of how extensive the Amoraim's erudition in the Mishnah was. His conclusion is that it was almost perfect: he finds few instances where the Amoraim either contradicted or ignored a Mishnah. It is possible, indeed likely, that those are instances in which the Amoraim in fact had a different reading of the Mishnah. In another chapter (pp. 946–979), Epstein meticulously collected all kinds of late additions to the Mishnah. Why not, then, attribute the few instances where it seems as if the Amoraim's knowledge of the Mishnah is deficient to variant readings of, or later additions to, the Mishnah?

3. D. Kraemer, who is writing a dissertation at the Jewish Theological Seminary, New York, entitled "The Literary Characteristics of Amoraim Literature," informs me that the ratio of apodictic to argumentational traditions of Rav and Shmuel approaches twenty-two to one. "Of the apodictic statements, twice as many prescribe fixed laws, according to the model of the Mishnah, as interpret earlier texts. By way of comparison, the ratio of apodictic to argumentational traditions of R. Yochanan and Resh Lakish is approximately two to one, still a significant margin. In contrast, however, more of these apodictic statements are explanatory than halakhic. Significantly, in the next generation, the model of preserved traditions diverges still further from the earlier Mishnaic precedent, and by the generation of Abaye and Rava the ratio of apodictic over argumentational traditions is substantially less than two to one, while the majority of the former is now explanatory."

4. Some biblically justified (that is, hermeneutically deduced) laws have the same authority as explicitly written laws (see my *Sources and Traditions,* Yoma, pp. 7–9), whereas logically justified laws may not have that same authority. Consider, for instance, "Punishment can not be decreed on the basis of a mere logical inference" (Mekhilta, Mishpatim, parshah 11 [p. 288] and parallels).

5. One may contest this, however, saying: had we had Midreshei Halakhah of the school of R. Akiba to the whole Pentateuch, the number of times R. Judah is mentioned in the Midreshei Halakhah would have been considerably higher. In the Sifra, the most typical Midrash of the school of R. Akiba, R. Judah is mentioned quite frequently. Nevertheless, it is doubtful that even then the number would have equaled that of the Mishnah.

6. See E. Z. Melamed, "Tannaitic Controversies Concerning the Interpretation and Text of Older Mishnaoth" (Hebrew), *Tarbiz,* vol. 21, 1950, p. 164.

7. B.T. Gittin 18a and P.T. Shabbath 6:3 (8c). Tannaitic statements cited by Amoraim using *lo shanu* are found in B.T. Shabbath 50a, Erubin 64b, Nedarim 53a–b, Chullin 123b, and P.T. Moed Katan, at the beginning.

8. First noted by R. Malachi Hakohen, *Yad Malachi,* Livorno 1768, passage 356.

9. See, for example, B.T. Pesachim 48a: "He was silent in our Mishnah but answered him in another Tractate (*Braitha*)."

10. By way of comparison, *The Records of the Federal Convention of 1787,* edited by M. Farrand, might be of interest. Both considered deliberations of lesser importance, not worthy to be preserved along with the conclusions. To quote the book jacket of 1937, revised edition, Yale University Press, New Haven: "The Federal Convention of 1787 engaged in the great and complex labor of framing the Constitution for the Union of the States. For many years afterwards, little

was known of its deliberations and nothing official was published. The variety of versions which began to appear thereafter tended to confuse rather than clarify the situation." Of striking similarity to the modern critical Talmud scholar is Farrand's attempt to sift through different versions of the deliberations, none of which was fully reliable. Farrand tells us of his travails in the introduction.

11. The exceptions are B.T. Ketuboth 51b; Baba Kama 87b, 116a; Niddah 24a.

12. Principally by the Tosafoth Baba Bathra 150b, s.v. *beram.* The list is incomplete. See the indexes to the volumes of my *Sources and Traditions,* s.v. *iteiveih.*

13. See, however, B.T. Rosh Hashannah 15b: *Iteiveih Resh Lakish le Rabbi Yochanan* (Resh Lakish asks R. Yochanan), and R. Chananel (ad loc.): "Yerushalmi (at the beginning of the fifth chapter of Shebiith):"

א״ר אבא ... איך מותיב ר״ש בן לקיש ומקבל ר׳ יוחנן מיניה ושתיק ליה ...

(Said R. Abba . . . Why is it that R. Shimon the Son of Lakish asks [R. Yochanan] and R. Yochanan accepts it and is silent . . .). This *iteiveih* seems to be real, though the exact form is in doubt.

14. See my article "The Reception Accorded to Rabbi Judah's Mishnah," in *Jewish and Christian Self-Definition,* ed. E.P. Sanders et al., Fortress Press, Philadelphia 1981, pp. 204–212.

15. With the exception of the language of contracts. This type of language, especially in marriage contracts, was treated with the same detailed attention as was the language of the Bible. This prompted P.T. Ketuboth 4:8 (28d–29a) to say of some rabbis (with an element of surprise) that they subjected contracts to Midrash:

עבדין כתובה מדרש.

16. See also P.T. Beitzah 2:1 (61b):

דרש רב חונא כהדא דר׳ שמעון בן אלעזר, דרש ר׳ יוחנן לטיבראי כהדא דר״ש בן אלעזר ... הורי ר׳ אבהו כהדא דר״ש בן אלעזר.

(R. Chuna *darash* like [the opinion of] R. Shimon ben Elazar, R. Yochanan *darash* to the Tiberians like [the opinion of] R. Shimon ben Elazar . . . R. Abahu *horei* like [the opinion of] R. Shimon ben Elazar).

Here the words *darash* and *horei* are used together, though not in the same sentence. The difference between the two is that whereas *darash* introduces a statement that was promulgated in public, *horei* refers to the rendering of a decision given to a practical question whether delivered in public or in private. See, however, Sifrei Deut., piska 155 (p. 207):

על מעשה הוא חייב ואינו חייב על הוריה

and Mishnah Sanhedrin 11:2:

״אינו חייב עד שיורה לעשות״.

("He is not culpable unless he gives a decision concerning what should be done"). *Horei* alone does not necessarily mean action.

17. This found its way into the dictionaries of A. Kohut and E. Ben Yehuda, s.v. *darash.*

18. For references, see C. J. Kasowski, *Thesaurus Talmudis,* vol. 5, p. 2438, and vol. 9, p. 446.

19. See J. M. Kosovsky, *Sinai* (Hebrew), Mossad Harav Kook, Jerusalem 1959, vol. 22, p. 234.

20. See also ibid., p. 235. That *amar* refers to a statement enunciated in the

Academy was already stated by R. Shmuel Sid(ilyo) (ca. 1530) in his *Killei Shmuel,* ed. S. B. D. Sofer, Jerusalem 1972, s.v. *a'mar,* par. 22, p. 20:
כל מקום דאמרינן אמר פלוני, פירושו שנאמר בבית המדרש.
("Wherever it says *amar* Peloni, it means that it was said in the Academy").

21. See *Piskei HaRid,* Shabbath, Mossad Harav Kook, Jerusalem 1964, p. 229:
כך היא המשנה לאמוראין כמו התורה לתנאים.
("[Exegetically] the relationship of the Amoraim to the Mishnah is similar to that of the Tannaim to the Bible").

22. However, when simple textual reading is involved, the usual phrase is
קורא בתורה ושונה משנה.
See my *Sources and Traditions,* Kiddushin, pp. 671–673.

5. *The Stammaitic Period*

1. R. Ashi died in 427; 501 is the date of Ravina the Second's death; 520 is the date of the death of R. Assi or R. Yose (depending on whether one follows the French or Spanish recension of the Epistle, p. 97). The first two dates are directly taken from R. Sherira Gaon's (966–1065) famous Epistle, ed. B. M. Lewin, Haifa 1921, pp. 94–95, whereas the third date follows I. Halevy's interpretation of R. Sherira (*Dorot Ha-Rishonim,* B. Harz, Berlin and Vienna 1923, vol. 3, p. 28). I have serious reservations about the accuracy of Halevy's date for R. Assi's or R. Yose's death. However, since any substitute date is less certain, I leave it unchallenged. The B.T. Baba Metzia 86a calls both R. Ashi and Ravina "the end of *hora'ah.*" R. Sherira presumably, as already noticed by H. Graetz (see his *Geschichte der Jüden,* 3rd ed., O. Leiner, Leipzig 1895, book 5, n. 2, pp. 347ff.; see also N. Bruell, *Jahrbücher für Jüdische Geschichte und Literatur,* Wilhelm Erras, Frankfurt am Main 1876, p. 26, n. 2), identified the R. Ashi of "the end of hora'ah of the Talmud" with R. Assi or R. Yose, whom he indeed called "the end of hora'ah."

R. Sherira's understanding of "the end of hora'ah" is the end of the Talmud. My understanding is the opposite: it means the beginning of the Talmud, that is, the beginning of the preserving of the "give and take," the deliberations. I interject the period of the Stammaim between "the end of hora'ah" and the Saboraim, diverging from R. Sherira's chronicle, on the basis of evidence presented elsewhere (the introduction to my *Sources and Traditions,* Shabbath, pp. 14–22). However, with respect to the time when the period of the Saboraim began, as well as what happened during the period, I do not dare to diverge from R. Sherira's chronicle. We are totally dependent on him—the oldest and most classical historian of the Talmud—for the history of the Saboraim.

2. See B. M. Lewin, *Rabbanan Saborai veTalmudam,* Achiever, Jerusalem and Tel Aviv, 1937, pp. 46–54.

3. See B.T. Berakhoth 36b and parallels. See also my *Sources and Traditions,* Shabbath, pp. 361–362.

4. At least twice (Yoma 5b, Ketuboth 3a), in connection with discussions of past events, the Gemara asks: "[What difference does it make?] What's past is past!" (See also Tosafoth Chagigah 6b, s.v. *ma'y.*) But this should not be inter-

preted as indicating impatience with discussions that had no practical application. As already noticed by the medieval commentators, the same question could have been asked in many other places in the Talmud but was not. Apparently, the Stammaim asked this question rhetorically when they had an answer to it. When they had no answer, they simply ignored it. The same is true of other similar questions (see my *Sources and Traditions,* Erubin, p. 208, n. 1).

Cf. E. E. Urbach, *The Jews, Greeks and Christians,* ed. R. H. Kelly and R. Scroggs, E. J. Brill, Leiden 1976, p. 120. His reference in note 12 to P.T. Kila'im 1:3 (27a):

מה דהוה עובדא הוה עובדא.

is not pertinent. Its meaning is similar to the statement in the Babylonian Talmud (Rosh Hashannah 14b, Ketuboth 7a, 27a) that one cannot necessarily deduce from a story that the law would have been different had the story been different. See also B.T. Sanhedrin 51b and Zebachim 45a.

5. For instance, the rule that "the law is like Rav in ritual matters (*issurim*) and like Shmuel in civil matters (*dinim*)" (B.T. Bechoroth 49b), even though Rav is not always right in *issurim* or Shmuel in *dinim.* A very instructive responsum on this subject is that of R. Y. Bachrach, *Chavath Yair,* Frankfurt 1699, no. 94, at the beginning.

6. For an example, see the introduction to my *Sources and Traditions,* Yoma to Chagigah, pp. 2–5, and ibid., Pesachim, pp. 477–480.

7. Introduction to my *Sources and Traditions,* Shabbath, p. 5.

8. B.T. Berakhoth 20a and parallels.

9. B.T. Sukkah 28a and parallels.

10. See the Introduction to my *Sources and Traditions,* Seder Nashim.

11. The question, of course, did not escape the attention of the medieval commentators. The Tosafoth (ad loc., s.v. *ella*) explain that the Gemara had to add "that subsequently there appeared witnesses" because without subsequent witnesses, the Mishnah here would not be adding to what it says later on in the tractate at Chapter 7:4. The mere law that confession exempts one from a fine is stated there too; there is no need for repetition. The Tosafoth raise the possibility (based on the Gemara, ibid. 13b) that the Mishnah first stated the law in general terms (befitting an old Mishnah that uses such anachronistic expressions as *hav* instead of *hayyav;* see ibid. 6b) and later on exposited it. But, say the Tosafoth, that would have required the exposition to be of greater length than the general term—which it is not. The Gemara, therefore, was forced to add the additional clause.

However, the Mishnah 7:4 is not reporting the law that confession exempts one from a fine as a law by itself, but as an example among many when a thief pays only twofold restitution, not fourfold or fivefold as required by the Torah. It is quite plausible that the Mishnah is first stating the law in general terms and then in 7:4, based on the first Mishnah, includes it among similar instances where the outcome is that the thief pays only twofold restitution. The Gemara's motive for adding the clause must be other than to avoid repetition.

12. C. Albeck, in his supplement to the Mishnah Baba Kama 1:3, s.v. *bifnei,* p. 408, has collected the sources on whether or not money damages are paid for tort.

13. L. Jacobs, *Teiku: The Unsolved Problem in the Babylonian Talmud,* Leo Baeck Publication, London, 1981, concludes from the stylistic uniformity of *teiku* that besides the bare posing of the problem, the discussion of the *teiku* is the working of later editors "who must have lived subsequently to all the propounders . . . not earlier than the latter part of the fifth century" (p. 294), which corresponds to the period of the Stammaim.

14. A beautiful example is B.T. Shabbath 52b. See my *Sources and Traditions,* ad loc.

15. Z. Frankel, *Introduction to the Palestinian Talmud* (Hebrew), Breslau 1870, pp. 32b ff.

16. Ibid., p. 35b. It should be noted that there are some layers of stam even in the Yerushalmi (less so—almost none—in the older parts of the Yerushalmi, that of Tractates Baba Kama, Baba Metzia, and Baba Bathra, generally referred to as Yerushalmi Nezikin). The custom in the academy was that the speakers' own ideas were conveyed without specific authorship, without quoting themselves as authors, whereas the ideas of their teachers were quoted attributionally, in their respective names. When the editors of the Yerushalmi decided to close the development of the text and to "freeze" it into a book, they recorded what went on in the academy at that particular time. The ideas of the then "present speakers" were therefore recorded anonymously (hence the existence of stammoth in the Yerushalmi). Had the editors allowed the text to develop further, the then "present speakers'" ideas would have been transmitted by their disciples attributionally, in their names. By arresting the further development of the text, the editors created an anonymous ring around the attributional material. But the ring was thin and not always significant; it was the result of a technical decision to record the "present speakers'" ideas anonymously. In contrast, the anonymous sections of the Babylonian Talmud are rich, multitiered and comprehensive, the result of a new awareness of the importance of the "give and take" and a desire to preserve and develop it. The difference is a qualitative one.

17. With gradations, however. The Mishnah remained much the same, despite occasional significant variations, but this is less true of the Braithoth. Those found in the Palestinian Talmud are usually closer to the original language than those found in the Babylonian Talmud. On the other hand, the Babylonian Talmud had a richer knowledge of Braithoth than the Palestinian Talmud. The apodictic statements of the Amoraim are often considerably different in the parallel sources yet resemble each other enough to be recognized as similar.

18. See D. Rosenthal, introduction to *Babylonian Talmud, Codex Florence,* Makor Publishing, Jerusalem 1972. See especially the first two lines on p. 2.

19. The fact that many sugyoth conclude with a statement of R. Ashi should not be construed as evidence that he was the redactor of the Talmud (see J. Kaplan, *The Redaction of the Babylonian Talmud,* Bloch Publishing Company, New York 1933, chaps. 5–6, especially pp. 75–79). On the contrary, the fact that R. Ashi is mentioned by name indicates that the redaction took place after his death and that it used earlier materials, including material of R. Ashi (though this is not the case with Rabbi, the editor of Mishnah). Furthermore, in a number of instances (see, for instance, my *Sources and Traditions,* Nedarim, pp. 326–327, Erubin, p. 27, Pesachim, pp. 304–305) the redactor of the Gemara misunderstood

R. Ashi because he did not have a complete or accurate version of R. Ashi's statement. If R. Ashi had also been a redactor, he most likely would not have lived much before the final redactor, and the latter would have been more thoroughly acquainted with his teachings. Those who maintain the semi-traditional position (aggressively defended by I. Halevy) that the redaction of the Talmud began with R. Ashi (died 427) and concluded with Ravina the Second (died 501) have the unenviable task of explaining why a literature of 200 years' duration (starting with Rav, who established this Academy or a semblance thereof in Sura around 220) needed more than seventy years for redaction.

It may be added that the statements of R. Ashi and subsequent discussions thereon do not display any recognizable difference from their predecessors. If he were a redactor, we would have expected his statements to betray traces of this activity. On the other hand, with the exception of Mar bar R. Ashi and Ravina the Second, the vast majority of the statements of the Amoraim who lived after R. Ashi are radically different from their predecessors. Little is recorded in their names, and it is of a different quality: it is simple, single-tiered, and does not form a link in the chain of a continuous sugya. Their statements are hardly ever followed by subsequent discussions. While their attributed contribution is best described as minor "touch-ups" to an already existing and organized Gemara, to whose anonymous redaction these Amoraim devoted most of their efforts, their overall literary activity must have been greater than these meager leftovers. Cf. N. Bruell, "Die Entstehungsgeschichte des babylonischen Talmuds als Schriftwerkes," in *Jahrbücher für Jüdische Geschichte und Literatur,* Wilhelm Erras, Frankfurt am Main 1876, pp. 67–68 nn. 106 and 107; and J. Kaplan, *Redaction of the Babylonian Talmud,* pp. 10–11.

20. See my *Sources and Traditions,* Rosh Hashanah, p. 358, n. 4.

21. This is a reconstruction by the Stam. Originally R. Yitzchak, an early fourth-century Palestinian scholar, most likely said only: "Why do we blow the *shofar* on Rosh Hashanah? In order to confound Satan." He, like some Tannaim before him and some Amoraim a bit after him, was in the habit of giving explanations of commandments (Cf. Z. Chajes' gloss, ad loc. His distinction between *lammah* and *mipnei mah* is not warranted. The Gaonim read here too *mipnei mah.* [See my *Sources and Traditions,* Rosh Hashanah, p. 380, n. 6.]) By the time of the Stammaim, this was no longer customary. They, therefore, interpreted R. Yitzchak's question to mean not why do we blow at all, but why do we blow twice, sitting and standing.

22. See my article, "Contemporary Methods of the Study of Talmud," *Journal of Jewish Studies,* vol. 30, no. 2, Autumn 1979, pp. 195–196. For an apologetic explanation, See *Tarbiz,* vol. 49, p. 192.

23. See my *Sources and Traditions,* Pesachim, pp. 477–480 (particularly note 11x).

24. I collected most of the instances in my *Sources and Traditions,* Nashim, Introduction, p. 14, n. 19.

25. For a beautiful example of the difference in the mode of learning between the pre-Stammaitic and post-Stammaitic periods, see B.T. Baba Kama 20a–b and 21a.

26. For some time it was thought that *Sefer Hayerushoth* by R. Saadiah Gaon

(882–942) constituted an exception to this rule. Recently, however, S. Abramson, *Inyanoth Besifruth Hageonim,* Mossad Harav Kook, Jerusalem 1974, p. 232, has shown that the present edition of *Sefer Hayerushoth* is only a shortened copy of an earlier, fuller one that contained proofs from the Bible and Talmud.

27. If the thesis developed in Chapter 2 is correct, that the school of R. Ishmael opposed the innovation of the Mishnah and insisted on the old way of transmitting laws together with their scriptural support, one may say that ultimately the school of R. Ishmael triumphed over the school of R. Akiba. We are observing a phenomenon not uncommon in the annals of intellectual history: esteem does not correlate with adherence. Rabbinic literature esteems R. Akiba and his school far more than it does R. Ishmael and his school; yet the mode of learning it finally adopted is closer to the school of R. Ishmael than it is to the school of R. Akiba. The hallmark of rabbinic learning is not Mishnaic style, the style so intimately connected with R. Akiba and his school, but Midrashic style, the medium of R. Ishmael and his school.

6. The Gemara as Successor of Midrash

1. J. Neusner was the first to call attention to the affinity of Midreshei Halakhah to Gemara by calling the Sifra, for instance, "a sort of Talmud in its own right" (*History of the Mishnaic Laws of Purities,* E. J. Brill, Leiden 1974, vol. 7, p. ix). See also B. Bokser, *Post-Mishnaic Judaism in Transition,* Scholars Press, Chico, Calif. 1980, pp. 441–443.

2. A notable example is the question "How do we know that circumcision is on that place?" (which is not found in the Midreshei Halakhah now extant but undoubtedly comes from there). In the B.T. Shabbath 108a this question is raised (and refuted by Midrashic expositions) by R. Yoshiyah and R. Jonathan, the students of R. Ishmael, while in the Tosefta Shabbath 15:9 it is raised (and refuted by Midrashic exposition) by R. Yose, a student of R. Akiba. The topic was apparently discussed in both schools. Of a similar nature is the question raised (and refuted by Midrashic expositions) by R. Chiya in Sifra Vayikra, Nedavah, chapter 6:3 (7b): "How do we know that an animal is to be slaughtered on the neck (and not on another part of the body)?" See also B.T. Chullin 27a.

3. R. Bultmann, *Der Stil der paulinischen Predigt und die Kynischstoische Diatribe,* Vandenhock and Ruprecht, Goettingen 1910, has called attention to the dialogical element in the Diatribe, which is defined by A. J. Malherbe, *Harvard Theological Review,* 731–732, Jan.–Apr. 1980, p. 231, as when "a speaker or writer makes use of an imaginary interlocutor who asks questions or raises objections to the arguments or affirmations that are made. These responses are frequently stupid and are summarily rejected by the speaker or writer." As Bultmann's title indicates, the dialogical elements are generally attributed to Greek influence, particularly Stoic. Dialogical elements are found profusely in Midreshei Halakhah, and while both may have Greek antecedents, it is possible, indeed likely, that the elements are natively Jewish. In comparing Paul with Epictus, Malherbe (ibid., p. 239) says: "Paul always provides a reason for his rejection of the false conclusion. Epictus does so only sometimes." In Midreshei Halakhah, too, there is always a reason for the rejection—further testimony to their affinity.

4. See also M. Weinfield, *Deuteronomy and the Deuteronomic School,* Oxford University Press, London 1972: "The most outstanding feature of Deuteronomic style is its use of rhetoric" (p. 3). J. Weingreen, in his book *From Bible to Mishnah,* Manchester University Press, Manchester 1976, pp. 143–154, calls Deuteronomy "proto-Mishna." Incidentally, some of Weingreen's conclusions, for instance, that "alongside the literary material preserved in the Hebrew Bible there existed a corpus of written extra-biblical law, history and folk tradition" (p. x) conform to the standard opinion of many historians writing in Hebrew, except that they believe that that extra literature was oral. See, for example, I. H. Weiss, *Dor Dor Vedorshav,* The Widow and Brothers Rom, Vilna 1904, first chapter.

5. In a few instances, the dissenting view is referring not to the direct statement of the *tanna kama* (the opinion of the previous Tanna), but to a *diyuk,* an inference which probably, because of brevity, was left out (since it was self-evident). See the indexes to the four volumes of my *Sources and Traditions,* s.v. *diyuk.* Of course what is self-evident to one may not be so to another, resulting in disagreements. A case in point is M. Baba Bathra 1:3 with respect to the *tanna kama*'s view: "If he fenced in the fourth side." See the Talmuds, ad loc., and parallel sources.

6. The medieval commentators often interpret the Gemara in a manner that implies that there is a lacuna. J. J. Weinberg's list in *Talpioth,* vol. 6, p. 610, is far from complete.

7. Cf. Z. Frankel, *Introduction to the Palestinian Talmud* (Hebrew), Schletter, Breslau 1870, pp. 21b, 30a.

8. In most places, however, the missing law is not as clearly implied in the context as it is in the example from Moed Katan. We may require the assistance of an Amora to bring it out. I am thinking in particular of Mishnah Chagigah 3:5: "From Modiith and inwards, men may be deemed trustworthy in what concerns earthenware vessels; from Modiith and outwards they may not be deemed trustworthy." How trustworthy were they in Modiith itself? The Mishnah does not tell us. The answer is provided in a Braitha quoted in B.T., ibid., 25b (at the end). According to Abaye, ibid., 26a, the answer is implied in the Mishnah. On our own, however, most likely we would not have discovered it from the Mishnah. Abaye's deduction is far from certain. See also B.T. Baba Metzia 51a: "What the Mishnah omits is explained in the Braitha . . . This too follows from the fact that the Mishnah states . . ."

9. See D. W. Halivni, "The Reception Accorded to Rabbi Judah's Mishnah," *Jewish and Christian Self-Definition,* ed. E. P. Sanders, et al., Fortress Press, Philadelphia, 1981, pp. 379–380 (n. 3).

10. See my *Sources and Traditions,* Nazir, pp. 402–403, for an instructive example.

11. See ibid. (note 9), pp. 206–207.

12. A beautiful example of this kind is Mishnah Shabbath 2:7. See my *Sources and Traditions,* Shabbath, pp. 96–97.

13. Or that R. Akiba used *perat le* in Sifra p. 98a and *lehozi et* in the Mekhilta of R. Ishmael, Mishpatim, parshah 10, p. 292. However, the drashah in the Sifra is attributed in the parallel sources in B.T. Nazir 61a and Menachoth 73b not to R. Akiba but to R. Yose Haglili.

14. And similar expressions in Aramaic found in the Babylonian Talmud and absent in the Palestinian Talmud, or vice versa. On the other hand, expressions like *lo shanu,* which are found in both Talmuds attributed to Amoraim of all generations (even to Tannaim; see supra, Chapter four, note 7), undoubtedly arose already in Amoraic times (if not earlier). This was true even though in some instances it can be proved that the expression does not belong to the Amora but was added later. When, for example, there are two versions of the same statement of an Amora and only one contains the expression *lo shanu,* it is plausible to assume that originally the Amora did not use that expression, that it is the result of an interpretation by a later disciple, while another disciple disagreed. For additional examples, see the indexes to my *Sources and Traditions,* vols. 2 and 3, s.v. *lo shanu.*

15. First mentioned by R. Yeshuah Halevy, *Halichoth Olam,* gate 2, chap. 2.

16. The words *teno rabbanan* preceding a Braitha usually signify that the content of the Braitha bears some resemblance to the previously cited Mishnah. Otherwise, it would say *tanya.* (The standard books on the "rules of the Talmud" give other distinctions between *teno rabbanan* and *tanya.* For a short summary, see S. B. D. Sofer, *Divrei Sofrim,* Jerusalem 1961, vol. 3, pp. 93a–94a.) Sometimes, however, the resemblance is not to the previously cited Mishnah but to the preceding Amoraic statements (for instance, Shabbath 25b, 115b [at the end]), which indicates that the words *teno rabbanan* were inserted by those who arranged the order of the Talmud. According to the author of *Seder Tannaim ve Amoraim,* ed. K. Kahana, Hermon Verlag, Frankfurt 1935, p. 9, par. 6c, the Saboraim arranged the order of the Talmud. Hence the words *teno rabbanan* are from them.

17. Even contradictory sources; see, for instance, J. N. Epstein, *Introduction to the Text of the Mishnah* (Hebrew), Magnes Press, Jerusalem 1948, pp. 1214–15, and my *Sources and Traditions,* Nazir, pp. 389–390.

18. See *Aruch Completum,* s.v. בחר, for the meaning of "highly selective" in connection with Tractate Eduyoth.

19. There are instances where a Saboraic source did not know an Amoraic source. See my *Sources and Traditions,* Sukkah, p. 197.

20. When, however, one statement within the same Talmud is in one place commented on and in another uncommented on, as in the Babylonian Talmud, Baba Kama 20a–b and 21a, we have to say that the reason for the difference is not lack of opportunity—the redactors could easily have integrated the two statements—but that the redactors of the commented statement were not familiar with the uncommented (chronologically earlier) one. Compilation and redaction are two distinct functions. It is therefore quite possible that after the redaction of the Talmud was completed, compilors continued to add occasional apodictic statements to the Gemara. Redaction being closed, the compilors left the apodictic statements uncommented on.

21. In the introduction to my *Sources and Traditions,* Shabbath, pp. 22–23, I explained the famous Braitha in B.T. Baba Metzia 33a (see also P.T. Shabbath 16:1 [15c]):

העוסק ... תלמוד אין לך מדה גדולה מזו. ולעולם הוי רץ למשנה יותר מן התלמוד.

which seems contradictory. "There is nothing more meritorious than the study of

Talmud"; yet "a person should always run to the Mishnah more than to the Talmud." I explain this passage to mean that the Talmud is richer than the Mishnah. The Talmud contains both Mishnah and Talmud, both definitive rulings and deliberations of rulings. The early rabbis, therefore, said: there is nothing more meritorious than the study of Talmud. Nevertheless, for practical reasons and also because the Mishnah is more reliable, later rabbis advised that a person should run to the Mishnah more than to the Talmud. To which R. Yochanan (ibid.) added "the Mishnah taught during the time of Rabbi." Only the Mishnah of Rabbi has the high degree of reliability that makes it preferable to the versatility of the Talmud; other collections of Mishnah are not that reliable and are not to be preferred over the Talmud.

22. B.T. Chullin 32b.

23. Z. W. Rabinovitz, *Shaare Torath Eretz Yisrael,* Jewish Theological Seminary, Jerusalem and New York 1940, pp. 340–343. For a different view, see S. Safrai, *Proceedings of the Seventh World Congress of Jewish Studies,* Jerusalem 1981, pp. 29–43.

24. This also explains why the formula

חד אמר וחד אמר

("One [sage] said this and one [sage] said that") is applied almost exclusively to Amoraic opinions. In the Mishnah or Braitha it is always clear who said what—as already noticed by R. Malachi Hakohen (d. 1785–1790?) in his book *Yad Malachi,* Passage 5. Tannaitic literature was transmitted with greater exactitude.

7. *The Legacy of the Stammaim*

1. For Bechor Shor, see S. Poznansky, *Commentary to Ezekiel and the Minor Prophets by R. Eliezer from Beaugency,* Mekize Nirdamim, Warsaw 1913, pp. 55–78 (Hebrew); for Rashbam, in addition to the standard book by D. Rosin, *R. Samuel Ben Meir als Schrifterklärer,* Breslau 1880, see also the highly stimulating article by E. Touitou in *Studies in Rabbinic Literature, Bible and Jewish History: A Book in Honor of E. Z. Melamed* (Hebrew), Bar Ilan University, Ramat Gan 1982, pp. 48–74, entitled "Rashbam's Exegesis in Light of the Historical Reality of His Time." The literature on Ibn Ezra is vast. I like to single out the article by U. Simon, "The Exegetical Method of Abraham Ibn Ezra as Revealed in Three Interpretations of a Biblical Passage," *Annual of Bar Ilan University,* vol. 3, pp. 92–138. Simon quotes the literature, and of particular interest to us are pp. 130–138, where he compares Ibn Ezra with the Rashbam with respect to the relationship between peshat and halakhah.

2. Like Philo, *On the Special Laws,* IV, 35.

3. So was the Mekhilta of R. Ishmael, tractate Mishpatim, at the beginning of parshah 15.

4. The other suggestions offered in the periodical *Hamayan,* no. 3, 1976, pp. 7–69; 1977, pp. 26–49, are unacceptable. The mutual criticism is justified.

For an interesting—though brief—mystical explanation, see Adereth Eliyahu, by the Gaon of Vilna, at the beginning of Parshath Mishpatim.

5. Depending on what the psalmist meant by the word *torah*—the keeping of God's commandment exclusively or, in a few places, also the study of Torah. The

question of meaning was raised by Y. Amir, *Teuda II* (Hebrew, with English summaries), Bible Studies, Tel Aviv University, 1982, pp. 68ff. That Psalm 119 presents a transition between the biblical and the rabbinic periods is satisfactorily proved by Amir (after citing the extensive literature on this Psalm, including two full-fledged books), based on other evidence.

6. See, for instance, Mishnah Aboth 3:11 ("even if he possesses Torah and good deeds") and Mishnah Peah 1:1 ("the study of Torah is equal to them all"). This Mishnah has often been misunderstood. Some take it to mean that the study of Torah is more important than the commandments it is contrasted with, namely, "honoring father and mother, deeds of loving kindness, making peace between man and his fellow." This is not so; some acts of loving kindness take priority over the study of the Torah. See B.T. Ketuboth 17a: "One interrupts the study of Torah for the sake of a funeral procession and the leading of the bride under the bridal canopy." This Mishnah can be understood only in light of another earlier Mishnah in Kiddushin 1:10. There the Mishnah says, "If a man performs a single commandment, it shall be well with him and he shall have length of days and shall inherit the land." What kind of commandment assures its practitioner such lofty rewards? That question was also asked by the author of Mishnah Peah (quoted above), and he answered: "These are the things whose fruits a man enjoys in this world while the capital is laid up for him in the world to come: honoring father and mother, deeds of loving kindness, making peace between man and his fellow. And the study of the Torah is parallel to them all" (see also B.T. Shabbath 127a, b). The commandment that assures such lofty rewards has to be of the type that keeps a man occupied almost all his life, such as honoring parents, doing deeds of loving kindness, or making peace between a man and his fellow. A chance mitzvah such as returning a lost object, or a seasonal mitzvah such as eating matzoh on Passover night, does not bring such rewards. Among the commandments, nothing is as timeless and as situationless as the mitzvah of studying Torah. From his cradle to his death, a person is obligated to study Torah under all conditions and in all circumstances. One who fulfills the single mitzvah of studying Torah (that is, spends all his free time in the study of Torah) is more assured of the reward mentioned in the Mishnah Kiddushin than he is by fulfilling any other mitzvah.

This is the meaning of the phrase "The study of Torah is equal to them all." For the study of Torah is truly a lifelong occupation, whereas other commandments, including honoring one's parents, deeds of loving kindness, and making peace between a man and his fellow, are not that demanding; there are times when one has no opportunity to fulfill them. This is not true of the mitzvah of studying Torah. It is omnipresent. (For a detailed explanation, see my *Sources and Traditions,* Kiddushin, pp. 661–663.)

7. B.T. Abodah Zarah 3b: "The first three hours of the day God studies Torah".

8. Some go beyond exhortation; they condemn it outright. The strongest condemnation is found in B.T. Yoma 72b. (See also B.T. Shabbath 31a–b.) R. Jonathan (a third-century Palestinian scholar) said: "Woe unto the enemies of the scholars [a euphemism, meaning the scholars themselves] who occupy themselves with the Torah, but have no fear of Heaven." Rava said to the sages: "I beseech

you, do not inherit a double Gehenom" (Rashi comments: The double Gehenom is the toil and labor that the study of Torah requires in this world and the punishment which will be meted out in the world to come for not having observed the commandments of the Torah). R. Joshua ben Levi (a colleague of R. Jonathan) said: "What is the meaning of the scriptural verse 'and this is the Law which Moses set [*sam* in Hebrew, which could also mean poison] before the children of Israel'? —if he is meritorious, it [the study of Torah] becomes for him a medicine of life, if not, a deadly poison." The analogy to "deadly poison" implies that one is better off not to study Torah at all than to study and not to practice. Indeed, it is so stated explicitly in Deuteronomy Rabbah 7:4, in the name of R. Simon ben Chalafta:

כל מי שלמד דברי תורה ואינו מקיים, ענשו חמור ממי שלא למד כל עיקר.

("Whoever studies Torah and does not observe [the commandments], his punishment is greater than the one who has not studied at all"). The same idea is expressed by Rava (ibid. Shabbath): "This may be compared to a man who instructed his agent: Take me up a *kor* of wheat [symbolizing the study of Torah] in the loft. The agent did. Did you mix in a *kor* of *chumton* [sandy soil containing a salty substance used for the preservation of wheat. In this analogy, it represents observance.] No, replied the agent. It would have been better had you not carried it up." A similar sentiment is expressed by R. Papa (a fourth-century Babylonian scholar) in his homily (B.T. Yebamoth 109b): "Scripture said: 'that ye may learn them and observe them' [Deut. 5:1]—whosoever is engaged in observance is also regarded as engaged in study. But whosoever is not engaged in observance is not regarded as engaged in study." It is possible, however, that R. Papa sees no value in study without practice, but unlike R. Joshua ben Levi, does not consider it as a "deadly poison."

This strongly condemnatory view of study without practice was not shared by all Talmudic sages. The Mishnah Aboth 3:9 quotes R. Hanina ben Dosa as having said: "He whose fear of sin comes before his wisdom, his wisdom endures. But he whose wisdom comes before his fear of sin, his wisdom does not endure." A man may not continue study for long without putting what he has studied into practice. But as long as he studies, he is fulfilling a commandment. It may not endure, but while it lasts, it is a worthwhile act. The answer given by the majority of scholars to the question quoted in the text, "What is more important, study or deeds?" was "Study is greater, for it leads to action." One may interpret their answer to imply that whenever study does not lead to action, either because (as we shall see later) the laws being studied are no longer relevant or because the person who studies them does not intend to put them into practice, such study is not greater than deeds. But neither is it inferior to deeds (and when in time of conflict, one may choose either one). Moreover, there is a statement in the P.T. Peah 1:1(15d) in the name of either R. Brachyah or R. Chiya from the village of Techumin (followed by two other sages, either R. Tanchuma or R. Yose the son of Zimra—all fourth-century scholars) that says:

אפילו כל מצוותיה של תורה אינן שוות לדבר אחד מן התורה.

("Even all the mitzvoth of the Torah do not add up in value to the study of a single thing from the Torah"). Clearly the author of this statement places the study of Torah over and above, and independent of, observance. This view did not go unchallenged. Together with it another view is quoted, in the name of one of the sages mentioned above and using the same formula. But instead of "all the mitzvoth of the Torah," this view has כל העולם כולו, "the whole world": nothing in the world compares in value to the study of Torah. This formulation does not necessarily, at least not explicitly, place the study of Torah above observance. The "whole world" may refer to the physical world, not to the spiritual fulfillment of commandments. Nevertheless, it is noteworthy that even the opposing view does not reverse the formula stating that "all of the Torah does not add up in value to the fulfillment of a single mitzvah." Even that view values Torah as much as it does mitzvoth. See R. Sh. Z. of Lyada, *The Laws of the Study of Torah,* 4.3.

See also Deuteronomy Rabbah 11:6:

ורצה בעושיה ולא אמר בעמליה ולא אמר בהוגיה אלא בעושיה, באלו שהן עושין את דברי תורה.

("Blessed art Thou O Lord, King of the Universe who has chosen this law and sanctified it and has found pleasure in them who fulfill it"). He did not say "in them that labor at it" (in its study), not "in them who meditate on it," but "in them that fulfill it," that is to say, "in them who carry out the words of the Torah." See *Dikdukei Sofrim,* Berakhoth, pp. 79–80. The famous statement by R. Simon, the son of R. Gamaliel, M. Aboth 1:7:

לא המדרש עיקר אלא המעשה.

("Not the exposition [of the law] is the chief thing, but the performance [of the law]") is not wholly condemnatory of learning without doing. In the words of the pseudo-Rashi, printed in the Vilna edition of the Talmud, doing (observing) mitzvoth is greater than studying mitzvoth and not doing them. But learning and not doing is greater than not studying and not doing.

According to R. M. A. Fano (1548–1620), *Assarah Mamoroth,* vol. 4, chap. 5, deeds are more important for the former sinner, study for the wholly righteous. Is this an attempt to reconcile contradictory sources or to elevate the status of study?

9. See, however, Mekhilta D'Rashbi (ed. Epstein-Melamed), p. 149; Aboth DeRabbi Natan (ed. S. Schechter), p. 44; and A. B. Ehrlich, *Mikra Ki-Peshuto,* Ktav, New York 1969, p. 172.

10. Indeed, R. Yonah, a fourth-century Palestinian scholar, inquired (P.T. at the beginning of Tractate Shebiith):

הרי פרשת מילואין, הרי פרשת דור המבול הרי אינן עתידן לחזור, מעתה יעקרו אותן מן המשנה? אלא כדי להודיעך.

("The investiture of Aaron the High Priest and the generation of the Flood will not occur again. Shall we excise them from the Mishnah? [No!] They are there to inform us [of past events]").

11. If the disagreement between the two High Priests mentioned in B.T. Yoma 59a (and parallels) is historical, then we have an example of a disagreement prior to the Shammaites and Hillelites. See *Tosaphoth Yeshanim,* ad loc. (found in the Vilna edition of the Talmud). See also Tosefta Sotah 7, 10–12.

12. A third example is found in Tosefta Negaim 6:1 in connection with a house afflicted with leprosy. See also P.T. Nazir 7:2 (52b): midrashoth amina (?).

13. In the Babylonian Talmud (not so in Tosefta Sanhedrin 11:6), the statement about the rebellious son is attributed to R. Simon, a mid-second-century Palestinian scholar who lived after the period of the Shammaites and Hillelites. In

the chronological sequence, I put this statement in the third stage after the recognition of the value of rejected views during the period of the Shammaites and Hillelites.

14. R. Yisrael Salanter, *Or Yisrael,* Vilna 1900, chap. 31, raises the question of why the Torah had to set aside laws that have no practical application in order to get reward for the study thereof. Does not he who studies laws that have practical application also get a reward? And he explains: When one studies laws that have practical applications, he is usually biased in favor of a particular conclusion. Since he is partial, the value of the learning is diminished, and therefore the reward is less. But he who studies laws that have no practical application is impartial and unbiased; he has no vested interest in which direction the conclusion will take. The value of that learning is complete, and therefore the reward is full.

15. It has since been pointed out to me that R. Joseph Kara, a colleague of the Rashbam (see Poznansky, *Commentary to Ezekiel and the Minor Prophets,* pp. xxiii–xxxiv) in his *Commentary on the Early Prophets,* Mossad Harav Kook, Jerusalem 1972, p. 47 (Hebrew) already made the connection between interpreting the Bible untraditionally and the phrase in the Talmud "to make the Torah greater and more glorious."

16. See supra, Chapter 3, note 50, in the name of the Maharal. A detailed analysis of the various meanings of *torah lishmah* and the relevant literature are to be found in N. Lamm, *Torah Lishmah* (Hebrew), Mossad Harav Kook, Jerusalem 1972. He broadly divides them into three categories (p. 135): (1) the functional—to learn in order to know how to behave; (2) the religious—to fulfill the commandment of studying Torah, which to the Kabbalists meant communion with God, the Torah giver; (3) the intellectual—to know and understand God's Torah (for the latter, see especially chap. 7, pp. 159–173).

Pertaining to the Talmudic period, it seems that there were two separate strands that intermingled later. One strand was that of the Sifra, at the beginning of Bechukotai,

הלמד שלא לעשות,

one who learns in order not to do (mitzvoth), which the P.T. Berakhoth 1:2 (3b) and parallels understand to mean when one uses learning to absolve him from doing mitzvoth. (I am learning and I do not have to stop learning in order to build a Sukkah or take a *lulav* on the holiday of Sukkoth.) Whoever says so, is severely condemned:

נוח לו שלא נברא

("It would have been better had he not been created"). An extension of the Sifra is Rava's statement in B.T. Berakhoth 17a:

שלא יהא אדם קורא ושונה ובועט באביו ובאמו וברבו ובמי שהוא גדול ממנו בחכמה ובמנין.

("A man should not study Torah and Mishnah and then despise his father and mother and teacher and his superior in wisdom and rank"). In Rava's case (unlike that of the Yerushalmi) the person's learning does not directly conflict with observance, but comes close to it. When people see a learned man being rude or not observing the law, it is as if he uses his learning against observance. In the same spirit, the Tanchuma, Eikev, 6 changes the statement of the Yerushalmi from

הלמד שלא לעשות

to "one who studies Torah and does not observe its commandments." The two statements are related. Nevertheless, R. Hiya bar Abba expresses the sentiment that God would have preferred the Jews to have abandoned the mitzvoth and studied the Torah to the reverse, keeping the mitzvoth and not studying the Torah:

השאור (המאור) שבה היה מקרבין אצלי.

Through Torah, "through its light or power of fermentation," they would have ultimately accepted the mitzvoth too. The converse is not necessarily true; observance may not lead to knowledge. (P.T. Chagigah 1:7 [76c] and parallels.)

The second strand was

עוסק בתורה שלא לשמה,

one who learns Torah for ulterior motives. The Sifrei Deut., piska 48 (113), defines one with ulterior motives as "he who says I will learn in order to be called a *chacham,* in order to head an Academy, in order to have my days strengthened in the world to come." Studying with ulterior motives was not condemned. A prayer was offered (Berakhoth 17a) for those who study *shelo lishmah* that they might soon study *lishmah.* Moreover, people were encouraged to study *shelo lishmah* because it will lead to *lishmah* (ibid. and parallels). Later, however, some types of *shelo lishmah* were also condemned (ibid.):

וכל העושה (העוסק) שלא לשמה נוח לו שלא נברא.

("Whoever studies *shelo lishmah,* it would have been better if he had not been created"), borrowing the phrase "it would have been better if he had not been created" from

הלמד שלא לעשות,

"he who learns in order not to do." The intermingling of the two strands is particularly pronounced in *Tractate Kallah,* ed. M. Higger, Moinester Publishing Company, Brooklyn, N.Y. 1936, p. 276, and among the medieval commentators, who attempted to harmonize the two different strands.

The use of the word *lishmah* in connection with the Rashbam is my own. He does not explain himself at all on this matter, nor does he tell us how he justified his counter-halakhic exegesis. In my usage, it is taken in the sense of fulfilling the mitzvah of studying Torah. It excludes—to use Lamm's categories—the functional and eliminates from the religious the mystical element, the communion with God. Studying is a mitzvah by itself; whatever the text suggests is Torah. And if this suggestion is counter to accepted halakhah, it should not be followed in practical guidance, yet whoever studies it is fulfilling a commandment. See J. Goldin, "The Two Versions of Abot de Rabbi Nathan," *Hebrew Union College Annual,* vol. 19, 1945–46, pp. 99–102.

Sources from the intertestamental period (including Qumran literature) in praise of study (Wisdom) were collected by B.Th. Viviano, *Study as Worship,* Leiden 1978, pp. 132–52. In these sources, as in the Bible, learning is not an end in itself. It provides knowledge toward achieving a higher goal, that of fearing God or keeping the law. Learning that leads to neither is frowned upon. See, for instance, Ben Sira, chapter 10.

17. For "the motives and goals of the Mishneh Torah," see I. Twersky, *Introduction to the Code of Maimonides,* Yale University Press, New Haven and London 1980, pp. 61ff. The Rambam's unappreciative attitude toward the "give and take" was a considerable factor.

18. See ibid., pp. 356–374. See also D. Hartman, *Maimonides: Torah and Philosophic Quest,* Jewish Publication Society, Philadelphia 1976.

19. In a famous responsum to his favorite pupil Joseph Aknin, Pe'eir Hador, chapter 142, Maimonides derides the worth of the discursive in the Talmud: "Do not waste your time with interpretation and discussion of the Gemara." See also my *Sources and Traditions,* Shabbath, introduction, p. 12, n. 24.

20. *The Rambam's Responsa and His Letters* (Hebrew), Leipzig 1859, vol. 1, chap. 140, p. 26.

21. See (among others) R. Malachi Hakohen, *Yad Malachi,* Keter, New York 1945 edition, p. 182 (rule 4 of the rules of the Rambam).

22. R. Joseph Karo's *Shulchan Aruch* comes close to it. He often omits the justificatory part of the Rambam, even when he quotes him. He could do so only because he first wrote a separate work, the *Beit Joseph,* to justify his *Shulchan Aruch.*

23. Compare Harav Hameiri's criticism of the Rambam's *Mishneh Torah* in his introduction to *Beth Habchirah,* Berakhoth, ed. S. Dikman, Machon Hatalmud Hayisraeli Hashalem, Jerusalem 1965, pp. 25ff.

24. R. Sh. Lurya (sixteenth century) accuses the Ibn Ezra: "That he encouraged heretics, Sadducees and people who are light in their beliefs" (*Yad Shel Shelomo,* at the end of the introduction to the tractate Baba Kama, Prague 1616).

25. In medieval times they rarely used the Bible as the chief source for a practical decision; see Y. Gilath, "The Exposition of Biblical Verses in the Post Talmudic Period," *Memorial Volume for Dr. D. Ochs* (Hebrew), Bar Ilan University, Ramat Gan 1978, pp. 210–231. For early medieval times, see the erudite study of A. Grossman, *The Early Sages of Ashkenaz* (Hebrew), Magnes Press, Jerusalem 1980, pp. 155ff.

26. Like, for instance, R. Yeshayeh Horowitz ("*Sehlah*"), R. Joel Sirkis, and R. Shmuel Eidlish (sixteenth- and seventeenth-century scholars). The relevant passages from their writings were collected by D. R. Rappel, *The Debate over Pilpul* (Hebrew), Dvir, Tel Aviv 1979, pp. 107–112.

27. The kind that R. Ephraim of Luntshits (sixteenth century) bitterly renounces:

שמו שמים על זאת שרב זקן ויושב בישיבה ישנה את הידוע לו ולאחרים כי יאמר חדשות אני מגיד וכך הוא פשט הגמרא והוא בעצמו יודע שאין הפשט כן.

("Be astonished, O you Heavens [Jer. 2:12] that an old scholar, a head of an Academy shall change what is known to him and to others. For he often announces: I have something new to say. This is the correct understanding of the passage in the Gemara [the correct *peshat*] when he so well knows that it is not the correct understanding."). *Amudei Sheish,* Prague 1618, p. 12.

28. J. N. Epstein, *Introduction to the Text of the Mishnah,* Magnes Press, Jerusalem 1948, pp. 595–672, examining anew the places in the Mishnah where according to the Gemara there is a "lacuna in the text" and concludes that in the overwhelming majority of cases, there is no need to say so, if one follows the peshat. See, however, Kuzari, book III, paragraphs 69, 72.

29. See E. Z. Melamed,

מפרשי המקרא דרכיהם ושיטותיהם

(*Bible Commentators*), Magnes Press, Jerusalem 1978, p. 453.

30. This is a free translation from the original. In the original, it is not clear whether he meant that one ought not to *interpret* a text against the Gemara that has practical applications, or that one should not *draw* practical conclusions from such an interpretation. He uses both words, *shelo yakhri'a veyifaresh* that "he should not decide and interpret." The difference would be whether or not one is allowed to interpret a text against the Gemara that has practical application if he eschews drawing practical conclusions from the interpretations. I am inclined to think that the author of the Tosafoth Yom Tov would have answered in the negative. He was so understood by later scholars, such as Meshulam Roth, *Lichvod Yom Tov,* Mossad Harav Kook, Jerusalem 1957, pp. 90–94 (reprinted in Roth's *Kol Mevasser,* Mossad Harav Kook, Jerusalem 1972, pp. 119–121, 128–129 as *Simchat Yom Tov*). The debate over whether or not one is allowed to interpret a text against the Gemara has flared up again recently in the periodical *Shematin* (published in Israel by teachers of religious subjects in the High Schools); see the issues of 1972, no. 31, pp. 63–65; no. 32, pp. 6–17; no. 33, pp. 36–41.

31. See, for instance, his commentary to Mishnah Sanhedrin 10:3.

32. In practical halakhah the opinion of the Babylonian Talmud prevails over that of the Palestinian Talmud. This is not necessarily the case, however, in matters pertaining to the correct version of a text. Sometimes the version of the Palestinian Talmud is preferable to the Babylonian Talmud version, according to R. Chaim Itter (1696–1743),

פרי תואר,

Solkiew 1770, chapter 119, note 1. This assertion puzzled R. Malachi Hakohen, *Yad Malachi,* in the section dealing with the difference between the two Talmuds, note 7 (Keter, New York edition, 1945, p. 177), and he exclaims: "Because of my limited knowledge, I do not know from where he gets this idea."

33. Despite the many exhortations against pilpul. My favorite one is that of R. Israel Isserlin (1390–1460), the greatest religious authority of his time, who once said, as reported by his disciple, R. Joseph, the author of *Leket Yosher* (ed. J. Freimann, Berlin 1903, p. 44): "May God forgive me! For in my opinion, pilpul does not deserve to have the benediction of Torah recited before its study."

Appendix: Use of the Word "Halakhoth"

1. Even if one is to accept the explanation that the law

אין מפטירין אחר הפסח אפיקומן.

("after the Passover meal, they should not disperse to join in revelry") is singled out in the Passover Haggadah as part of the father's instruction to his wise son because it is the last law, and even if the intention is that the father should teach his son all the laws up to the last one (see M. Friedman's comment to his edition of the Mekhilta, Vienna 1870, p. 22b, n. 23), it would still not follow that the author of that passage in the Passover Haggadah had our Mishnah and its order. This law is not the last law in our Mishnah Pesachim 10:8; a few other laws follow it. It is, however, the last law pertaining to the ritual of the eating of the paschal lamb. It is last in *procedure,* not last in text.

2. For a fuller explanation of this Braitha, see P.T. Shabbath 2:7 (5b) and S.

Lieberman, *Tosefta Ki-fshutah,* Jewish Theological Seminary, New York 1962), pp. 35–36.

3. I am basically following M. Friedman's distinction between Mishnah and halakhoth as he developed it in the introduction to his Mekhilta, chap. 6, pp. 37–40. I do not accept his interpretation of the disagreement between R. Meir and R. Judah (discussed later in this appendix). In his overview of Halakhoth and Mishnah, Friedman for some reason omitted B.T. Berakhoth 11b and its parallel P.T. ibid. 1:5 (3c). In light of what I said above, I am inclined to accept the Palestinian Talmud's version:

ר׳ חונה אמר ... מדרש צריך לברך, הלכות אין צריך לברך.

("R. Chuna says . . . he who studies Midrash must recite the benediction [before learning]: he who studies halakhoth does not need to recite the benediction [before learning]"). Halakhoth in the sense of practical laws are less Torah than Midrash (which also contains laws). One does not have to recite a benediction—according to R. Huna—before studying halakhoth, whereas in the Babylonian Talmud we follow the reading of the

רא״ה: ור׳ אלעזר אמר למשנה צריך לברך, למדרש אין צריך לברך.

(see *Dikdukei Sofrim* ad loc.); ("R. Aharon Halevy: And R. Elazar said: Whoever studies Mishnah must recite the benediction, and he who studies Midrash does not need to recite the benediction"). Mishnah (which also contains drashoth) is more Torah than Midrash. Before studying the latter—according to R. Elazar—one does not have to recite a benediction.

4. The phrase בכל יום ("every day"), which is found in the printed edition of the prayer books and at the end of B.T. Niddah, is an "import" from an earlier statement in B.T. Berakhoth, 4b:

כל האומר תהלה לדוד בכל יום, מובטח לו שהוא בן עולם הבא.

("Whoever recites Psalms, chapter 145, every day (according to some readings: three times a day] is sure of a share in the world to come").

5. Called by R. Hillel (a twelfth-century scholar) in his commentary on the Sifrei (ed. S. Koloditzky, Mossad Harav Kook, Jerusalem 1946, vol. 3, Deuteronomy, p. 45): *dinin.* The editor's suggestion to read *dayeinu* is unnecessary.

6. Only the school of R. Ishmael (or close to it) would call Midrash לחם ("bread," the main food staple) and halakhoth על כל מוצא פי ה׳ ("everything that proceeds from His mouth"); Sifrei Deut., piska 48, p. 113. This makes *halakhoth* less important. The school of R. Akiba probably would have reversed this and called Mishnah "bread" and Midrash "everything that proceeds from His mouth." Similarly, only the school of R. Akiba would say

הלכה ומדרש, נזקקין להלכה.

("In the Academy when one has to discuss both halakhah [Mishnah] and Midrash, he should start with halakhah"); Tosefta Sanhedrin 7:7. The school of R. Ishmael probably would have said one should start with Midrash.

7. I have since seen that J. Neubauer, *HaRambam al Divrei Sofrim,* Mossad Harav Kook, Jerusalem 1957, p. 123, gives a similar interpretation of the disagreement between R. Meir and R. Judah. For a clever interpretation of this disagreement (arguable both ways), see N. Bruell, "Begriff und Ursprung der Tosefta," *Jubelschrift zum Neunzigsten Geburtstag der L. Zunz,* L. Gerschell, Berlin 1884, pp. 101–104.

Index of Passages Cited

Bible

Mekhilta

Sifra

Sifrei Numbers

Sifrei Deuteronomy

Mekhilta D'Rashbi

Sifrei Zutta

Mishnah

Tosefta

Palestinian Talmud

Babylonian Talmud

Deuteronomy Rabbah

Ecclesiastes Rabbah

Tanchuma

General Index